BESTSELLING
BOOK SERIES

Travel Planning Online
For Dummies

MW00988564

Tips for Mobile Computing

- **Watch your laptop carefully.** Thieves prey on expensive notebook computers. Don't leave yours alone for a second.

- **Know what equipment you need to connect.** Make sure you have the right adapters for connecting to the phone lines in your destination city.

- **Beware of digital phone lines.** Many laptops can be damaged by a connection to a digital line. Ask the hotel's staff or invest in digital line tester.

- **Find an Internet service provider.** You can find lists of ISPs on the Web that can help you get a connection anywhere in the world.

- **Think about buying an acoustic coupler.** If you travel outside your country, especially to the developing world, these old-school modems work on any phone.

- **Get a comfy computer bag.** Don't mess around with trying to squeeze your laptop into luggage that wasn't designed for delicate electronics. Get a quality bag — your back will thank you, as will your notebook.

Tips for Better Surfing

- **Bookmark good sites.** Bookmarking makes it easier to check with sites that offer good bargains daily.

- **Open more than one browser window at a time.** While you're waiting for those beautiful pictures to download, you could be reading about ticket prices in another window.

- **Make sure your credit card number is safe.** A little lock symbol in your browser window means that your sensitive data is protected.

- **Switch off your graphics.** Doing so can significantly increase the speed of your surfing.

- **Familiarize yourself with search options.** Most search engines let you refine your search by entering keywords in a certain way (for example, in quotes). On most sites, you can click an Options button to find out the search engine's requirements.

Tips for Getting Cheaper Airline Tickets

- **Buy your tickets well in advance.** That means 21 days or more before your flight.

- **Purchase tickets at the very last minute.** You can subscribe to weekly e-mails direct from airlines to stay up on last-minute bargains.

- **Stay over a Saturday night.** What the heck — it could be fun!

- **Don't fly on holidays.** Make sure you know of any holidays in your destination area.

- **Don't be afraid to fly any and all airlines, great and small.** The fares vary widely.

- **Fly the same airline on all flight segments of your flight.** Using two airlines sometimes doubles the cost of a ticket.

- **Look for flights with plenty of seats remaining.** The airline may offer a bargain rate in order to fill up the plane.

...For Dummies®: Bestselling Book Series for Beginners

Travel Planning Online For Dummies®

Cheat Sheet

Benefits of Travel Planning Online

✔ **Get tons of free destination info.** No matter where you want to go, you can find information on the Internet to help you explore the area.

✔ **Make travel plans on short notice.** Don't panic — you can take care of all of your travel arrangements online at the last minute.

✔ **Never miss a travel bargain.** Use the Internet to keep abreast of the latest fare wars, promotions, and discounts through e-mail newsletters and a good list of bookmarks.

✔ **Comparison shop.** You can explore the different options offered by a variety of travel companies, travel agents, and suppliers, all from the comfort of your home.

✔ **Get expert travel advice.** The Internet provides a terrific way to find experts on every travel topic. Send an e-mail and get a quick response.

✔ **Communicate with other travelers.** Travel-related newsgroups, mailing lists, and chat rooms enable you to get accurate and up-to-date travel advice.

✔ **See what you're getting.** Before you book, you can see destinations, hotel rooms, cruise ships, and so on through photos, slide shows, and movies.

✔ **Generate precise maps for driving.** You have no excuse for getting lost anymore.

✔ **Get health and safety information.** Before you head off into the sunset, get the latest travel advisories off the Internet.

✔ **Track flights.** Never wait at an airport again — go online and find out if your plane is on time.

✔ **Manage awards programs.** Download awards program management software to keep track of your awards.

✔ **Figure out how much things cost.** Online currency converters and exchange rates make it possible for you to tell a rupee from a franc.

IDG BOOKS WORLDWIDE

...For Dummies®: Bestselling Book Series for Beginners

TRAVEL PLANNING ONLINE
FOR
DUMMIES®

TRAVEL PLANNING ONLINE FOR DUMMIES®

by Noah Vadnai

IDG Books Worldwide, Inc.
An International Data Group Company

Foster City, CA ♦ Chicago, IL ♦ Indianapolis, IN ♦ New York, NY

Travel Planning Online For Dummies®

Published by
IDG Books Worldwide, Inc.
An International Data Group Company
919 E. Hillsdale Blvd.
Suite 400
Foster City, CA 94404
www.idgbooks.com (IDG Books Worldwide Web site)
www.dummies.com (Dummies Press Web site)

Library of Congress Catalog Card No.: 98-87911

ISBN: 0-7645-0438-X

Printed in the United States of America

10 9 8 7 6 5 4 3 2

1B/RV/QS/ZZ/IN

Distributed in the United States by IDG Books Worldwide, Inc.

Distributed by Macmillan Canada for Canada; by Transworld Publishers Limited in the United Kingdom; by IDG Norge Books for Norway; by IDG Sweden Books for Sweden; by Woodslane Pty. Ltd. for Australia; by Woodslane (NZ) Ltd. for New Zealand; by Addison Wesley Longman Singapore Pte Ltd. for Singapore, Malaysia, Thailand, and Indonesia; by Norma Comunicaciones S.A. for Colombia; by Intersoft for South Africa; by International Thomson Publishing for Germany, Austria and Switzerland; by Distribuidora Cuspide for Argentina; by Livraria Cultura for Brazil; by Ediciencia S.A. for Ecuador; by Ediciones ZETA S.C.R. Ltda. for Peru; by WS Computer Publishing Corporation, Inc., for the Philippines; by Contemporanea de Ediciones for Venezuela; by Express Computer Distributors for the Caribbean and West Indies; by Micronesia Media Distributor, Inc. for Micronesia; by Grupo Editorial Norma S.A. for Guatemala; by Chips Computadoras S.A. de C.V. for Mexico; by Editorial Norma de Panama S.A. for Panama; by Wouters Import for Belgium; by American Bookshops for Finland. Authorized Sales Agent: Anthony Rudkin Associates for the Middle East and North Africa.

For general information on IDG Books Worldwide's books in the U.S., please call our Consumer Customer Service department at 800-762-2974. For reseller information, including discounts and premium sales, please call our Reseller Customer Service department at 800-434-3422.

For information on where to purchase IDG Books Worldwide's books outside the U.S., please contact our International Sales department at 317-596-5530 or fax 317-596-5692.

For information on foreign language translations, please contact our Foreign & Subsidiary Rights department at 650-655-3021 or fax 650-655-3281.

For sales inquiries and special prices for bulk quantities, please contact our Sales department at 650-655-3200 or write to the address above.

For information on using IDG Books Worldwide's books in the classroom or for ordering examination copies, please contact our Educational Sales department at 800-434-2086 or fax 317-596-5499.

For press review copies, author interviews, or other publicity information, please contact our Public Relations department at 650-655-3000 or fax 650-655-3299.

For authorization to photocopy items for corporate, personal, or educational use, please contact Copyright Clearance Center, 222 Rosewood Drive, Danvers, MA 01923, or fax 978-750-4470.

About the Author

Since his travel-filled childhood, **Noah Vadnai** has never been one to pass on the opportunity for a good trip. A year living and studying among travel-happy Israelis in Jerusalem convinced him of the value of a sturdy backpack — that same pack has journeyed with him on all of his travels throughout the Middle East, Southeast Asia, Nepal, China, and all over North America.

After graduating from the University of Rochester with a highly marketable degree in Religion and Classics, Noah's "career" has been a journey in itself: A stint working as a tree surgeon gave way to less callusing (but no less arduous) work as a film and video production lackey. The Associated Press was then kind enough to grant him work as a photo editor in New York City for two years, but wanderlust took hold when a friend called from Tel Aviv, suggesting that he quit his job and blow his savings on a one-way ticket to Nepal. A year and many digestive traumas later, Noah was back in New York working as the Travel Channel Producer for NetGuide, an online Internet directory and guide. The next destination? Fortunately, there is no available guidebook.

ABOUT IDG BOOKS WORLDWIDE

Welcome to the world of IDG Books Worldwide.

IDG Books Worldwide, Inc., is a subsidiary of International Data Group, the world's largest publisher of computer-related information and the leading global provider of information services on information technology. IDG was founded more than 30 years ago by Patrick J. McGovern and now employs more than 9,000 people worldwide. IDG publishes more than 290 computer publications in over 75 countries. More than 90 million people read one or more IDG publications each month.

Launched in 1990, IDG Books Worldwide is today the #1 publisher of best-selling computer books in the United States. We are proud to have received eight awards from the Computer Press Association in recognition of editorial excellence and three from Computer Currents' First Annual Readers' Choice Awards. Our best-selling ...For Dummies® series has more than 50 million copies in print with translations in 31 languages. IDG Books Worldwide, through a joint venture with IDG's Hi-Tech Beijing, became the first U.S. publisher to publish a computer book in the People's Republic of China. In record time, IDG Books Worldwide has become the first choice for millions of readers around the world who want to learn how to better manage their businesses.

Our mission is simple: Every one of our books is designed to bring extra value and skill-building instructions to the reader. Our books are written by experts who understand and care about our readers. The knowledge base of our editorial staff comes from years of experience in publishing, education, and journalism — experience we use to produce books to carry us into the new millennium. In short, we care about books, so we attract the best people. We devote special attention to details such as audience, interior design, use of icons, and illustrations. And because we use an efficient process of authoring, editing, and desktop publishing our books electronically, we can spend more time ensuring superior content and less time on the technicalities of making books.

You can count on our commitment to deliver high-quality books at competitive prices on topics you want to read about. At IDG Books Worldwide, we continue in the IDG tradition of delivering quality for more than 30 years. You'll find no better book on a subject than one from IDG Books Worldwide.

John Kilcullen
Chairman and CEO
IDG Books Worldwide, Inc.

Steven Berkowitz
President and Publisher
IDG Books Worldwide, Inc.

Eighth Annual Computer Press Awards ≥1992

Ninth Annual Computer Press Awards ≥1993

Tenth Annual Computer Press Awards ≥1994

Eleventh Annual Computer Press Awards ≥1995

Dedication

"And so each venture is a new beginning/A raid on the inarticulate."
– *T.S. Eliot*

This book is dedicated to my family, who instilled in me the love of travel and knowledge, which will continue to guide me throughout my life. Mom, Dad, Liza, Magda, Ellen and Winnie — thanks and much love.

Author's Acknowledgments

Thanks very much to Mary Goodwin, a patient and thorough editor who loves Apricot Ale. And thanks to all the other hard workers at IDG Books Worldwide, Inc., for helping put this book together. To Lisa Swayne, my agent (I *love* saying that!), thanks for knowing that I could write this book. Edward Hasbrouck and the participants of the Infotec-Travel electronic mailing list, thanks for the much needed travel industry guidance.

Big thanks to everyone who helped me stay the course during a long summer of writing in a tiny apartment (and in an even smaller bedroom): C. Elise, Danny, Liza, Nina Renee, Julian, Sianfoulkes (sic),Tomas, T-Brown, Mal, Rosen, E², Jeremiah, Joc, Petey Wheatstraw, Papa Bill, Mellow Man, Jimmy James, Simeond, all of my NetGuide peeps, Moo, Ad-Low, Doris, Lapkin, Sohn, Lael, Vito, and all the other peoples on the L.E.S. and 'round the world.

An extra big *merci* to Elise and Becky Barna, who played a large role in my transition from civilian to author. And to Mixmaster *Mei-yo:* Mikey, thanks for showing me how to ride a bus — always remember your Flagyl.

Peace!

Publisher's Acknowledgments

We're proud of this book; please register your comments through our IDG Books Worldwide Online Registration Form located at http://my2cents.dummies.com.

Some of the people who helped bring this book to market include the following:

Acquisitions, Editorial, and Media Development

Senior Project Editor: Mary Goodwin

Associate Project Editor: Andrea C. Boucher

Acquisitions Editor: Jill Pisoni

Copy Editors: Rowena Rappaport, Billie Williams, Phil Worthington

Technical Editor: Dennis Teague

Media Development Editors: Joell Smith, Marita Ellixson

Media Development Coordinator: Megan Roney

Associate Permissions Editor: Carmen Krikorian

Editorial Manager: Kelly Ewing

Media Development Manager: Heather Heath Dismore

Editorial Assistant: Paul Kuzmic

Production

Project Coordinator: E. Shawn Aylsworth

Layout and Graphics: Lou Boudreau, Linda M. Boyer, Angela F. Hunckler, Jane E. Martin, Brent Savage, Deirdre Smith, Rashell Smith, Kate Snell

Proofreaders: Kelli Botta, Laura Bowman, Michelle Croninger, Nancy Price, Rebecca Senninger, Janet M. Withers

Indexer: Liz Cunningham

General and Administrative

IDG Books Worldwide, Inc.: John Kilcullen, CEO; Steven Berkowitz, President and Publisher

IDG Books Technology Publishing: Brenda McLaughlin, Senior Vice President and Group Publisher

Dummies Technology Press and Dummies Editorial: Diane Graves Steele, Vice President and Associate Publisher; Mary Bednarek, Director of Acquisitions and Product Development; Kristin A. Cocks, Editorial Director

Dummies Trade Press: Kathleen A. Welton, Vice President and Publisher; Kevin Thornton, Acquisitions Manager

IDG Books Production for Dummies Press: Michael R. Britton, Vice President of Production and Creative Services; Cindy L. Phipps, Manager of Project Coordination, Production Proofreading, and Indexing; Kathie S. Schutte, Supervisor of Page Layout; Shelley Lea, Supervisor of Graphics and Design; Debbie J. Gates, Production Systems Specialist; Robert Springer, Supervisor of Proofreading; Debbie Stailey, Special Projects Coordinator; Tony Augsburger, Supervisor of Reprints and Bluelines

Dummies Packaging and Book Design: Patty Page, Manager, Promotions Marketing

♦

The publisher would like to give special thanks to Patrick J. McGovern, without whom this book would not have been possible.

♦

Contents at a Glance

Cartoons at a Glance

By Rich Tennant

"OK kids, pick your in-flight snack—cheese sticks or corn nuggets."

page 113

"Hint? It's not a hint. I just thought I'd create a little atmosphere as you get ready to research our next vacation. Well, hasta la vista."

page 5

"I love these online travel tips, like how not to look like a tourist. Imagine – I was gonna get off the plane in India with a goofy camera around my neck."

page 209

When I reserved this thing online, I thought a dromedary was the name of a late model Chevy station wagon. Now, which one of your agents do I see to get a refund?

page D–1

After spending 9 days on 22 different sites and reading 26 online brochures, Dave had an acute attack of "Toxic Option Syndrome."

page 273

"This afternoon I want everyone to go online and find all you can about Native American culture, the history of the old west, and discount air fares to Hawaii for the two weeks I'll be on vacation."

page 289

Fax: 978-546-7747 • E-mail: the5wave@tiac.net

Table of Contents

Chapter 4: Great Adventures Begin on Your Desktop 71

Chapter 5: Reading Is Fundamental, Even Online 93

Part III: Plugging In to Plan and Prepare Yourself 209

Chapter 10: Healthy, Wealthy, and Wise 211

Introduction

· ·

Travelers today are lucky. Not only do they have safe, high-speed transportation, but they also have access to boundless information and services on the Internet. Gone are the days when you booked way-too-expensive transportation to a place you knew nothing about, arriving only to realize that you packed all the wrong clothes. Thanks to the Internet and *Travel Planning Online For Dummies,* you can always know what you're getting into.

I Know Who You Are

I even know where you live! In all seriousness, I figure that because you're reading this book, you probably enjoy traveling. Further, you know a bit about using the Internet and have heard about the Internet's value for travelers. And while neither you nor I are dummies (I've been called worse), I assume that you haven't had much experience using the various components of online travel planning. Don't let lack of experience worry you — I take the time to explain many procedures, such as buying plane tickets, in a clear, step-by-step manner. If you get bored, you can always skip ahead.

Travel Planning Online For Dummies isn't geared towards any one particular type of traveler. Rather, it contains useful information for leisure travelers, business travelers, independent travelers, traveling families — you get the idea. Everyone who travels can benefit from using the Internet and reading this book. (I look up travel stuff on the Internet even when I don't have a vacation in sight — just to vicariously enjoy the many trip possibilities.)

How to Use This Book

Although I'd be happy if you did, I don't expect you to pick up *Travel Planning Online For Dummies* and read it start to finish. Use this book as a reference — each chapter can be read without knowing information from any of the other chapters. When you want to know about, say, how to find a restaurant in New York, turn to Chapter 2 and start reading.

Use the Index and the Table of Contents and you'll have no trouble finding the topics that interest you. Or just throw the book up in the air and start reading on the page where the book falls open. However, if you prefer this method of reading the book, please wait until you get the book home from the bookstore.

How This Book Is Organized

I divide this book into five parts. Each covers topics that loosely fit under the title of each part. Or at least that was the plan.

Part I: Investigating Your Destination Online

Part I shows you how to research all sorts of destinations and vacations using the Internet. You get introduced to city guides, online travel guides, all sorts of online travel reading, and restaurant databases. Part I also talks about how any traveler, with any set of interests and needs, can find tours, travel agents, and information to make his or her perfect trip happen.

Part II: Turning Your Computer into a Travel Agent

Part II explores the most revolutionary aspect of online travel — online travel agencies and electronic travel commerce. This part shows you how to buy plane tickets, book hotel rooms, and rent cars using the "Big Four" online travel agencies. You also get information about train travel and the details of finding accommodations online. And, (drumroll, please) I include a chapter that's all about using the Internet to find travel bargains and low fares.

Part III: Plugging In to Plan and Prepare Yourself

Part III examines the Internet tools that can enhance your travels, including weather forecasts, detailed and interactive maps, ATM locators, and much more. I also explain, in this part, how to tap into the vast pool of travel experts known as your fellow travelers. I also tell you about travel newsgroups, chat rooms, and mailing lists in this part.

Part IV: The Part of Tens

This part offers two quick lists of helpful hints. The first chapter in this part runs through time-honored advice for getting cheaper airfares. The second section suggests ways to make your Web surfing and time on the Internet more efficient (and fun).

Part V: Appendixes

The two short appendixes in this part get you up to speed on the travel offerings on America Online, the world's largest commercial online service, and on the CD-ROM that comes with this book.

The Travel Planning Online For Dummies Internet Directory

Somewhere toward the end of the book, you see a section of yellow pages. In these yellow pages you find a collection of great travel Web sites, reviewed and organized by topic. (You'll also find the directory in an interactive format on the CD-ROM, included with this book. If you're online when you use the CD, you can click on the Web links to bring you directly to the sites that I review.)

Icons Used in This Book

Throughout the book, you find cute little illustrations that denote various pieces of pertinent advice and special items of interest.

Highlights useful advice or a shortcut. Following these tips saves you time, money, energy, and aggravation. I've been planning trips online for years, and I gladly pass my hard-earned experience on to you.

Points out things that you won't want to forget as you plan your trip online. I hope that you don't get sick of hearing about the stuff next to this icon, but I assure you that these items are very important.

Egad! Avoid these pitfalls at all costs — or else you may find yourself on a slow train heading somewhere you don't want to go.

Denotes stuff that you don't really need to know to successfully plan a trip online, but you may find the technical details interesting. Please feel free to breeze right by this information.

Indicates that you can find an item on the CD-ROM that comes with this book.

I'm Here for You

I'd love to hear about your travel experiences, online or otherwise. Or if you have an online travel-related question, feel free to drop me a line at Nvadnai@hotmail.com. Talk to you soon — happy trails!

A Word about the Internet

The Internet changes at an unbelievable rate — no one really knows where it's headed. While Web sites redesign themselves and newsgroups come and go, the specific descriptions and instructions that make up a good part of this book will remain useful, if not exact, for travelers who want to get a grasp of the vast resources for them on the Internet. And of course, there're always future editions. . . .

Part I
Investigating Your
Destination Online

The 5th Wave   By Rich Tennant

"Hint? It's not a hint. I just thought I'd create a little atmosphere as you *get* ready to research our next vacation. Well, hasta la vista."

In this part . . .

*W*hen you come right down to it, traveling is all about the destination. This part shows you how to access the Internet's amazing amount of destination information. I give you tips on how to use city guides and how to find detailed information about any and every place on Planet Earth. I also include information about how to use the Internet to plan all sorts of trips; from finding the right tour operator to the best places to read expert advice. I even show you where to get a tasty bite to eat.

Chapter 1

Scouting Out Locations Online

· ·

· ·

*A*fter you know where to look for information about destinations on the Internet, you have access to many different perspectives, not just to the perspective of someone trying to sell you a trip. You also expose yourself to a wider variety of destination options; places you may never have dreamed of visiting you suddenly see in a new light. Or for a business junket or a short journey, you can easily obtain first-hand advice about an unfamiliar city and how to do business there.

Destination info is tucked away all over the enormous storehouse of information that is the Internet. You just have to know where to find it. This chapter shows you the ins and outs of finding quality online information about cities, countries, resorts, and every other type of place your travels may take you.

Your Keys to the City: Using Online City Guides

A new and unfamiliar city can be one of the most daunting places to navigate for a just-arriving traveler. Unless you have a friend or relative living in each city you visit, you are dependent on your wits and a city guide for all the decisions you make. The city guides you find on the Internet can save you from buying three or four different (heavy) books about your destination; but the Internet will not save you from visiting your Aunt Carol and Uncle Peter if they've promised to "show you the town."

A quality online city guide directs you to all a city has to offer, including the following:

- ✔ Places to eat
- ✔ Sights to see
- ✔ Nightlife options
- ✔ Movie timetables
- ✔ Sporting events
- ✔ Art galleries and exhibitions, festivals, and theater performances
- ✔ Neighborhoods to check out (and those to avoid)

Online city guides provide a terrific alternative to the singular voice of the guidebook. A good online city guide grabs your attention with

- ✔ A good, clean design
- ✔ Easy site navigation
- ✔ A clear editorial voice
- ✔ Photographs
- ✔ Links to related Web resources

But the most important advantage an online city guide offers over a conventional, print guide is that online information gets updated all the time. The city information you find on the Web is often the most current available. Try finding a movie timetable in a print guidebook!

Dozens, and in many cases hundreds, of guides for every city on the big, blue marble of planet Earth are on the Web. In this section, I tell you about all kinds of city guides great and small.

Several major commercial efforts for city guides are currently establishing themselves in cities across the U.S. and in other countries. These city guide networks generally maintain staffs comprised of local editors, critics, and writers in each selected city, offering first-hand knowledge of the city in a standardized format. This way, if you're familiar with one city's guide, you won't have to figure out a whole new system to read another city guide that's part of the same network.

The major city guide networks all have some serious investment behind them (for example, Microsoft backs the Sidewalk guides, which you can read more about later in this chapter). Creating and maintaining up-to-date, comprehensive, and accurate information about a place as big as say, New York City, is extremely expensive. For almost every city, there exist small, non-commercial sites that are maintained by people that are passionate about their hometown, or the city in which they reside. But a big, commercial city guide undoubtedly outperforms a guide produced by one dude in his basement when he gets home from his 9 to 5 each day.

In the following sections, I detail the many features of the four biggest online city guide networks, allowing you to get a feel for their many features.

CitySearch

CitySearch (www.citysearch.com), Figure 1-1, currently publishes guides for 13 cities worldwide, most of which are in the U.S. (including New York, Los Angeles, and Washington and also smaller cities such as Nashville and Austin). City search also currently offers guides to Melbourne and Sydney, Australia and Toronto, Canada. To access any city's guide, click the appropriate place on the map.

CitySearch provides a lot of editorial advice, meaning it doesn't just tell you a club's address and give you no details to go on. For most of its listings, editors visit the place they're writing about and then relay the ambiance, the prices, the type of people that go there, and other relevant information to you. CitySearch also makes excellent use of photography to illustrate restaurants and venues it reviews.

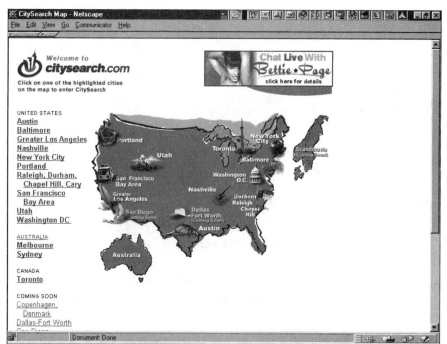

Figure 1-1:
The
CitySearch
home page.

Getting around each site is a fairly simple affair. Use the category links (Arts & Entertainment, Eat & Drink, Community, Sports & Outdoors, and so on) on the left hand side of each guide to move through the sections that interest you.

Each page of each guide has a search box in the upper-left-hand corner labeled, "What Are You Looking For?" Use the search box at any time during your use of CitySearch to quickly perform a search for anything and everything.

Each CitySearch guide features a section specifically for visitors to its city. This section contains editors' picks for special events, activities, or sights that may be of particular interest to a visitor to the city. For example, I recently visited CitySearch New York's Visiting the City section and found a description of a ride on the Staten Island Ferry, a free ride with great views. I live in NYC and I can't agree more with this editor's choice for an inexpensive New York activity.

CitySearch has a customizable newsletter that you can set up to let you know about upcoming events and happenings in a city, and can prove a useful feature if you pass through a city with any regularity. To set up your newsletter, follow these steps:

1. **Click Personalize CitySearch at the bottom left of a guide's home page.**

2. **Register for a free account by entering your name, address, and e-mail address and then click Register Me!**

3. **Choose your preferences.**

   You are now on the "Scout Page" where you select the content of your newsletter.

4. **Click My Searches.**

   You then select the categories that you want to be kept informed of. Place checks next to the categories that interest you.

   Create several search pages — one for restaurants, one for nightlife, and so on. Using multiple search pages makes it much easier to digest the information you get.

   Click Add New Search when you are done.

5. **Click Performer Alert and enter your favorite musicians, dancers, and so on.**

   When they come through town, you'll get an e-mail.

6. **Click Newsletters and select the CitySearch newsletters you want to receive.**

   CitySearch mails out newsletters about every aspect of a city's life — place checks next to the newsletters that interest you. Check out the newsletter especially for travelers, called Visiting the City.

CitySearch is expanding rapidly; Dallas/Fort Worth, San Diego, and Scandinavia (you didn't know it was a city, did you?) are all coming soon. Maybe your destination city is next.

Digital City

Digital City (www.digitalcity.com), Figure 1-2, currently covers more than 36 American cities on its WebGuides (including New York, Los Angeles, New Orleans, Chicago, Cleveland, and Chapel Hill) and the same 36 (or so) cities on America Online. Digital City is owned by America Online (see Appendix A), meaning they have a lot of resources to produce complete guides.

These guides generally act as comprehensive "Yellow Page"-type directories, with varying degrees of editorial content. Click the map of the U.S. to access a guide for the city you are traveling to.

For each city, you find what you're looking for by going to the category of your interest. Looking for a restaurant in Denver? Click Restaurants in the Entertainment section (restaurants are *so* entertaining) and you're presented with a list of links to online restaurant directories for Denver and some links to actual restaurants' Web pages.

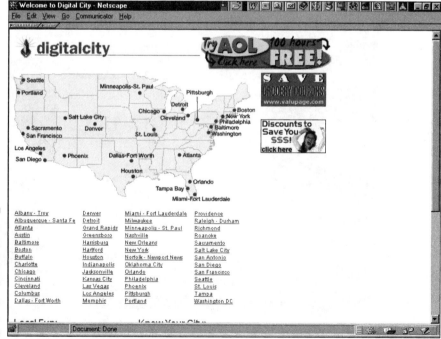

Figure 1-2: The Digital City national network of online guides.

Digital City guides have varying degrees of editorial content (restaurant reviews, movie critiques, and so on); bigger cities tend to have more in-depth guides. Some of Digital City's guides offer unique, first-hand reviews of the features they cover; other guides are made up of only collections of links to other sites' directories. In New York's guide, for example, the writers review restaurants, bars, and all the other stuff critics critique, while Denver's guide is mostly composed of reviewed Web sites. (This discrepancy is probably dictated by what the other online guides in the city are offering.) All in all, Digital City WebGuides are not as authoritative and useful as city guides that consistently write their own reviews.

Sidewalk

The Sidewalk city guides (www.sidewalk.com), Figure 1-3, currently focus on ten cities, including Boston, New York, San Francisco, Seattle, and Houston, with more planned for the near future.

These complete guides (sponsored by Microsoft) offer insight into all aspects of a city's life through painstaking reporting and well-crafted reviews. Click the name of a city on the Sidewalk home page to access a specific guide.

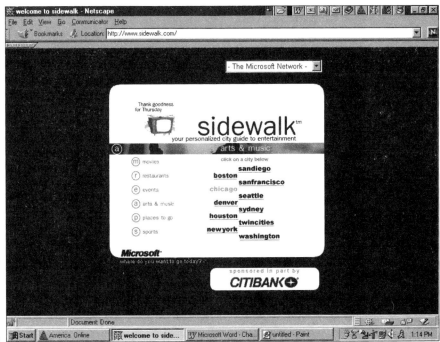

Figure 1-3:
The
Sidewalk
home page.

Microsoft prides itself on its ability to create well-designed software that has a high level of functionality. The Sidewalk guides are no exception. You can access all the information you need on Sidewalk by using any of the following methods:

- ✔ **Using the Fast Finder:** If you know what you are looking for, type an appropriate keyword into the Fast Finder (the search box on each guide's home page) and away you go.

- ✔ **Browsing:** Using the horizontal navigation bar at the top of each guide page, click the links to Movies, Restaurants, Arts & Events, Places, Sports, and Traffic View to peruse the offerings.

- ✔ **Searching:** Each Sidewalk guide offers a series of links that guide you through a search. Click Find a Movie, Find an Event, or Find a Restaurant to use the clever system of search boxes that search by neighborhood, price range, and other criteria.

   For example, say that you want to search for a restaurant. Click Find a Restaurant (on any guide). Using the five pull-down menus, select a neighborhood, a cuisine, a price range, and a star rating. (Each variable is optional. If you just want to search in a specific neighborhood, just select a neighborhood.) When you are ready, click the Go! button and the site presents you with a list of restaurants that match your specifications.

One of the coolest things about Sidewalk is its ability to let you customize the site, making it easy to find the things that interest you. It takes a little time to customize the offerings, but if you plan on visiting a city often, you should spend the time. To customize any Sidewalk guide, follow these steps:

1. **On the right side or at the bottom of any guide's home page, click the link called Customize Now.**

   The next page explains the personalization services.

2. **Click Next to continue.**

   Sidewalk now leads you through pages of choices for restaurants, movies, music, and so on.

3. **Click the boxes next to the things you wish to know about and click Next when you are ready to move on.**

   When you have selected all your choices, the site asks you to enter your favorite performers or events into the Personal Agent — I entered Kenny G. and Gloria Estefan. When your choices are coming to town, Sidewalk sends you an e-mail notification. Can't wait for that e-mail!

   The site displays your picks at the bottom of the home page. Each time you visit, the site updates the information. You can update your choices at any time, by selecting Change Custom Options.

TimeOut

The TimeOut guides (www.timeout.co.uk), Figure 1-4, are the most global of the major city guide networks, currently operating in 22 cities worldwide, including Amsterdam, Barcelona, Las Vegas, Miami, Prague, and Tokyo.

TimeOut (both in print and online), is targeted towards a young, trendy, urban audience and the tone of the writing is best described as hip and in-the-know. Though it may not be as in-depth as CitySearch and Sidewalk, TimeOut's online guides complement its well-known print versions in many of the featured cities and draw on the pithy content from those publications.

The most valuable section of each online TimeOut guide is the Events section, which lists the goings on for the next two weeks. The site organizes the listings by categories, which include Art, Children, Clubs, Comedy, Dance, Film, Music, Sports, and Theatre.

You may also want to check out the City Guide section that contains "detailed, critical listings on accommodations, sightseeing, arts, entertainment, and eating and drinking in the city." I couldn't have said it better myself.

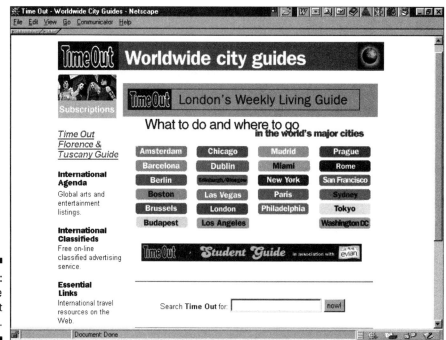

Figure 1-4:
The
TimeOut
home page.

Small online guides are like a good friend

The large, commercial city guides have one major downside; they are large and commercial. Sometimes they feel a little stilted — kind of like your mother trying to tell you what's cool. For example, say you're headed to San Francisco to make a business contact and relax for a few days. Aside from a short stint on the Haight in 1969, you haven't a clue what's going on in the city by the Bay. But you're still hip and want to find some good nightlife. San Francisco Sidewalk (`sanfrancisco.sidewalk.com`) offers some insight, but seems a bit sterile.

Instead of missing out, I recommend doing a search on one of the search engines to find some less commercial city guides. Virtually every city has a host of guides maintained by local people, some are for profit (they sell ads) and others are created just for the fun of it.

Using city guides that aren't part of huge, multimillion-dollar initiatives has the following advantages:

- ✔ **A small guide may have an opinionated, local viewpoint.** Only someone who hangs out regularly in a club really knows what the scene is like. Critics from a commercial guide probably visit only once. The same holds true for restaurants and other venues; locally produced guides are full of insider advice.

- ✔ **A small guide can cater to a specific type of traveler.** A guide produced by a young Web aficionado speaks to young people better than a guide produced by a middle-aged, baby-boomer.

- ✔ **Many small guides have no annoying advertising.** Because commercial guides depend on advertising dollars to pay the bills, they often inundate you with all sorts of ads. Small, local guides are generally produced just for love and won't annoy you with pop-up ads.

- ✔ **Small guides have the ability to cover more off-beat topics.** Guides come in all shapes and sizes. Some guides just talk about bars. Some just talk about restaurants. Some just talk. It's all up to the person creating the guide.

Because the smaller city guides don't generally have an advertising budget, you're probably not going to have their names on the tip of your tongue. Yahoo! (`www.yahoo.com`), the ubiquitous Web directory, provides one of the best tools for locating the wide range of city guides. You can either enter your search words directly into the search box (San Francisco guide, for example) or click the Travel heading to drill down through Yahoo's directories.

I usually frame my search terms in quotation marks, which limits the search to the exact words entered into the search box — this method works in most search engines and directories.

The epitome of efficiency: MetaCrawler

MetaCrawler (www.metacrawler.com) is perhaps the most powerful search engine on the Web. Instead of maintaining its own database of Web sites and newsgroups, MetaCrawler simultaneously searches the databases of Yahoo!, Infoseek, Lycos, Excite, AltaVista and others. The results are then organized by relevance. I've had excellent results with MetaCrawler when searching for travel information.

To use MetaCrawler, click the Power Search link on the left of the page to customize the search parameters to your needs. You can also launch the MiniCrawler, which opens a small browser window that you can keep open while you search. And if you get bored, see what other people are currently searching using the MetaSpy — but beware; some of the search terms can be naughty.

Also keep your eyes open for local street papers that have Web sites; these are often very useful for getting the flavor of a city. The same type of searches on Yahoo! or a search engine should turn these up, or see Chapter 5 for more detailed info on using online newspapers to get travel info.

The following two Web sites provide great examples of these smaller, intimate city guides (and they come in really handy if you just happen to be planning a trip to Boston or San Francisco).

Cave Mole's Guide to Boston

You can get a feel for the tone of Cave Mole's Guide to Boston (www.junie.com/cavemole.htm) by reading the attached disclaimer: "Yes, this page is a one person operation, if I'm a little slow with the updates, it's because I am out trying to maintain some semblance of a life." Since she has no advertisers to please, the producer of this irreverent guide doesn't hold back her true feelings about the bars, clubs, and other places she reviews. If she doesn't like a place (and she has problems with many), you know it immediately.

SF Station

SF Station (sfstation.com/), Figure 1-5, is my favorite guide to the Bay Area. The site's stated mission is "to utilize the tools of technology and the Internet to bind the community of San Francisco together." SF Station draws on the vast pool of resources in the Bay Area (lots of good Web designers live out there) to produce a very slick, very useful guide to the San Francisco area.

SF Station has many of the same features as do the big city guide network sites, but in addition captures more of the essence of San Francisco with its editorial advice and cutting edge design. This independent city guide gives you the best of both worlds; a very comprehensive, searchable database with lots of local flavor. Though independent guides that can do both are somewhat of a rarity, more and more are being produced in cities 'round the world.

Figure 1-5:
The
SF Station
home page.

Show Me the Way! Destination Guides Abound on the Web

Whether you're headed to England or New England, or just poking around for cool places to visit, you can find many sites on the Web devoted to guiding travelers to all sorts of destinations. Old-fashioned paper guides can't even begin to compete with the capabilities of a digital guidebook (except that the offline versions are more portable). In contrast to the online city guides, online destination guides cover entire countries and are geared solely towards travelers.

Like all information on the Web, destination guides offer the following features that set them apart from offline destination guides:

✔ **They save you money.** Although you could go out and buy a guidebook for each place you're interested in visiting, almost every online guide-book is free of charge.

✔ **They feature full color photos.** Brochures have just a few enticing photos, at best. Get a true feel for your destination with online slide shows, Webcams, and virtual tours. (Chapter 11 tells you more about Webcams.)

✔ **They are available 24 hours, seven days a week.** Whenever wander-lust strikes, the Internet provides instant gratification. Try finding a travel agent at four in the morning.

✔ **They give you access to exotic and unusual destinations.** Even if you are searching for info about a tiny island in the middle of nowhere, chances are you can find at least a few pages about it on the Web.

✔ **They are more up to date.** Most offline destination guides come out only once a year, but the online guides can be updated anytime, most of them offering new content every day.

Destinations 'r' us

In the past few years, many sites have been developed to guide travelers to destinations around the globe. You can find quality destination information primarily at three types of sites:

✔ Guidebook sites that complement a line of printed travel literature, such as the Lonely Planet guidebooks (www.lonelyplanet.com.au). (See the next section about online guides with books to match.)

✔ Destination directories that are used as guides to the vast destination information on the Internet — City.Net (city.net) is one of the best.

✔ Full service online travel agencies often have complete online guide-books as part of their sites — LeisurePlanet (www.leisureplanet. com/TravelGuides/Travelguide.asp) is a good example.

None of these types of guides are inherently superior to the other. I gener-ally use a combination of all three to give me a feel for the destination. Because I always try to travel on the cheap, I usually start with Lonely Planet Online, guides that are designed for budget, independent travelers. These guides also have good lists of Web links, for further researching.

If you don't know the first thing about a potential destination, start with a well-established, professional guide that can provide an overview, and then move on to smaller, non-commercial guides that can provide more focused and diverse info.

Online guides with books to match

If you're an experienced traveler, you may have a line of offline guidebooks that you use and have grown to trust. The good news is, your esteemed series of travel literature is probably published in one form or another on the WWW. The bad news is, your computer is really heavy and not very fun to travel with. (See Chapter 13 for info about using laptops and staying connected while traveling.)

In all seriousness, virtually every successful travel series has a Web site; some offer more free information than others. For example, Rough Guides (`www.roughguides.com`), a popular line of guidebooks, offers their complete guides, totally unabridged, on the Web, while Fodor's offers only a portion of their offline content online.

Fodor's Guides

Fodor's Guides (`www.fodors.com/`), Figure 1-6, have been around for 60 years and are now the largest publisher of English-language travel information in the world.

While the Fodor's site doesn't come close to covering the enormous number of destinations that their print guidebooks cover, the site does allow you to design your own guides to 99 of the most popular vacation destinations. You choose the specific info you want included and the custom guides draw from a database of detailed and professionally written advice from the Fodor's staff. The site also has a massive database to help you find hotels, B&Bs (bed and breakfasts), and restaurants. Or drop in on one of the discussion forums and connect with other travelers.

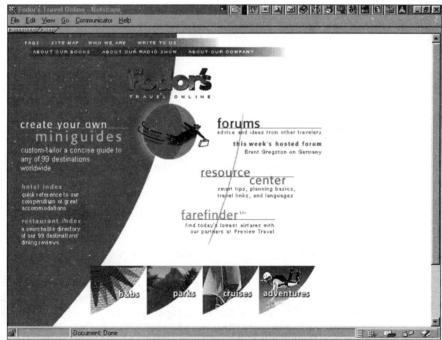

Figure 1-6:
The Fodor's
home page.

To access any of the information about the 99 destinations on the Fodor's site, you must click Create Your Own Miniguide on the home page. Then follow these steps:

1. **Pick a destination from the alphabetical list.**

2. **Select the types of info you wish to retrieve about the destination.**

   Your choices include Where to Stay, Fodor's Top Picks (editors' choices for activities and sights), Eating Out, Essential Information (travel tips and contacts), and destination overviews. Click the boxes beside each choice to select. You can choose one, all, or some.

3. **Click Continue.**

4. **Select the price range and other factors you desire for your accommodations, or select to view Fodor's choices for the destination.**

   You must make similar choices for the other categories of info.

5. **When you're all set, click Create My Miniguide.**

   The result is a guide tailored to your needs.

Although currently you can't reach the hotel and restaurant properties listed on the site directly from Fodor's online (there are no links), try searching for the name of the hotel in a search engine (use quotations around your search term) to see whether the hotel has a Web site of its own.

Lonely Planet Online

First published in 1973 with a single guidebook to Southeast Asia, Lonely Planet guides (www.lonelyplanet.com.au/lp.htm), Figure 1-7, are now absolutely ubiquitous among backpackers and independent travelers all over the world.

These books have reached Bible status because they are exceptionally well-written and useful. The same can be said for Lonely Planet Online. And, while the site certainly provides information with independent travelers in mind, Lonely Planet Online is an extremely useful starting point for anyone looking to get a handle on a destination.

Click the Destinations sections and you are presented with a map of the world and a search box. After you zero in on your destination, you see that Lonely Planet's often imitated, budget traveler-oriented style background and touring advice is laid out in a simple text format. Each guide also contains terrific photography interspersed in the selection. And at the end of each online guide is a link list of geographically related Lonely Planet guides and the subWWWay, a useful list of links to other Web resources for your destination.

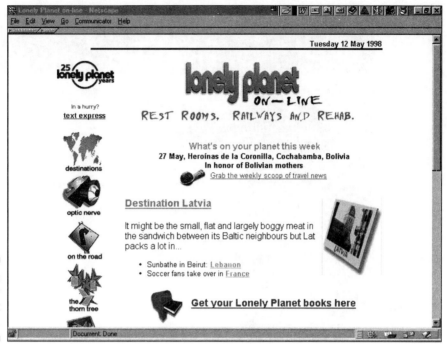

Figure 1-7:
The Lonely
Planet
home page.

Also, check out Lonely Planet Online's other sections for destination info and general travel advice: On the Road (travel literature), The Thorn Tree (a very active forum where travelers, primarily of the backpacking variety, post their questions and observations), and Health (surprise! this section talks about health issues).

The Rough Guide to Travel

After years of residence on the Wired Magazine site, the Rough Guide to Travel (www.roughguides.com/Travel), Figure 1-8, finally has its own URL and a snazzy site all its own.

The Rough Guides publish an excellent print guidebook series that decided to take an innovative approach to complement its print guidebooks — it publishes the entire, unabridged versions of all its travel guides (more than 100 titles) online, free of charge.

Rough Guide to Travel is divided into a travel guide and a travel magazine. To find a destination in the travel guide portion of the site, follow these steps:

1. **Click the Go to Rough Guides Search to bring up the search page or enter a keyword directly into the box provided for a quick search.**

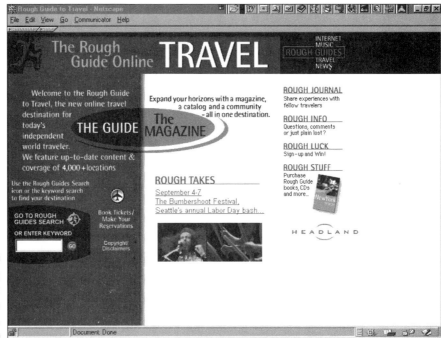

Figure 1-8:
The Rough
Guide home
page.

2. **From the pull-down menus, select the country, city, or state for which you want info.**

   You can also select from a menu of places that Rough Guide recommends or just enter keywords or destinations. When you have the search ready, click the corresponding Go button to perform the search.

   Each country, state, or region that has its own guide page starts with a written overview of the country or state, with a few photos. From there, use the labeled icons on the top of the overview to navigate through the various types of destination info. Lodging, dining, nightlife (called scene), and other aspects of travel have their own sections — some are quite brief, but usually give a feel for that aspect of the destination. You also find a link to the Journal section, a discussion forum for travelers to converse about the destinations.

To use the magazine portion of the site, click Magazine in the center of the home page. The magazine consists of features articles related to the travel experience, usually with somewhat offbeat topics. When I visited, I read an article about the quirky, seldom visited sides of London, a visit to the Gaza Strip, and a story about the wildlife in South Africa (bats!).

Using online travel agencies' destination guides

The major online travel agencies have recognized that in order to be successful, they need to provide travelers with as many resources as possible, all in one place. They have spent huge amounts of money and time developing not only state-of-the-art booking applications, but also online guidebooks where their customers can shop around for trips and destinations. Many of the major sites have partnerships with established travel guides and draw on this content for their own guide sections.

The agency sites constitute another excellent source of destination information. You probably won't find exotic or unusual destinations described in great detail, but these guides are certainly valuable for the early stages of a search or to get a feel for a place.

Many of these online travel agencies also have areas where you can connect with other travelers and travel experts in chat rooms. (Read more about chat rooms in Chapter 12.)

Expedia's World Guide

Expedia (expedia.msn.com/wg/), Figure 1-9, may have the best site design of all the major online agencies.

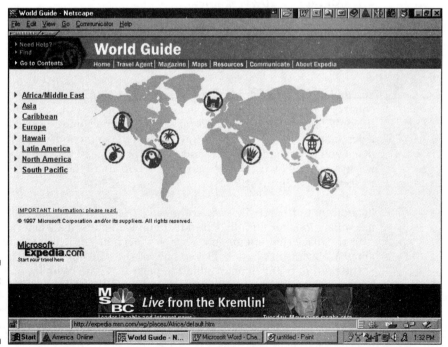

Figure 1-9:
The World Guide page for Hawaii.

You find the destination information in two main sections. The first is the World Guide, which includes about 300 popular destinations. The World Guide covers all your favorite vacation regions with its attractively designed guide pages. You can find basic background information, travel essentials, and some nice photography.

The second area on Expedia for exploring places that strike your fancy is the Worldwide Links, an enormous index of links to destination info on the Internet. Use the alphabetical listing to find places as obscure as Malawi, Africa, and as familiar as New York City (only sometimes I'm not sure which is more exotic). This index contains at least 10,000 links.

Internet Travel Network's Travel Guide

Internet Travel Network's (ITN's) Travel Guide (`www.itn.net/cgi/get?style/public/tg_index`) draws its destination information from the World Travel Guide, a factual and somewhat basic collection of information.

This guide is a good stop if you just need to know some facts about a country, such as a short history, an overview of the types of available accommodations, and the names of the primary resort areas. Don't expect a lot of editorial advice. Use the world map to find the region of your interest.

You also get the writings of Lee Foster, an award winning travel writer, and some valuable links to other Web resources. Everyone loves a valuable link!

LeisurePlanet's Travel Guides

LeisurePlanet's Travel Guides (`www.leisureplanet.com/TravelGuides/Travelguide.asp`), Figure 1-10, is one of my personal favorite destination guides, primarily because of its fantastic and quick-loading slide shows for its many featured destinations.

You find a ton of well-informed and professional travel writing here about a country's background, climate, accommodation, health, and other info. Use the pull-down menus (those boxes with the arrows on the right side) to find a destination or use the box below the pull-down menu to search for the place you have in mind. Then press Go. You can also browse through the world's regions by using the links on the bottom of the page that correspond to your area of interest.

In addition to the terrific slide shows, Leisure Planet offers you live views of many locations around the world through Webcams, live cameras set up all over the place that update images every few minutes. (You can read more about Webcams in Chapter 11.) You get to the cams by clicking the Cam logo at the bottom of the main destination page . . . if you're lucky, maybe you'll see someone you know!

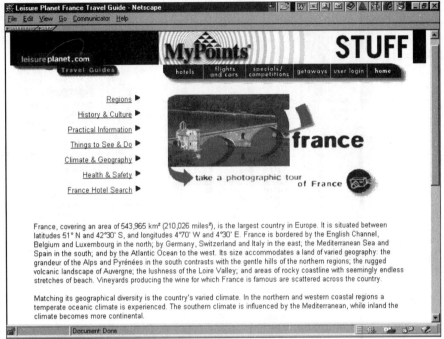

Figure 1-10:
The
LeisurePlanet
Travel
Guides
home page.

Preview Travel's Destination Guides

You can find Preview Travel (destinations.previewtravel.com), Figure
1-11, on the Web and on AOL. This guide is co-produced with Fodor's Guides
and contains the same, solid travel writing you find on the Fodor's site
(which you can also read about earlier in this chapter). Especially cool is
the Custom Guide option that allows you to create a custom guide by
checking boxes that correspond to the info you desire.

Scroll through the destinations in the box in the center of the home page.
Hit Go! when you find the destination you're looking for. The guide pages
offer in-depth info about all aspects of a trip. You can easily locate restaurants, accommodations, transportation, and practical info. You can also use
the photo gallery and local maps to see where you're headed.

Preview takes its destination guide a step further by providing links that
automatically search the lowest airfares to the destination you're investigating. You can also reserve hotels and cars for each destination with no
problem.

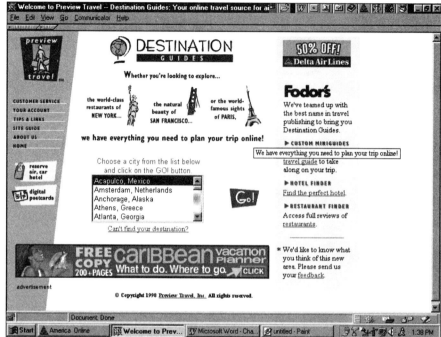

Figure 1-11:
The Preview
Travel
Destination
Guides page.

Travelocity's Destination Guides

Travelocity (www2.travelocity.com/destg/) features Lonely Planet's guidebook information in its destination section — the info is virtually identical to that you find on the Lonely Planet Web site, just arranged a bit differently and not quite as in-depth. Use the map of the world to find your place of interest. The guide pages feature tabs at the top of the page (as in your address book) that denote the different varieties of information. Clicking a tab opens that section.

Travelocity's guide pages do not offer the same level of detail found on the Lonely Planet Online Web site, but offer more of an overview. But you can get a good feel for the place and then go and check the price of a ticket — or move on to another guide when you find a place you dig.

Ladies and Gentlemen, Start Your (Search) Engines

The major search engines have evolved into more than just searchable databases. You can still use them to search for any destination on the planet, but now they have built specific travel sections where you can find out about various places you may want to visit. The large search engines offer the following features:

- ✔ **LookSmartTravel** (`www.looksmart.com`): At LookSmart, you start with broad terms, such as travel and vacations, and drill down to specific terms, such as a specific destination. After you get to the country or city you're interested in, you are presented with a list of sites that relate to the topic.

- ✔ **Infoseek Travel Channel** (`www.infoseek.com/Travel/`): The Places to Visit section of Infoseek allows you to choose from a list of general travel directory sites containing destinaton guides or to use Infoseek's hierachical directory of regions and countries to find your exact place of interest. For example, the listing for Asia contains a list of subjects about Asia. Choosing Travel brings you to a list of sites about Asia travel with short reviews.

- ✔ **Lycos World City Guide** (`cityguide.lycos.com`): Lycos presents you with a clickable world map. As you may have guessed, you click the region you're interested in to bring you to a more detailed map that eventually leads you to a city guide. This city guide is composed of a few paragraphs of descriptive text and a list of links broken down into categories. The links are not necessarily exclusively for the city; they may pertain to the country as a whole.

- ✔ **Yahoo! Travel** (`travel.yahoo.com/`): The Yahoo! travel section uses content from various well-known travel publications to provide its travel section with gusto. The destination info is the same you find at the Lonely Planet Web site, but in addition, Yahoo! provides current weather reports for most destinations, a destination spotlight that's updated often by way of National Geographic Traveler (see Chapter 5), and articles about categories of activity and lifestyle travel, courtesy of *Travel and Leisure* magazine.

Pointing You in the Right Direction: Destination Directories

Editors who are experts on the travel resources on the Web compile online destination directories. These wonderful people spend all their time scouring the Web for the best resources and then cataloging them so you can access the solid information quickly and easily.

A good destination directory points you to a large variety of sites, all of which have been deemed worthwhile for a traveler researching a trip or vacation.

Destination directories lead you to many diverse types of sites, including the following:

✔ Official country sites (governmental sites, visa, customs and passport info, and so on)

✔ Maps and weather information sites

✔ Culture and language information sites

✔ Lodging sites

✔ General travel and tourism sites

By using destination directories as a starting point, you always know where to quickly find destination info for any country or city. After you know a few good starting points, you can easily surf on to more related sites by using links. When you find a good piece of information, either add a bookmark to your browser's files, or print out the information and compile your own guidebook. (I talk more about bookmarking in Chapter 15.)

The following two guides are great resources to use when you want to find quality Web sites that pertain to a destination.

City.Net

One of the most useful starting points for a traveler researching a destination is Excite's City.Net (`city.net`), Figure 1-12. City.Net has listings for over 5,000 destinations. You can either search for a specific destination or browse the listings by clicking the map of the world.

City.Net provides links to high quality content on the Internet, broken down into categories (Government, Newspapers, Travel and Tourism, and more). The top of each guide page has links that move you through that specific guide page.

I usually go right for the Travel and Tourism link, which leads me to an editor's choices for online guides pertaining to the selected country or city. Click these links and you move out onto the Web, away from City.Net, to an online destination guide about your place of interest.

I use City.Net all the time when I'm trying to get a feel for what's out there on the Internet for a specific destination. When I visit City.Net, I know that, at the very least, it points me to a few excellent destination guides, from which I surf onward using links provided by that guide. City.Net also features current weather and maps for many destinations as part of the site — useful for all sorts of journeys.

Figure 1-12:
The City.Net
home page.

NetGuide's TravelGuide

NetGuide (www.netguide.com/Travel), Figure 1-13, as you may guess from the name, is a guide to the best content on the Internet. The travel section, which holds a special place in my heart (I am the former producer), has an ever-expanding list of destinations in the section called Destinations.

Click your destination and NetGuide presents you with a short article that contains links to noteworthy and valuable sites about that country or city. Within each article about a destination are hand-picked links to outstanding destination guides on the Web. The article also describes what to expect from each site, so you don't waste time surfing to sites that won't provide the travel guidance you're looking for.

The TravelPage

The TravelPage (www.travelpage.com/dest.htm), Figure 1-14, is a comprehensive resource for travelers, developing original travel content as well as pointing you to other sites that provide travel information. In the Destinations section you choose your destination from a world map.

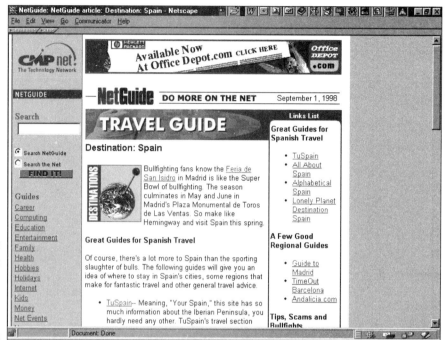

Figure 1-13:
The
NetGuide
TravelGuide
home page.

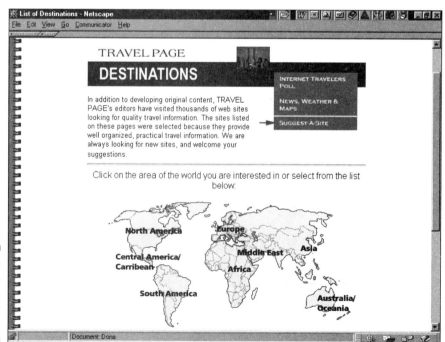

Figure 1-14:
The
TravelPage
Destinations
page.

Your destination has links chosen by the TravelPage's editors. I like the choices because they point to a wide range of sites that describe different cities in the countries listed, ensuring a wide breadth of info.

Yahoo! Travel Directory

Yahoo! (www.yahoo.com/Recreation/Travel/), Figure 1-15, is my hands-down favorite way to find destination guides and travel information on the Web, simply because of its completeness. Almost every site worth its server has a listing on this king of Web directories.

After clicking Travel on the main Yahoo! page, go to the Regional section to find listings for countries and cities. Countries have individual listings. Or you can drill down through the regional directories to find the place you're looking for. Because Yahoo! doesn't represent an editor's top choices, you may end up sifting through more sites than you'd like, but Yahoo! is the most complete listing of destination related sites on the Internet.

Figure 1-15: The Yahoo! Travel Directory page.

Chapter 2

From Laptop to Tabletop: Finding Restaurants

● ●

In This Chapter

▶ Using search engines and directories to find eateries

▶ Reading restaurant review databases

▶ Getting restaurant advice from people on the Internet

▶ Locating restaurants for people with special diets

● ●

*T*raveling sure works up an appetite. Lucky for you, people all over the world eat food and operate restaurants where you can get a square meal. The days of wishing you knew a good restaurant in Chicago or Paris are over. The Internet is full of resources that find and tell you about restaurants all over the world.

Sizing Up the Field: Using Search Engines to Locate Restaurants

No doubt this section will make you hungry. Search engines are an all-important Web resource that are the key to finding everything on the Web — and restaurants are no exception.

A well-aimed search on a search engine reveals everything from individual restaurants' Web pages to citywide restaurant directories and databases. The following sections show you a sample search on three major search engines.

Seeking nourishment on Infoseek

You can use the search technique I show you in this section on just about any search engine. All the search engines are fairly similar; I focus on Infoseek here because I find it easy to use and I like some of its features for restaurants a little more than those of some of the other engines.

Other search engines behave in much the same fashion as Infoseek, so it pays to try your search on a few engines just to see how the results differ — unless you're getting really hungry and need to just go eat.

The following technique turns up everything that Infoseek can find about restaurants in your destination area. This type of search can be very helpful if you aren't sure what kind of establishment you're looking for:

1. **On the Infoseek home page, type the name of the city you're interested in and the word** restaurants, **both words preceded by the + sign. You can also try framing the search words in quotation marks.**

   For example, say you're looking for restaurants in Chicago. Try typing **+Chicago +restaurants**. The plus signs tell the search engine to retrieve pages that have both terms, but not necessarily next to each other. You can also try **"Chicago restaurants"** in the search box. This searches for pages that have the two words next to each other and generally returns a smaller number of hits.

   Notice that I put a space between **+Chicago** and **+restaurants**. This space lets the search engine know that it needs to search for two words. If you don't use the space, the search will probably return nothing or gibberish.

2. **Click Search.**

   The search returns all the pages it can find that contain these two words together. In this case, the search returns over 700 listings for restaurants in Chicago (Figure 2-1). Of course, you may appreciate the number of listings if you truly want to see everything that's out there.

3. **If desired, narrow your search.**

   Infoseek offers you a few different ways to narrow the field a little:

   • **Click the Best Bets link at the top of the page:** The Best Bets links are comprised of topics related to your search terms and can help you narrow your search.

   • **Search the returns:** Above the search box on your results page, you see two small check boxes, one labeled New Search and the other one Search Only Within These Pages. Click the latter option and enter a search term into the search box.

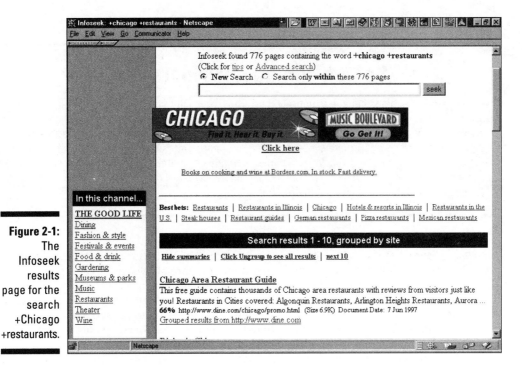

Figure 2-1:
The
Infoseek
results
page for the
search
+Chicago
+restaurants.

For example, maybe you want to find a place to eat some of Chicago's famous deep dish pizza. Enter Pizza into the box, click the Search Only Within These Pages option, and click Search. Your results will all have the word Pizza in them and it will be a much more manageable list.

- **Start a new search using more specific keywords:** Using the search methods described in the first step, add words to narrow your search to specifics. Perhaps you are looking for restaurants in a specific neighborhood. Try searching **+Lincoln Park +Chicago +restaurants** to find eateries in that Chicago neighborhood. Now you're getting much closer to some sites you can sink your teeth into.

Yahoo! for food

Basically, you can use the same search technique on Yahoo! as you do on Infoseek (see the preceding section for the details). However, if you do your search using Yahoo! (www.yahoo.com), you may come up with better results. Yahoo! usually provides the best results when doing a general restaurant search because it's a directory and not a true search engine.

Search engine idiosyncrasies

No two search engines behave in entirely the same way. While variety is the spice of life, it would be very nice if the same search procedures worked the same in every search engine. If you plan on using the Web for any significant amount of time, I highly recommend spending a bit of time and clicking the Search

Tips, Help, and Advanced Search Help buttons that all search engines (including Yahoo!) have next to their search boxes. I guarantee that the more you know about how these search engines operate, the more efficient your time on the Web will be.

But what does this directory business mean? Well, the folks at Yahoo! put the listings into categories; then their software allows you to search the categories, either by searching for keywords (as in a search engine) or by moving through the hierarchies of categories and subcategories until you find the specifics you are searching for. In contrast to search engines (like Infoseek) that compile the site listings in their database by automation, the listings in Yahoo! are submitted by Web masters and evaluated by Yahoo! producers. The result is a database of high-quality sites with a minimum of chaff.

The +**Chicago** +**restaurants** search on Yahoo! returns category listings and site listings (Figure 2-2). The Yahoo! search also returns entries with the words Chicago AND restaurants, some of which may be helpful. Read the short descriptions before you click the entries. (I think I hear your stomach rumbling.)

Let your stomach do the walking: The Yellow Pages

Another great place to find restaurants in the U.S. is the online yellow pages, called BigYellow (www.bigyellow.com).

BigYellow is produced by Bell Atlantic, one of the largest telephone companies in the U.S., and has cataloged businesses from every state in America into a single database. For hungry travelers on the go, BigYellow functions very well as a means to find basic info (addresses and phone numbers) for specific types of restaurants in any city or town.

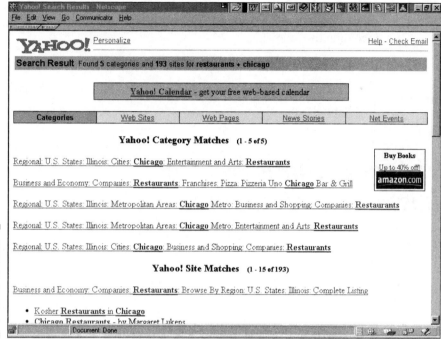

Follow these steps to search BigYellow for restaurant information:

1. **Under Big Topics, click Dining.**

   You find this link under the Big Topics heading on the left side of the page.

2. **In the Find Dining search box at the top of the page, select a type of food and a location.**

3. **Click Find it!**

   BigYellow presents you with the fruit of your labor. BigYellow's restaurant listings contain the names, addresses, and phone numbers of all the establishments that meet your chosen criteria.

To generate a map for directions to a selected restaurant, click the little graphic of the Earth that precedes each listing. The restaurant is marked by a red X on the map. You can zoom in and out for more or less detail by clicking Zoom In or Zoom Out (makes sense, no?).

Unfortunately, the restaurants listed in BigYellow are not reviewed, but you do get contact information and the site generates maps so you can locate the restaurants. (If you're interested in finding a review of the restaurant, check out the next section, "Virtual Feeding Frenzy: Restaurant Databases.")

In addition to BigYellow, all the major search engines have links to similar directories that can also locate basic listings for restaurants around the U.S., including the following:

- ✔ Infoseek Yellow Pages (`yp.microsoft.com/infoseek`)
- ✔ Lycos/Excite Yellow Pages by GTE (`yp.gte.net/sform.phtml`)
- ✔ Yahoo! (`yp.yahoo.com`)

Virtual Feeding Frenzy: Restaurant Databases

A while back someone had the brilliant idea to gather together as much information about restaurants as possible, city by city, compile it into a database, and then publish that database on the Web for travelers to use. Since the initial idea, uncountable numbers of restaurant databases have come into existence. Some are the products of well-known guidebook companies with large staffs of editors and critics, and others are the brain-child of one person that really loves sushi restaurants.

These databases vary in terms of quality of the reviews and the frequency of the listing updates, but most of these restaurant databases contain one or more of the following features:

- ✔ Reviews
- ✔ Menus
- ✔ Locations and maps
- ✔ Phone numbers for reservations

And the best part about a database — it's searchable. So if you find yourself in Portland, Oregon with a craving for Indian food, you can turn to one of the restaurant directories and a find a nearby restaurant in your budget. You can usually search for a restaurant a number of ways:

- ✔ By cuisine type
- ✔ By location
- ✔ By price range
- ✔ By amenities
- ✔ Alphabetically

The following sites are examples of high quality restaurant databases. Though each is produced with a slightly different working philosophy, all can find you a place to eat (and maybe even a film to see afterward). Also, check the Online Travel Planning For Dummies Internet Directory of Web sites in this book for more excellent restaurant guides.

CuisineNet

Although CuisineNet (www.cuisinenet.com), Figure 2-3, covers only 16 cities within the United States (including Atlanta, Houston, Los Angeles, and New York), it's the prototype for a slick and useful restaurant database.

The reviews in CuisineNet are written and edited by professionals, and I have found their reviews to be quite trustworthy. If you plan to visit (or live in) one of the cities covered by CuisineNet, your taste buds will thank you for a visit to this site.

To search the database for the perfect restaurant, just follow these steps:

1. **Choose a city by clicking the graphic that represents the city.**

   The appropriate city page appears offering the following search options:

   • The default setting allows you to perform a search using your own criteria. Use the search box to search by cuisine, location, price, restaurant name, or amenities. You can also check a box if you want the search to return only restaurants with online menus.

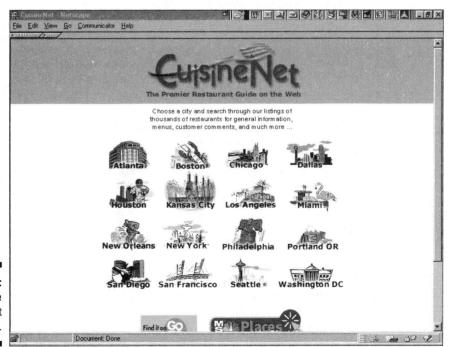

Figure 2-3:
The
CuisineNet
home page.

- Using the tab above the search area, click Alphabetical to see a complete listing for the city listed — you guessed it — alphabetically.

- Click the Top Picks tab to see a weekly selection of CuisineNet picks for a certain topic — when I last visited it was Top Picks for Dinner and Movie experiences.

- Click the Browse by Cuisine tab to select a genre of cuisine. You can then browse the reviews.

2. **Select your search method and then click Search.**

   Your search returns a list of restaurants; a short description of each restaurant tells you its price range, address and phone number, and customer ratings by number.

   Click the restaurant's link and you can read a critic's review as well as some actual diners' comments (feel free to post your own).

   If your search returned a large number of restaurants, you can sort them to reflect your preferences using the button above the listings. Choices include Restaurant Name (default, alphabetical), by Food Rating, and by Price. Click the corresponding button to reorganize the list.

Each city's restaurants page also offers the following links on the navigation bar at the top of the page:

- **Café:** Read entertaining and factual articles with names like "Cream Soda: A Love Story" to "The Trouble with Truffles."

- **Digest:** The Diner's Digest provides info about various aspects of the food experience. Read about famous chefs, ingredients, and, the most important meal of the day, breakfast.

- **Market:** Buy stuff from the famous eateries of your selected city.

- **Search:** Brings you back to the home page.

Feel free to add your own reviews of restaurants that exist in the database, or create a new listing if you don't find your favorite restaurant listed. On the city's search page, click the Recommend a Restaurant tab. You then need to fill out a survey. When you complete the survey, click the Submit Survey button. You are now a restaurant critic.

Fodor's (also known as Food-or's)

For a global culinary experience, your pals at Fodor's Guides (www.fodors.com/ri.cgi), Figure 2-4, are hard to beat. Fodor's database of restaurants covers all 99 worldwide destinations that its well-known travel guidebooks cover.

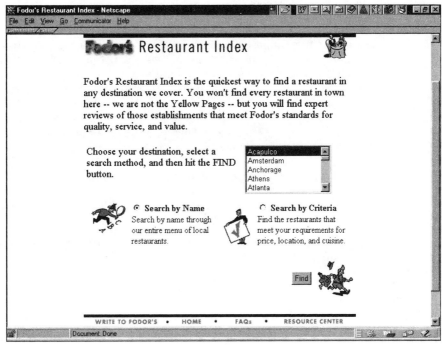

Figure 2-4:
The Fodor's
Restaurant
Index home
page.

You can search by a variety of criteria and every restaurant has a review, a fact that few of the big restaurant directories can boast of. To find restaurants on the Fodor's site, follow these steps:

1. **Click the Restaurant Index at the bottom left corner of the home page.**

2. **Select a city or region from the scroll down list.**

3. **Choose whether you want to search by criteria (such as location, price, or cuisine) or by restaurant name by clicking the boxes next to these two choices.**

4. **Click the Find button.**

   If you choose to search by criteria, the next screen gives you a choice of locations, price ranges, and cuisine. Select your choices by clicking the boxes next to the criterion. Then click Find to search the database.

   If you chose to search by name, Fodor's retrieves an alphabetical listing of eateries in the selected city.

   When you have a list of restaurants, click the name of the restaurant to access the review with contact information. A red star denotes a highly recommended restaurant.

The Sushi World Guide

In addition to commercial restaurant databases, you can tap into loads of small, independent, online restaurant guides. Often, one person with a passion for food produces such a database. These smaller restaurant guides don't cover as many restaurants, but the info is not filtered by an editor with an eye on the bottom line, so the reviews are the heartfelt opinion of the site's producer (for better or for worse). The Sushi World Guide (sushi.to), Figure 2-5, is a good example of this type of guide, providing guidance on the world's best sushi restaurants.

To find a good sushi restaurant at the Guide, follow these steps:

1. **Click the link called The Restaurants — it's labeled The heart of this web site.**

2. **From the list of regions, on the left side of the page, select where you want to find raw fish.**

3. **Select a country and a city.**

   The site presents a list of the appropriate restaurants in alphabetical order. Click the restaurant name to see the review. A red box next to the name means that the info has been updated recently.

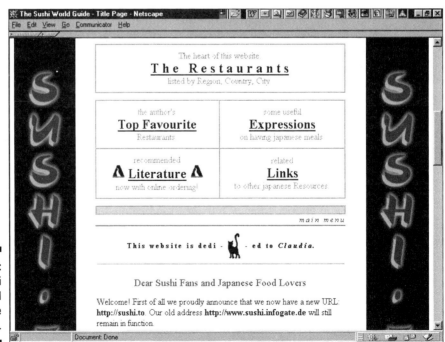

Figure 2-5:
The Sushi
World
Guide home
page.

The restaurant listings contain, at the very least, the address and phone number. Most have one or more reviews by the Sushi World Guide Crew or written in by devotees of the restaurant. Some even have links to more info. To return to the home page, scroll to the bottom of the page.

Please Recommend a Good Restaurant

The Internet is a community. Rest assured, someone in the community knows the perfect restaurant for you and yours to enjoy on your travels. But how do you know who to ask? You can't just send an e-mail out into Cyberspace asking for a good Italian restaurant in London. But you can post a question about Italian restaurants in London to a Usenet newsgroup and hope for responses.

People new to the Internet often overlook newsgroups. Although these online forums are one of the oldest components of the Internet, because of the Web's popularity and media attention, you may not realize how active and useful newsgroups still are for finding out firsthand information about restaurants. (For detailed instructions on how to use the Usenet, consult Chapter 12.)

Extra! Extra! Eat all about it

Most daily and weekly newspapers have restaurant sections where their critics review a wide range of eateries. And nowadays, most newspapers have a Web site where reviews are archived.

To find restaurant reviews in local online newspapers, you first need to find the local online newspapers. The following two sites locate papers all across the globe and are very easy to use:

✔ **AJR NewsLink** (www.newslink.org/news.html): Go to this site to find links to nearly every online newspaper in the world, from *The New York Times* to college campus monthlies.

✔ **Newspapers Online** (www.newspapers.com/): Another comprehensive newspaper resource. If it's published online, you can find a link for it here.

After you find a newspaper that covers your destination, you need to find the section that has the restaurant reviews. Many papers' online sites have an actual dining section. If you don't see a section devoted exclusively to eating, try the Living, Entertainment, or Guide sections.

For more about online reading material, take a look at Chapter 5.

The following sections detail a few useful restaurant newsgroups on Usenet and how to find them.

Deja News and rec.food.restaurants

Your best bet for finding someone online to recommend a restaurant is a popular newsgroup called `rec.food.restaurants`. The postings in this newsgroup are frequent and the participants knowledgeable. Basically, the ingredients are fresh!

Chapter 12 explains the nuts and bolts of using newsgroups, but if you already know your stuff, I recommend using Deja News (`www.dejanews.com`) to find newsgroups that pertain to restaurants. You can search in Deja News to find restaurant related discussion forums (such as newsgroups) or use its newsreader capabilities to read and post to `rec.food.restaurants` (or any other forum).

`Rec.food.restaurants` is full of people discussing places to eat in a variety of cities and countries. Post your own questions or answer others if you know a good restaurant.

Newsgroups for specific locales or cuisines

You can also access newsgroups in which people discuss eateries in a specific city or a certain type of cuisine. On the Deja News home page, click Interest Finder (a feature that finds discussion forums about a given topic), enter **Restaurants** into the search box, and click Search. Deja News then returns a list of newsgroups in which people are discussing restaurants.

A sampling of restaurant-related newsgroups:

- `seattle.eats`: Discusses Seattle restaurants.
- `la.eats`: Covers Los Angeles restaurants.
- `rec.food.veg`: Talks about where to find good veggie eats.
- `alt.food.sushi`: You guessed it! Sushi restaurants.
- `alt.food.barbeque`: Barbecue is tasty!

In addition to newsgroups that were created just for discussions of food and eateries, you can also gather info from the people who participate in forums dedicated to discussions of specific cities or countries. To find such discussion forums, use the Deja News Interest Finder and enter keywords that will find groups about locations. For example, entering "Quebec" into the Interest Finder pulls up many groups, including `soc.culture.quebec`.

Locating Restaurants for Special Diets

Many of you are very particular about what food goes into your body. I'm not talking about finicky eaters who don't like brussels sprouts. I mean vegetarians, folks who have dietary restrictions due to religious convictions, and so on. For you, traveling outside of your community is a greater challenge than for someone like me who eats anything that doesn't eat him first.

With the Internet, you can find the food you like almost anywhere in the world. The following sections offer specific sites for those who are particular about their dining experience. (For more information on finding specific types of restaurants, take a look at the section, "Please Recommend a Good Restaurant" earlier in this chapter. You can use the same methods as you do with search engines and yellow pages to find restaurants that fit your dietary needs.)

Vegetarians

Traveling as vegetarian can be very challenging in some parts of the world. To avoid having a diet of strictly bread and cheese while traveling, do a little prep work on the Web and find restaurants that cater to veggies before you go.

Those of you who avoid eating animals or animal products should definitely bookmark the following sites:

- ✔ **The World Guide to Vegetarianism** (`www.veg.org/veg/Guide/`): This site has listings of veggie-friendly establishments all over the world — and they're arranged by country. The World Guide to Vegetarianism is the foremost vegetarian guide on the Web.

- ✔ **A Guide to Eating Vegetarian in the United Kingdom** (`www.cms.dmu.ac.uk/~cph/Veg/veg-uk.html?glasgow`): Not a very ornate page, but it is searchable and good for vegetarians headed toward jolly old England.

- ✔ `Rec.food.veg`: This is a Usenet newsgroup devoted to vegetarian eating and lifestyle. A good place to ask for restaurant recommendations. (See Chapter 13 for more on newsgroups.)

- ✔ **Vegetarian Society of Colorado Dining Guide** (`www.vsc.org/dining/`): This guide covers only Colorado.

Kosher

If you keep kosher and like to travel, you simply must bookmark these pages:

- ✔ **The Kosher Restaurant Database** (`www.shamash.org/kosher/krestquery.html`): Search this enormous database of Kosher restaurants worldwide.

- ✔ **Kosher Restaurants in Chicago** (`condor.depaul.edu/~scohn/NTJC-Fd.html`): Surprise — kosher restaurants in Chicago!

- ✔ **KosherLink** (`www.kosherlink.com/`): A database of Kosher restaurants in the New York metropolitan area.

Chapter 3

Vacations for Everyone on the Internet

. . . .

. . . .

*T*ravelers come in all shapes and sizes. The amazing variety of people in the world is well represented on the Internet — no matter who you are or what kind of traveling you like to do, the Internet provides information to help you plan your trip.

In this chapter, I tell you where you can find information to plan a trip that suits your lifestyle. I also explain how to find tour operators and travel agents who can take you on that trip you're dreaming about — whether it be a nice family vacation to Disney World or a decadent, all-inclusive package to Hedonism II in Jamaica.

Getting Professional Assistance for Focused Needs

Sometimes you just want to kick back and have someone do all the planning for your vacation. No running around comparing hotel brochures, trying iffy restaurants, or studying bus maps. You want an all-inclusive vacation or a tour operator (a company that organizes and conducts tours for customers) who can make all the arrangements for you. Or maybe you just want to find a good travel agent who specializes in planning a certain type of trip. Look to the Internet to help you get the travel planning help you need.

Tour operators and travel agents are two different professions, but both have a similar goal: to help you have a good vacation. The Internet is a terrific way to find yourself the right travel agent, the person who can analyze your needs and connect them with the right components of a trip. The same goes for tour operators.

Hundreds and hundreds of travel agents and tour operators have opened up shop on the Web. You need a good directory to browse through the Web pages for many travel professionals, a listing that enables you to check many options all in one place.

The Yahoo! guide to tour operators

Almost every conceivable type of tour known to man (and woman) has a listing on the Yahoo! directory of tour operators (www.yahoo.com/Business_and_Economy/Companies/Travel/Tour_Operators/), Figure 3-1.

Figure 3-1:
The Yahoo!
directory
of tour
operators.

The site arranges the trips by category (the categories include everything from agriculture to whale watching), which makes searching the trips very easy. To find a tour operator to fit your needs, just click through the categories. For example, say you're interested in agriculture; click the Agriculture link. The search results in a listing of agricultural tours all over the world, such as the agricultural safaris in South Africa. Following the agricultural example, click Agricultural Safaris. The link takes you to a page complete with a summary of the tour as well as contact information.

The Yahoo! directory of tour operators presents a very broad listing, but the short descriptions allow you to scan the companies and quickly pick out the ones that fit your needs. Bookmark sites as you go so that you can return easily when you want to compare.

Using professional directories

Some sites have been developed specifically to find you tour operators, resorts, and travel agents online. Most of these sites make a commission by connecting travelers with vacation companies, so professional directory sites make it a policy to work only with quality companies.

Reputability tests

You can usually get an idea of a tour operator's (or any other company's) trustworthiness and competency by looking for a few features on its Web site and asking a couple of questions, including the following:

✔ **Does the company provide its history in an "About Us" page?** While it's true that anyone can make up an illustrious past for themselves, you should still read a company's description of itself. If for no other reason, you may need this description if you consult the professional tourism groups I talk about in the next bullet.

Read with a wary eye towards outlandish claims. Check to see how long the company has been around. If the company is a new startup (just a few months old), you

may want to give them a little time to iron out the kinks.

✔ **Is the company associated with any tourism groups?** The American Society of Travel Agents (ASTA) is one of the biggest travel associations. (For more on ASTA, see "ASTAnet" later in the chapter.) ASTA member agencies are generally reputable and adhere to a code of ethics. If you have a complaint with an ASTA member, you can file a complaint with the organization and it will act on your behalf.

✔ **Ask the company for a client referral list.** Most importantly, talk with other travelers who have used the company's services. A good referral is more valuable than any sales pitch or guarantee.

Travelon

Travelon (`www.travelon.com`), Figure 3-2, bills itself as "Your Guide to the Best in Travel."

The site divides its list of tour operators into three main categories:

- ✔ Adventure and specialty travel
- ✔ Cruises
- ✔ Package vacations

You can search each of the categories for the type of tour operator you want by clicking the appropriate button and then selecting which facilities/activities, what country, and what price range you desire, from the pull-down menus that appear. Travelon searches its database and returns listings for tour operators and resorts that fit the bill.

Figure 3-2:
The
Travelon
home page.

Travelon lists only established travel suppliers (tour operators, resorts, cruises) so you can feel fairly confident that what you see is what you'll get. But as always, when selecting companies to work with, approach with an ounce of skepticism and ask many questions. (See the sidebar "Reputability tests" in this chapter for some hints on how to tell the good companies from the bad guys.)

Resorts Online

Resorts Online (www.resortsonline.com) connects you with resorts all over the world that fit your interest. Choose from the list of resort categories you find on the home page and then click the world map to tell the database where to look for resorts.

When you find a resort that sounds interesting, Resorts Online gives you a link either directly to the resort or to another directory that can give all the details and where you can possibly make reservations online.

Many sites offer the same services as Resorts Online. Check the directory section of this book for more useful tour and resort-finding directories. (Chapter 4 has useful advice for finding vacations and trips geared toward certain activities.)

ASTAnet

Though ASTA stands for the *American* Society of Travel Agents, agents from around the world belong to this mammoth organization; agents and travel professionals from 165 countries to be exact. The motto of ASTA is "Integrity in Travel." ASTA is the largest travel industry trade association (the largest trade association in the world, to be exact) and it holds its members to a high standard.

Because it has so many listings, the ASTA site (www.astanet.com) is one of the most valuable sites on the Web in terms of finding quality travel agents. From the ASTAnet home page, click Travelers to access the information geared towards you, the one doing the traveling (Figure 3-3).

From this page you can access the site's database, which contains over 27,000 listings of travel companies, one of which should match your needs.

To find a travel agent, follow these steps:

1. **In the top-left corner of the Travelers page, click Find a Travel Agent.**

2. **Choose from the pull-down menu which kind of travel company you are looking for.**

3. **Choose a specialty (family travel, for example) and a destination. (Entering a company name and a location are optional.)**

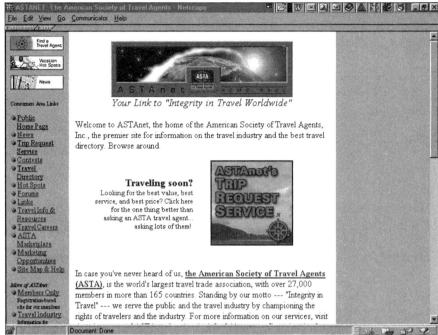

Figure 3-3:
The
ASTAnet
Travelers
page.

The results list the names, addresses, and contact info for the travel agencies that meet your given criteria.

ASTAnet offers more than its database of agents. You also get travel news, travel contests, a directory of travel, and links to travel resources. Find links to this information on the home page.

Resorting to Resorts

Most established resorts have a Web site that you can visit to check out prices, amenities, and photos. A Web site offers a lot more depth than any paper brochure, as the following sites quickly demonstrate. (A quick search on Yahoo! or any of the other major search engines turns up tons of listings for other resorts.)

Club Med online

Club Med (www.clubmed.com), Figure 3-4, is perhaps the most well-known of all-inclusive resort chains. If you are considering a Club Med vacation, the Club Med Web site is a mandatory part of your visit.

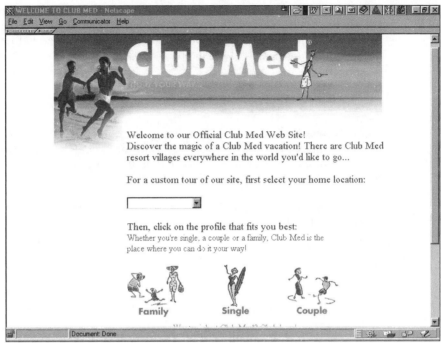

Figure 3-4:
The Club
Med home
page.

The site is extremely easy to use, if a bit slow to load. Follow these steps, clicking Go after each step, to find the right Club Med vacation for you:

1. **Select your home location from the pull-down menu on the home page.**

   The site offers its services in several different languages.

2. **Choose how you want to access the site's information.**

   The second page gives you a few choices of ways to find the right Club Med for you. You can a) pick a specific club from the pull-down menu of Club Med village locations, b) click the Village Directory to find a club that has what you want by selecting from a list of options, or c) click Good Deals to choose from the current Club Med specials.

   After you click Go, the site presents you with a village page. On the right of a village page, you find links to specific types of info about the resort. You also get an overview photo; click More Shots, next to the photo, to see more images of the resort.

You can find out prices, weather, and deals about the resort by clicking the corresponding links at the bottom of the page.

My ideal vacation has a circus school (I desperately need clowning lessons), no children (they scare me), and highly comfortable accommodations (I deserve pampering after this book). The database returned not just one, but a bunch of choices that fit my needs.

Sandals Resorts

Sandals Resorts (www.sandals.com), an "ultra-inclusive" experience, are for couples only. One price pays for everything at Sandals' dozen or so locations. After all, what's more romantic than never having to whip out the credit card to pay for anything?

Select a resort by choosing an island (Sandals has resorts on four Caribbean islands) or by clicking directly on the resort name that interests you. Photos of each resort help with your selection.

If you are in doubt about the romantic nature of these one-price-for-love vacations, check out the Romantic Testimonials. This section offers first-hand experiences from real-life couples. It also has advice on how to plan your Sandals honeymoon; excuse me, "Weddingmoon," as Sandals calls it. Sandals wants you to kill two birds with one stone — get married and have a honeymoon all at a Sandals resort. That's so beautiful, I think I'll cry. (See "Planning Your Honeymoon in the Information Age" to hear more about that.)

Finally, the Sandals site helps you find a travel agent to book your trip (if you live in North America). Enter your zip code for the United States or select a city if you live in Canada (if you live anywhere else, you are out of luck). The database finds expert Sandals agents right in your neighborhood.

Planning Your Honeymoon in the Information Age

Congratulations and *mazel tov*. You're getting married. But what about the honeymoon? You want to make the most of this once in a lifetime opportunity (well, unless you're Johnny Carson or Elizabeth Taylor, and then you get several shots at it) by researching a romantic getaway on the Internet. Pull your love seat up to the monitor and snuggle up close with your honey.

Honeymoons.com

Honeymoons.com (`www.honeymoons.com`) gives you lots of advice about honeymoon planning and the advice is expert, because it comes directly from Susan Wagner, a 15-year veteran of honeymoon planning and the ex-producer of the honeymoon section in *Modern Bride*.

The site focuses on a couple dozen romantic destinations in Mexico and the Caribbean for honeymooners; just click a destination's name on the home page to see the pertinent information.

If you want information about honeymoon possibilities beyond the destinations listed on the home page, this site is probably not going to be a lot of help. However, Ms. Wagner does supply her contact information, and perhaps, if you ask nicely, she can point you in the right direction.

1travel.com honeymoons

1travel.com (`www.1travel.com/honey.htm`), one of the Internet's top travel agencies, has some great honeymoon packages, many of which are very reasonably priced. 1travel is a full-service online travel agency, but the service has carved a nice niche for itself by compiling lists of travel package suppliers and tour operators that specialize in certain types of vacations.

To access the honeymoon listings, scroll to the bottom of the 1travel.com home page to the Specialty links and click on Honeymoon. The 1travel.com honeymoon page contains loads of rental properties, resorts, yachts for hire, cruises, and other amazing-sounding honeymoon ideas. Click any of the listings to get the full scoop on the honeymoon offering and who to contact if you're interested. 1tsravel updates this list frequently so check back to find different trips.

Modern Bride

The Honeymoon Planning section at the *Modern Bride* site (`www.modernbride.com/honeymoonplanning/index.html`) has lots of valuable info to help you in your search for the perfect romantic sojourn. Check out hints about how to avoid travel scams (all travelers benefit from this advice) and the honeymoon FAQ (frequently asked questions list). The site also offers information about popular destinations, B&Bs, budgeting for your honeymoon, and cruises.

Planning Family Vacations Online

Whether you want to pack the family into the minivan and drive to an amusement park or make reservations at Disney World, consult the Internet for some good ideas for airing out the family.

Starting with Yahoo!

If you are just trolling for family travel ideas, I recommend starting your research at that king of directories, Yahoo! (www.yahoo.com). Yahoo! is the best all around directory of topics on the Web, simply because it contains an enormous amount of sites, broken down into categories and subcategories.

Go to the Travel category (www.yahoo.com/Recreation/Travel) and then click Family Travel. You find only about a dozen links here, some relating to advice on how to make your journeys with the kiddies more enjoyable and others that are about destinations and all the other stuff that goes into a family trip. Use these links as a starting point to research family trips.

Yahoo! also has a category specifically listing amusement and theme parks (www.yahoo.com/Entertainment/Amusement_and_Theme_Parks/). Nearly every park with a Web presence has a listing here. This is a terrific way for you and the family to know what to expect from the park and the trip to the park. All the places that kids dig to visit are represented on Yahoo! — zoos, national parks, sports arenas, and so on. Try searching Yahoo! for these and any other keyword that you can think of.

TIP

Stop hitting your sister!
Or, how to make family travel more fun

Maybe you're new to parenting or maybe you just *know* that there *must* be a better way to keep those youngsters entertained and happy during the inevitable boredom of the trip itself. Before you lose your mind playing one more game of 20 Questions, check out some solutions on the Internet:

✔ **Family Fun Magazine's Great Traveling Games** (family.disney.com/Categories/Travel/Features/family_1998_04/famf/famf48games/famf48games9.html): The URL is long, but so are car trips without games. This guide has some good games.

✔ **About Family Vacations and Travel** (www.cyberparent.com/trip): A few good ideas reside here, from drawing charades to some thoughts on how to prepare for trips with the family.

✔ **Sesame Street's Travel Boredom Busters** (www.ctw.org/parents/weekly/1896/189601t1.htm): Seven games to keep them amused and keep your sanity.

Family vacation helpers

All parents attempting a journey with the kids should pay a visit to the resources I talk about in this section. The sites offer comprehensive help, allowing you to spend quality time on just a few sites, rather than surfing around endlessly for family-travel info (leaving you more time to actually spend with your little ones).

The Family.com travel category page

Family.com (`family.disney.com/Categories/Travel/`), Figure 3-5, is a Disney site, so you know they understand about kids. But the site also knows about parents and their travel planning needs.

The featured stories at this site mostly deal with trips in the U.S., but the information is usually timely with regard to the season.

This site also has loads of archived feature stories about family vacations. Select a topic from the pull-down menu and then select your child's age. The database then finds stories that apply to your family's needs (whether you have a toddler or a young adolescent), all written to get you and your family excited about the prospect of a trip and detailing what to expect from various family-oriented destinations.

Figure 3-5:
The Family.com Travel page.

The section called Road-Tested Vacations (the link is at the bottom of the page) is a collection of stories about actual trips that real families have taken and enjoyed. The trips are organized by region, so if you are headed to a particular region of the U.S., check out what other families have done.

Travel with Kids from the Mining Co.

The Travel with Kids page at the Mining Co. (`travelwithkids. miningco.com/`), Figure 3-6, is the most complete guide to family-related travel resources I've come across. The site features links to all sorts of family travel–oriented info.

First and foremost, like all Mining Co. pages, the Travel with Kids section has terrific links organized by category. Click any category and you are presented with a list of hand-picked (by the page's dedicated guide) Web links. The categories include:

- **Budget Travel:** Links about how to travel inexpensively with your family.
- **California With Kids:** You guessed it, stuff to do with the kids in Cali.
- **Car Trips:** Driving around with the young 'uns.

Figure 3-6:
The Mining Company Travel with Kids page.

✔ **Fun Places With Kids:** Links to aquariums (kids *love* fish!), amusement parks, and so on.

✔ **Gear and Games:** Be prepared for fun!

✔ **Vacation Ideas:** Links to help you come up with fun travel ideas.

The home page presents timely features under the heading In the Spotlight. Click a link to read the story and find out all sorts of info. Make sure you have some paper for your printer cause the stuff you'll find just begs to be printed.

Family Travel Forum

The Family Travel Forum (www.familytravelforum.com/) provides a one-stop information center for all questions regarding travel with the family unit. While you must spend $48 to receive the ten complete newsletters the site puts out, you can still get loads of free, useful information at the site as well, including the following:

✔ **Links to online family travel sites:** Lots of good links to family travel resources on the World Wide Web.

✔ **Family travel deals and discounts:** Check here for some hints and advice about places you can visit without spending a fortune. You can get ideas for regions all around the world.

✔ **An interactive forum where you can post and read about other parents' experiences:** Click Open Forum to post messages and read about others' family trips.

✔ **News and feature stories about family travel:** Click Family Travel News to see the latest news affecting family travel. Recent features included listings of the most popular amusement parks in many countries of the world, listings of worldwide festivals of interest to families, and America's top 20 beaches.

Walt Disney World

Well, of course I have to write about this destination — this place is the be-all and end-all of family vacations. Here's a hint: It starts with a *diz* and ends with a *knee*. The official Walt Disney World site (www.disney.com/ DisneyWorld/index2.html), Figure 3-7, lets you plan, reserve, and purchase tickets for your trip to the Mickey Mecca.

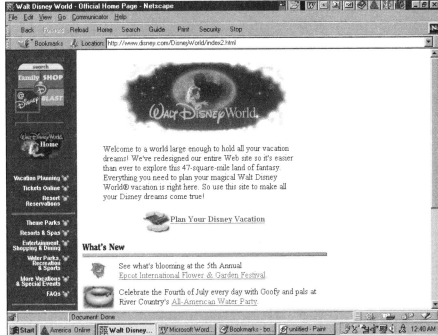

Figure 3-7:
The Walt
Disney
World home
page.

The site offers the following services to make your road to the Magic
Kingdom that much easier:

- ✔ **The Resort Recommender:** Input your needs and desires and the site
  tells you which of the Disney resorts is right for you.

- ✔ **Ticket purchase:** Get your tickets to any Disney theme park. All you
  need is a credit card. All transactions are conducted over a secure
  server, meaning there is little or no safety risk. (See Chapter 6 for more
  information on secure servers.)

- ✔ **Accommodation reservations:** You fill out a form online and a Disney
  representative then calls you back or e-mails you within 72 hours. You
  may also use the online form to modify existing reservations.

Of course, if you are more comfortable speaking with a live Disney agent, the
site provides that contact information, as well.

In addition to making the actual arrangements, the Disney site is an excellent place for both you and your kids to check out the many attractions Walt
Disney World has to offer, with updated seasonal events and listings. No
doubt your kids have already visited this site many times; if you have any
questions, ask them!

But if you're seeking additional opinions about Disney's resorts and vacations, check out the following sites:

- ✔ **Deb's Unofficial Walt Disney World Information Guide** (`www.wdn.com/dwills/contents.htm`): Well, the name says it all. Here you find information on all aspects of Disney World and its attractions, resorts, and amenities.

- ✔ **Brian Bennett's Disney Trip Planning Resource Net** (`members.aol.com/DVClubber/dvchome.htm`): This site contains loads of info about both Disney World (in Florida) and Disneyland (California). Maintained by a true Disney aficionado, this site offers everything from trip planning to boycott information.

- ✔ `rec.arts.disney.parks`: This newsgroup features discussions of Disney theme parks. Ask a question and it's sure to be answered. (See Chapter 12 for an in-depth look at newsgroups and how to use them.)

- ✔ **Disneyguide Theme Parks Web Ring** (`www.webring.org/cgi-bin/webring?ring=wdw21&list`): A Web ring is a collection of sites about a specific subject connected together by a loose affiliation that allows surfers to navigate through all the participating sites by way of links at the bottom of each page. This is the master list of all the Disney-related sites in the Disney Web ring. Click away!

Online Resources for Traveling Seniors

Seniors hold an enormous percentage of all adult passports and account for the majority of luxury travel and cruises, so the travel industry wants to attract seniors' business. Traveling seniors are also entitled to some serious discounts. Ahh, now I have your full attention. Almost all major airlines offer price breaks and incentives on travel for people over a certain age. Find out about all these great offerings and deals on the Internet.

Seniors who have lots of flexible time should also use the Internet to keep track of timely discounts. (In Chapter 9, I talk about how to find discounts and follow last-minute travel specials.)

Airline programs for seniors

In order to make flying more attractive to your distinguished demographic, most airlines offer discount programs for seniors.

One such program is the United Airlines' Silver Wings Plus seniors program (www.silverwingsplus.com/), Figure 3-8. This program is fairly representative of most airlines' offerings for seniors, though the United Airlines site has more information than most and more discounts on travel products other than air travel.

Members over the age of 62 are entitled to many benefits at this site, including the following:

- ✔ Discount airfares from United and its partners (generally 10 percent off most fares)
- ✔ Discount cruises from selected cruise lines
- ✔ Discount hotel rooms from selected hotel chains

A two-year membership to Silver Wings Plus costs $75 U.S. dollars and a lifetime membership is $275 U.S. dollars. To sign up, just fill out the online application and pay with a credit card. (The connection uses a secure server, so don't worry about the safety of your credit card information.)

Figure 3-8:
Silver
Wings Plus
home page.

The following airlines offer varying amounts of information about their programs for seniors on their Web sites:

- ✔ **American Airline Senior Fares** (www.americanair.com/aa_home/servinfo/senior.htm): The site tells about 10 percent discounts on most fares and other price breaks on travel products.

- ✔ **Continental Airlines' Freedom Trips and Freedom Passport** (www.flycontinental.com/products/senior/): Continental offers you two levels of membership in their senior travel program. Freedom Trips are designed for people who travel a few times a year. Purchase a book of discount travel certificates for a fee. The Freedom Passport allows unlimited discount fares for a given period, depending on the level of passport you purchase.

- ✔ **TWA Senior Travel Pak** (www.twa.com/html/vacation/toursp.html): The deal for seniors here is very similar to the other airlines. You must purchase coupons to cash in on the deals.

- ✔ **US Airways' Senior Travelers** (www.usairways.com/travel/fares/sen_trav.htm): US Airways' Senior page has very limited information, but you do get a toll-free number to call if you want more information. Seniors flying on US Airways are eligible for a 10 percent discount on most fares within the U.S. and Canada. You can buy a coupon book for travel outside the U.S.

Tour operators for seniors

A few tour operators design and run trips specifically for seniors that are interested in more than just going to Vegas for some gambling (not that there's anything wrong with a good Vegas junket). The following Web sites can connect you with tour operators that are eager to help you plan a trip that satisfies any interest you may have.

Elderhostel

Elderhostel is a unique and wonderful enterprise (my grandma has been on a few trips with it). Elderhostel (www.elderhostel.org/) is a 25-year-old not-for-profit that provides educational adventures for adults over 55 years old.

A search through the Elderhostel catalogs reveals trips and experiences as varied as a course in Tai Chi and acupuncture in Arizona to a study of Mayan civilization in Honduras and Guatemala. You can search the massive catalog by keyword by clicking Search the Catalog in the left-hand column of the site.

If you are new to Elderhostel, click Elderhostel Experience on the home page to discover what makes Elderhostel different from a traditional vacation. You find links for Testimonials from Elderhostel participants, information about the level of the Academics, details on Accommodations and Food, as well as the different program options.

ElderTreks

ElderTreks (www.eldertreks.com/) is a Toronto-based travel agency that specializes in designing active vacations for people over 50. The site is extremely well designed and provides you with tons of tantalizing information about the trips they offer. Hiking in the Gobi Desert? A journey through Irian Java? A far cry from shuffleboard aboard the Pacific Princess.

For starters, you can see the tour offerings by clicking the regional destination names on the photo of the signpost on the home page, or use the navigation bar at the bottom of the home page to browse through the various sections of the site:

- **All About ElderTreks:** Find out about the philosophy and mission of this unique travel agency.

- **Travelers and the Media Speak:** Testimonials from the pages of the popular press and from the mouths of happy ElderTrekkers.

- **How to Book:** Details the booking conditions and cancellation policy. If you are ready to book, write an e-mail or call the toll-free phone number.

- **Highlighted Departures:** Trips that are not conducted every year. This year there are groups going to Mongolia for 18 days as well as an Alaska trip for a week.

- **Scheduled Departures:** Regularly scheduled trips. Each is rated in terms of physical activity. Click a destination to find out the nuts and bolts, including prices and dates of departure. There are trips to Southeast Asia, Central Asia, Central America, North America, and many other regions.

Call or e-mail for a brochure. I can hardly wait till I'm 50!

SENIORCOM

The SENIORCOM Travel Section (townsquare.senior.com/travel) is a good way to find information on the Web for seniors who like to travel. The travel page has links organized by categories of travel information:

✔ **Travel News:** News articles that pertain to senior travel are posted here from various publications. Click the headline to access the full story.

✔ **Community Calendar Trips & Tours:** Looking for a trip? This updated listing has some good ones.

✔ **Airlines, Cruises, Rental Cars, and Lodging:** Find out about transportation and accommodations through these well-chosen links. Many focus on the interests of seniors.

✔ **Discounts:** This section is, unfortunately, a bit light on information. Check back to see if it gets updated!

✔ **Destinations and Tours:** Links to some great destination Web sites and tour operators that specialize in trips for adults.

If you are a frequent traveler, this is a wonderful way to find good resources on the Web that specialize in travel for seniors.

Internet Resources for Women Travelers

Like almost every other industry, travel could, until recently, be said to be skewed towards men's needs. Well, no longer. Female travelers have found a home on the Internet; a multitude of sites have arisen that speak exclusively to women travelers.

The online resources for women travelers range from tour operators that run trips solely for women to magazines for women travelers to travel guides with a feminine focus. Most of the sites are produced and run by women, so they know your oft-overlooked concerns, frustrations, needs, and desires as travelers, including:

✔ Safety issues

✔ Trips just for women

✔ Means to connect with other women travelers

✔ City guides for women

✔ What to wear in foreign countries (for fashion, comfort, and for safety)

Finding female-friendly travel Web sites

More and more women are discovering the joys of traveling, a fact that is reflected by the number of Web sites specifically designed for female adventurers. There's even a search engine devoted to women's sites and interests called Femina (`www.femina.com`). Femina's travel section (`www.femina.com/femina/RecreationandLeisure/Travel/`) boasts a long list of excellent travel resources just for women.

The Yahoo! travel section also has a category for women (`www.yahoo.com/Recreation/Travel/Women`) that contains links to many sites relating to women travelers. There are also sub-categories: Lodging and Tour Operators. Sites such as Christine Columbus (`www.christinecolumbus.com`) — a play on Christopher Columbus — sells products for women travelers while Travelgrrl (`www.travelgrrl.com`) provides a storytelling forum. When you find a site you like, check to see if that site offers links to other women's travel sites. The hours fly by as you surf from site to site.

Tour operators and guides for women

Want to go on a trip with other women? The following companies run a wide range of active trips exclusively for women, an experience that is bound to be different from a standard tour.

Wild Women – A Tour Company

There's nothing like a little adventure to break you out of a stagnant routine. Wild Women (`www.wildwomenadv.com`), a tour company started by two women (Martha and Carol), wants to show you the way. Just a visit to this irreverent and fun-loving site should get you psyched to do some traveling. The site offers the following sections:

- **Current calendar of tours:** 1998 has seen tours go to Spain to discover the mysteries of Tarot, spicy cookin' in Mexico (Red Hot Mamas), a tour of Ireland (Erin Go Braghless), and a trip to Egypt (Queens of the Nile), to name a few. Each trip consists of a small group of women on a mission for fun.

- **Advice for recovering good girls:** Join this online forum of women empowered by the freedom of traveling. Post your thoughts or just read along with the lively debate.

- **Facts about Wild Women adventures:** To make reservations, call the toll free number or print out and mail or fax the reservation form (click Reservations).

If you are a woman and like to travel, spend some time clicking through this site. I'm not even female and I got a big kick out of it.

Rainbow Adventures

Check out the array of adventurous trips offered for women over 30 by Rainbow Adventures (www.rainbowadventures.com), **Figure 3-9**; this is one beautifully designed site.

As of this writing, Rainbow Adventures offers 22 different active vacations. Explore the wide range by using the interactive map of the world:

1. **Click Trips for 1998 (or whichever year it happens to be) to access the interactive map.**

   The trips are denoted by numbers on the map of the world. They are also color-coded to show which season each trip departs.

2. **Select a trip by clicking the number.**

   Read the descriptions (including dates and prices) and check out the photos. When you decide on a trip, enter you name and e-mail address in the box provided on each trip page to receive info about that particular adventure. Don't forget to hit the Submit button to send the request.

Other features of the Rainbow Adventures site include links to other women-oriented sites, a guest book, press clippings, and a section of trips for women that are "Born to be Wild."

Figure 3-9:
The Rainbow Adventures home page.

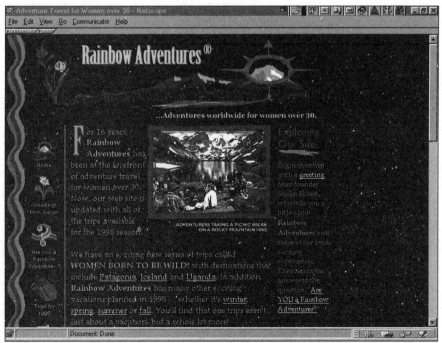

Accessible Journeys: Resources for Disabled Travelers

As is true for many special interest sites on the Web, many of the online resources for disabled travelers are created by people for whom the subject is very close to home. Disabled travelers can now easily access information to broaden their travel opportunities; from finding a specialty travel agent to meeting other travelers that share the same challenges to finding accommodations that are wheelchair-accessible.

Access-Able Travel Source

Access-Able Travel Source (`www.access-able.com`), Figure 3-10, is the foremost authority on the Web for folks with disabilities. The founder of Access-Able Travel has multiple sclerosis and created the site to share her love of travel with other disabled travelers.

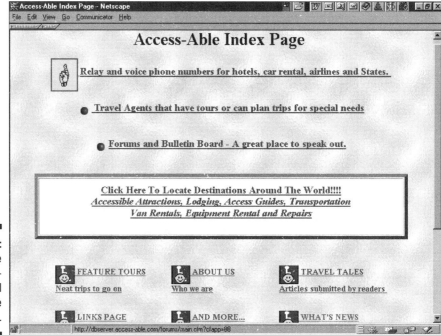

Figure 3-10:
The Access-Able Travel Source Index Page.

Whether you want to find out which cruise ships are wheelchair-accessible or find a travel agent, Access-Able can help. Peruse the site and its massive links page to find virtually every worthwhile site relating to special needs travel, including:

- ✔ Travel agents who specialize in trips for disabled persons
- ✔ Destination information
- ✔ Travel tales from other travelers
- ✔ A monthly newsletter
- ✔ A forum for discussing issues
- ✔ Equipment rental
- ✔ Relay phone numbers (for the hearing impaired) for hotels, airlines, and car rental

Connecting with other disabled travelers

Other travelers who share your needs can greatly enhance your travel experiences by relating their knowledge (and vice versa). Exchange travel stories and advice at the following places:

- ✔ **The AbleTravelers mailing list:** An e-mail mailing list for the purpose of networking with disabled travelers. Request subscription info by sending an e-mail to Ted@dts.org. (See Chapter 12 for more info about interactive e-mail mailing lists.)
- ✔ **The TravAble mailing list:** A valuable e-mail mailing list for first-hand information. Request subscription by sending an e-mail to TRAVABLE-request@MAELSTROM.STJOHNS.EDU
- ✔ misc.handicap: A Usenet newsgroup dedicated to discussion of great destinations and other topics about making travel more accessible. (See Chapter 13 for more on using newsgroups.)

Chapter 4

Great Adventures Begin on Your Desktop

● ●

In This Chapter

▶ Finding the perfect cruise online

▶ Locating festivals, concerts, and events with the Internet

▶ Investigating golfing, skiing, fishing, and camping vacations

▶ Virtual adventures in Cyberspace

● ●

Adventure travel means different things to different people. An Alaskan cruise may seem fairly staid to some, but to others, it's a trip and a half. Whether you are a mountain climber or someone who likes to explore the far reaches of a cruise ship (or maybe a bit of both), the Internet has the information to make your active trip happen.

This chapter talks about using Internet resources to find and research active vacations, adventurous travel, and trips that excite — and doesn't everyone need a little excitement?

Cruising on the Internet

Personally, I've never been on a cruise (unless the ferry to Martha's Vineyard counts). I do know that many people consider cruising to be the ultimate vacation. A big, fancy boat loaded with food, games, and entertainment sailing the high seas — sounds pretty good, right?

With all the cruise lines operating today, the Internet is a remarkable resource to help you research and choose cruises. You can check out a specific cruise line's Web page (they almost all have one) or you can conduct research on one of the various sites that are devoted to cruising. The Internet is also a great means of connecting with experienced cruisers who have firsthand knowledge of many different boats.

Finding the official cruise line sites

All the major cruise lines now have an online presence to promote their cruises; start researching a cruise on these official sites.

To locate the official site of the cruise line you're interested in, you can enter the name of the cruise line into a search engine such as Lycos (www.lycos.com), Infoseek (www.infoseek.com), or HotBot (www.hotbot.com). While these searches invariably return many links other than the actual official cruise line sites, you can easily pick them out.

To find a specific site in the listing, look either at the description provided by the search engine or scan the list of URLs (Web site addresses), checking the *domain name* (the name between the *www* and the *.com*). The official sites usually use their company names in the domain portion of the URL. For example, if you want to visit the Carnival Web site, scan the listed URLs for the word "carnival" — you know that you've reached the right place when you see the URL www.carnival.com.

You can also use a travel site that maintains a link list of cruise lines Web sites. For example, the Travel Page's Cruise Page (www.travelpage.com/cruise.htm) has an exhaustive listing of official cruise line sites, reviews of boats, and other sites relevant to cruises. The Cruise Page even lists sites of former cruise lines — perhaps you're curious as to what became of, say, the Club Med cruise ships.

The best of the big lines

Not surprisingly, the successful cruise lines tend to have better Web sites than their competitors. Aside from appealing design, a quality cruise line site has a few standard features, including the following:

- ✔ **Photos:** A picture is worth a thousand words — seeing your boat and the facilities it offers is better than reading a comparison chart that blandly lists the features of various cruise ships.

- ✔ **Destination information:** Describes the places its cruises visit.

- ✔ **Boat descriptions and cabin information:** A good cruise line site makes it easy to compare the different levels of service available with regard to cost, amenities, and activities.

- ✔ **Travel agent references:** These references aid you in finding an agent to help you plan the cruise.

The sites I discuss in this section offer all of these services and more. See you on board!

Royal Caribbean Cruise Line

Royal Caribbean Cruise Line (`www.rccl.com`), Figure 4-1, is one of the most popular and successful cruise operators in the world. And the line doesn't just cruise the Caribbean, as a visit to its Web site quickly reveals.

Some of the key features of this site include:

- ✔ **Destinations:** Takes you to information on the many regions for which Royal Caribbean offers cruises, what these regions have to offer in terms of travel experience, and the prices of the various packages.

- ✔ **Accommodations & Activities:** Provides information on different ships and the many classes of rooms available. This section also discusses cuisine (pick the ship with the best food!) and activities for adults and children.

- ✔ **Getting Your Feet Wet:** If you've never been on cruise, check here for info about destinations, details on how to book a cruise, and answers to frequently asked questions.

- ✔ **Loyalty Program:** Royal Caribbean rewards its repeat guests with an alumni program that includes discounts based on the number of your previous cruises, a magazine, and special on- and off-board promotions.

- ✔ **Info & Extras:** Send a free Royal Caribbean cyber-postcard or take a "CyberCruise" — a feature that shows you photos and descriptions of a typical RCCL cruise.

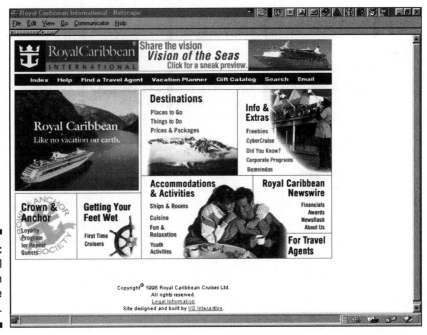

Figure 4-1:
The Royal Caribbean Cruise Line home page.

The Royal Caribbean site illustrates all of its pages with vivid photography and descriptions, making your decision on which boat to choose much easier. Captain Steubing would approve.

Carnival Cruise Line

The Carnival Cruise Line site (`www.carnival.com`) greets you with animation of a cruise ship moving slowly across a beautiful background. If this isn't enough to get you in the mood to cruise, click any of the following buttons for even more enticement:

- ✔ **Ships:** Takes a look at the Carnival fleet. Here you find a listing of each of the boats, from Ecstasy to Paradise (with names like those, the cruises have a lot of pressure on them); the site includes the embarkation point for each boat. Click the boat's name to explore the boat's features — you get photos of each area of the boat accompanied by short descriptions of the boat's features.

- ✔ **Cruises:** Here you find the cruises organized by region – click the cruise that interests you for schedules, ports of call, and a map of the route. For prices, the site may refer you to an official Carnival travel agent. Kathie Lee Gifford's phone number is not provided.

- ✔ **Fun:** Examine all the fun aspects of a Carnival cruise — spas, food, nightlife, and more. Click a link to find out about a particular feature of a Carnival ship.

- ✔ **Contact:** Want to contact Carnival with any questions or concerns? This section provides e-mail addresses for reservations, pricing, and guest relations.

- ✔ **FAQ:** Answers to frequently asked questions about Carnival cruises.

Norwegian Cruise Line

Norwegian Cruise Line is a very popular choice with cruisers. The Norwegian Cruise Line page (`www.ncl.com`), Figure 4-2, has a very attractive design and is easy to navigate, even without a first mate.

Check out the following features for a cargohold-full of information:

- ✔ **Destinations:** Explore all the places that Norwegian cruises go. Click a destination to view the boats, ports of call, and dates. Or click the Year at Glance for an overview of all NCL cruises for the given year.

- ✔ **Fleet:** Click the big ship on the home page and then select a boat to learn about each ship's amenities. You can get photos of the different classes of cabins, info about the boat's destinations, and facts about the vessel.

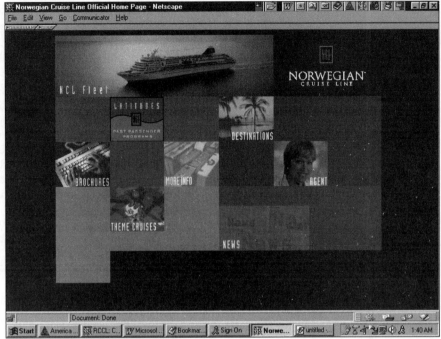

Figure 4-2:
The
Norwegian
Cruise Line
home page.

✔ **Latitudes:** Latitudes is the NCL loyalty program for repeat guests. If you've been on at least one NCL cruise, you're eligible to become a member. Benefits include special promotions, a periodic newsletter, and more.

✔ **Theme Cruises:** Each year, NCL plans special cruises that have a sports or musical theme. Check here for the dates and info.

✔ **More Info:** Find out about NCL's additional vacation offerings, such as Shore Tours and cruise facts to know before you go.

✔ **Special Offers:** This is the place to look for cruise bargains on NCL cruise packages. Listed on the left of the screen are links to various promotions, discounts and special cruises. These specials are updated periodically, so check back often if you're looking to save some money on a specific cruise.

✔ **News:** Check out the latest NCL press releases and company info.

Booking a cruise online?

You may have noticed that none of the major cruise lines allows you to reserve and book cruises online. This is due in part to the complexity of cruise reservations — there are so many variables, cabin types, ships, dates, routes, packages, and so on.

However, if you really want to book a cruise online, you can. At first glance, it seems that all "Big Four" online travel agencies (Expedia, Internet Travel Network, Preview Travel, and Travelocity) offer online cruise reservations. But when you follow through all the steps, only Preview Travel (www.previewtravel.com) allows customers to actually reserve and book (pay for) a cruise completely online. All the others let you browse through cruise listings and select a cruise, but when it comes time to pay, you must wait for a sales representative to call or e-mail you. I'm not saying this is a bad thing — on the contrary, I don't think online booking of cruises is very wise, given the complexities. But Preview Travel does allow you to purchase a cruise without ever speaking to a living agent. (See Chapter 6 for full details about using online travel agencies.)

Independent cruise resources

In addition to the official cruise line sites, many sites exist on the World Wide Web that can help you plan a cruise. The resources you find at these independent sites differ from what you get at an official site in the following ways:

- ✔ You get links to many official cruise line sites (including lesser known lines) as well as links to Web pages about cruising.
- ✔ You can read critical commentary and reviews of specific cruises and boats.
- ✔ You have means of connecting with travelers that have been on cruises.
- ✔ You can find out about cruise discounts for a variety of cruise lines.
- ✔ You can read up-to-date news from the cruise industry.

Cruise sites that are not affiliated with any specific cruise line make valuable bookmarks for both novice and experienced cruisers because these independent sites contain unbiased information about a variety of cruises. The following are a few of the best.

Travel Page Cruise Page

As a comprehensive cruise resource, the Travel Page Cruise Page (www.cruisepage.com), Figure 4-3, has links to nearly every cruise line on the planet, discount cruise information, and reviews of over 9,000 cruises — all free for the asking.

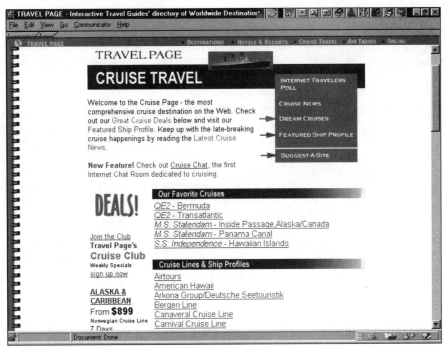

Figure 4-3:
The Travel
Page Cruise
Page.

The Travel Page Cruise Page works well as a jumping-off point when you research a cruise. You can move quickly between official sites by using the very complete list of links, making it very easy to compare and contrast the offerings of many cruise lines.

The Travel Page's boast that it's "the most comprehensive database of cruise information on the Web" is well earned. In addition to the Cruise Lines & Ship Profiles information, you can also check out the following features at the site for even more information:

- ✔ **Cruise News:** Gives you the latest on what's happening in the world of cruises, whether it be a new boat, a hot price on a cruise package, or a problem with a certain ship.

- ✔ **Cruise Talk:** Drop in and chat in this area designed specifically for cruise lovers to discuss their cruising adventures.

- ✔ **Dream Cruises:** Offers expert editorials on the best cruises operating today.

- ✔ **Featured Ship Profile:** Each month the Travel Page features an in-depth review of a specific cruise ship. An editor actually takes a cruise on the selected boat and reports back with an opinionated review that covers the itinerary, cabins, and other ship amenities.

You can also check out the cruise bargains in the left-hand column, which has current listing for the best in cruise values. Sign up to receive the free, weekly e-mail newsletter that details the latest cruise news and discounts. (Chapter 9 tells you more about getting discounts on cruises.)

CruiseOpinion.com

Do you wish you could talk to someone who has been on the cruise you are considering? CruiseOpinon.com (`www.cruiseopinion.com`), Figure 4-4, enables you to cut through advertising hype and sales pitches.

With a database of over 1,300 reviews written by actual cruisers, you get unedited, firsthand knowledge of specific boats and itineraries. You can also check out reviews for specific ships, as well as take the opportunity to offer your own reviews of your past cruises.

At the bottom of the home page, the date of the last update is displayed as well as the number of newly added reviews and the total number of reviews in the database. To get information about a specific ship, including a review from someone who has been on the cruise, follow these steps:

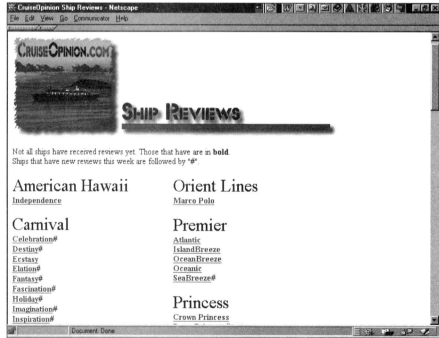

Figure 4-4:
The Cruise-
Opinion.com
Ship
Reviews
page.

1. **Click the Ships button to go to the review database.**

   On this page you find listings of cruise lines and the names of the ships in their fleets that have reviews in the database.

2. **Click the ship you're interested in.**

   You can view photos, a ratings chart, and posted reviews about the boat. The chart rates all the ship's features, from the dining room to the staff, on a scale of 1–100, which corresponds to the average of the reviewers' responses.

3. **In the Comments box at the end of the page, click a respondent's name to read the review.**

   Each review contains numeric ratings (1–100) for the ship's major features and services as well as commentary on many aspects of the cruise.

   Feel free to write to the reviewer using the provided e-mail address. And don't forget to post your own review if you have a favorite cruise.

CruiseFun

CruiseFun (`www.cruisefun.com`), Figure 4-5, offers very current info about a wide range of cruises and ships. The site is produced by Travel Incorporated, an Illinois-based travel agency that also produces the Cruise News Daily (`www.reply.net/clients/cruise/cnd.html`), a listing of the latest cruise news happenings.

Consult CruiseFun for the latest cruise news and passenger reviews of cruises, or click Cruise Search to find the perfect cruise for you, using criteria that you select.

One of the most useful aspects of the CruiseFun site is the Portfolio feature. Creating a portfolio of the cruises that interest you enables you to quickly access the cruise info you desire, easily compare various cruises, and receive e-mail notification of deals and promotions.

To set up a personal cruise portfolio, follow these steps:

1. **Click Portfolio at the top of the home page.**

2. **Register to become a member of CruiseFun.**

   Joining costs you nothing.

3. **Peruse the detailed listings of cruise lines and their specific ships.**

Figure 4-5:
The
CruiseFun
home page.

4. **When you see a cruise that strikes your fancy, click Add to Portfolio or Request a Quote.**

Requesting a quote puts the wheels in motion to receive price information from CruiseFun about your selected cruise. You will be contacted by the method you selected when you filled out your CruiseFun membership form (e-mail, phone, or fax).

Each time you visit CruiseFun, you can click View Portfolio to immediately access the cruises that interest you. From time to time, CruiseFun will contact you via e-mail about deals on the cruises in your portfolio.

Finding Festivals and Events Online

Sightseeing is fun. But sometimes you want to go beyond just looking around.

Before your next trip, consult one of the many festivals and events databases on the World Wide Web. Whether it's an outdoor concert in Golden Gate Park or the Australian Film Festival, the Internet is the perfect medium for finding interesting stuff to do at your destinations.

Feeling festive?

Festivals take place in every season all around the world. Don't miss the cornflake, foreign film, or wine festival at your destination just because you didn't know about it! Search for and locate these (and more appealing) events on the Web instead.

Festivals.com

Festivals.com (`www.festivals.com`), Figure 4-6, is the premier festivals and events database on the Web. The site lets you search for events at your destination. For example, say you're going on a trip to Quebec for a long weekend in Montreal. Here's how you would go about using Festivals.com to find some fun and interesting events in the area:

1. **Click the map of the world to enter the Festival Finder.**

2. **You can then use either the map of the world (click Canada, then Quebec) or type** Montreal **and a date into the search box.**

   The database displays the events for the coming months in the province of Quebec, many of which are located in Montreal.

   If the festival or event has a Web site of its own, you can click the name of the event to visit the page.

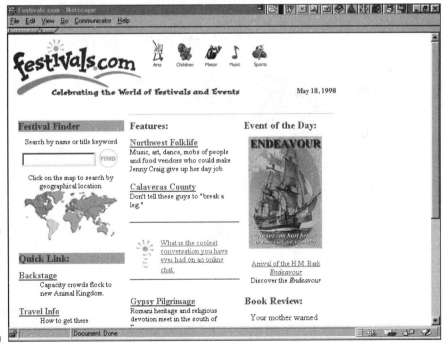

Figure 4-6:
The Festivals.com listing page for Quebec, Canada.

Festivals.com also has some other helpful resources. You can read the latest on noteworthy events or find a book about an event's subject. The site also provides, for your clicking pleasure, a list of online travelers' resources on the Travel Assistance page.

(Festivals.com is a trademark of RSL Interactive, Inc. All contents on Festivals.com are copyrighted property of RSL Interactive, Inc., Pier 55, Suite 288, 1101 Alaskan Way, Seattle, WA, 98101.)

CultureFinder

Does your idea of culture contain less county fair and more ballet? Then CultureFinder (www.culturefinder.com), Figure 4-7, is the site for you. Billing itself as the "online address for the arts," CultureFinder maintains a database of dance recitals, theater events, gallery openings, ballet recitals, and more. The listings cover over 550 cities in the United States and several European cities.

Begin your search by using the Calendar. Tell CultureFinder what type of event you're looking for and when it should be happening. You can also search by many other ways, such as geographic location, venue, organization, and so on. Or use the pull-down menu to select a city's entire culture calendar.

Figure 4-7:
The
CultureFinder
home page.

Also, if you're headed to Boston, Chicago, Los Angeles, New York, Philadelphia, San Francisco, St. Louis, or Washington D.C., CultureFinder has a complete city guide to aid you in cultural expedition. Go to CityGuides and select your city of interest. These guides list the current week's happenings, complete with phone numbers and addresses to venues (cultural events are broken down by category).

Next time you visit a new city and feel like you should nourish your artistic side, pay a visit to CultureFinder. Sign up to receive the free e-mail newsletter that highlights events around the world.

culturekiosque

The culture*kiosque* (www.culturekiosque.com), Figure 4-8, is the place to find "news, features, criticism, and interviews about art exhibitions, concerts, opera stars, jazz, dance, CDs and CD-ROMs, international cuisine, and technology," to quote the site's own description.

Most of the listings pertain to events in Europe, with a few for the U.S. and Canada; well-known critics from the Western world's leading magazines, newspapers, and journals write the reviews.

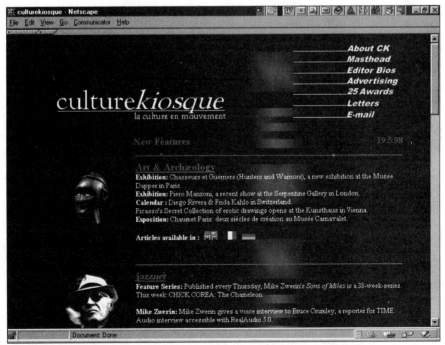

Figure 4-8:
The culture-*kiosque* home page.

culture*kiosque* breaks the arts down into categories, so if you're looking for Jazz in Vienna, go to the jazz section (jazz*net*) and then go to the Calendar section to find what you're looking for. Most articles are available in English, French, and German.

The master Calendar section (accessible from the bottom of the home page) is a good way to get an overview of all the events featured on the site. The listings appear alphabetically by country.

Online city guides as event finders

Online city guides offer another terrific way to locate events and festivals all over the world. Any online city guide worth its electrons has at least one section that lists current events and goings-on about the city. (Consult Chapter 1 for detailed information on how to locate and use online guides to the world's cities.)

The Sidewalk guides (www.sidewalk.com) are a good example of online city guides that provide event information. Each day, every Sidewalk guide (the site provides guides for many American cities) highlights editors' choices on the home page about the best upcoming events. Because the editors live and work within the city they are writing about, the choices are generally very well informed. Other city guides work in a similar fashion to point out the best events a city has to offer.

Using the Internet to Find Active Vacations

Do you have a passion for an activity that lends itself well to travel? Perhaps you've played all the golf courses within a 50-mile radius of your home. Or maybe the trout in your local streams and rivers just aren't biting like they used to. Whichever activity you want to enjoy on your next vacation, the Internet has the information to plan an active vacation — even if your activity is ordering daiquiris on the beach.

Trolling for activities

If you want to find a specific activity in a specific location, you can try using one of the popular search engines such as Excite (www.excite.com), Infoseek (www.infoseek.com), Lycos (www.lycos.com), or Hotbot (www.hotbot.com) to find the information you want.

Your search involves the following basic steps:

1. **Go to your favorite search engine.**

2. **In the search box, type the activity and the destination, framed in quotation marks.**

    For example, type **"fishing"** and **"Idaho"** — the quotes tell the search engine to find sites that have these two words next to each other. You can also try searching with the same two words separated by the + sign (**fishing + Idaho**). This tells the database to find sites that have both these words in their description.

 However, using search engines to locate sites in this manner can be very time consuming, because these general searches tend to turn up lots of sites that aren't very useful. For example, the fishing + Idaho search yields hundreds and hundreds of sites on Lycos. A better way to find quality sites of interest is to use a site that focuses on your activity or is a directory listing for special interest travel. I just happen to know a few good ones. . . .

Name your pleasure

So you want to go somewhere warm and play golf on a world-class course, but you need a place where the kids can have a good time as well? Surely a golf resort exists that fits the bill, but how to find it?

Yahoo! is a good place to start:

1. **Go to the Yahoo! travel section and find the subcategory that fits your activity.**

    For example, if you're looking for a golf resort, look under the subcategory called Resorts@ (www.yahoo.com/Business_and_Economy/Companies/Travel/Lodging/Resorts).

2. **Dig through the subcategories, clicking the links that seem most suited to your activity.**

    In the case of the golf resort, you find further subcategories of specific types of resorts, including a category for ski resorts (www.yahoo.com/Business_and_Economy/Companies/Sports/Skiing/Ski_Areas), a category for golf resorts (www.yahoo.com/Business_and_Economy/Companies/Sports/Golf/Resorts), as well as tennis resorts (www.yahoo.com/Business_and_Economy/Companies/Sports/Tennis/Resorts).

3. **Click any one of the subcategories to see listings of specific types of resorts.**

You can also use the site's capability to search within only the Resorts@ category (a pull-down menu next to the search box lets you choose "All of Yahoo!" or "just this category") and search specifically for the keywords that describe your desired location or other criteria.

An individual resort's site may not yield the best information you can find. A directory-type site devoted to your interest is the easiest and most surefire way to locate resorts or destinations that fulfill your requirements. You may be surprised at how many sites cater to folks looking for a specific type of vacation.

Virtual AdVentures

Virtual AdVentures (virtualadventures.com) operates and maintains a few sites that cover some of the most popular active vacation genres, including the following:

- ✔ Fly Fishing Travel Online (flyfishto.com)
- ✔ Golf Travel Online (gto.com), **Figure 4-9**
- ✔ Mountain Travel Online (mountainto.com)
- ✔ Ski Travel Online (skito.com)

Figure 4-9:
The Golf Travel Online home page.

The premise behind these sites is to provide travelers with all the resources needed to research, plan, and book active vacations over the Internet. Each site is very well-designed, easy to use, and has a similar look and feel.

All the Virtual AdVentures sites allow you to pick your destination from a pull-down menu or to search for what you want by using keywords. Narrow the search for your ideal resort by choosing from locations within the state or country you select.

Each listed property has a rundown of the features and amenities offered, as well as maps, photos, prices, and reviews from travelers. You can book some of the properties online; all can be booked by calling the toll-free number provided by the site and speaking to a representative.

During the summer months Ski Travel Online folds into Mountain Travel Online. Skiing is not that much fun in the summer when there's no snow.

The Great Outdoor Recreation Pages (GORP)

GORP (www.gorp.com), Figure 4-10, is without a doubt one of my favorite sites on the Web. GORP contains thousands of pages about the great outdoors and the wonderful things you can do in it. The site provides fantastic information on virtually any outdoorsy activity you can name.

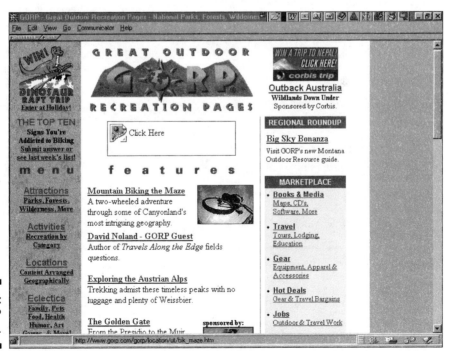

Figure 4-10:
The GORP
home page.

GORP hosts many smaller outdoor travel sites and also produces its own content. You browse through the offerings by clicking the links on the left-hand side of the home page. Each section has regularly updated, highlighted features as well as subcategories for further browsing. At any time during your visit to GORP, you can click Search (you see a search button on almost every page) to find listings that match specific keywords or phrases in the database.

Researching foreign study and work opportunities online

Studying or working in a foreign country can be one of life's most rewarding experiences. An extended stay in an unfamiliar land transcends the normal travel experience; you discover a country on a much deeper level than a traveler who just passes through.

Most exchange programs and student travel agencies now have sites on the Web where you can browse and check prices and offerings. The following highly-recommended sites focus on the study abroad experience:

✔ **Studyabroad.com** (www.studyabroad.com): A massive clearinghouse of information pertaining to educational opportunities around the world.

✔ **Council on International Educational Exchange** (www.ciee.org): The Council is a "nonprofit, non-governmental organization dedicated to helping people gain understanding, acquire knowledge, and develop skills for living in a globally interdependent and culturally diverse world," according to the About Council page on the Web. Founded in 1947, Council has a great reputation among educators and students worldwide for providing unique educational travel opportunities for students and teachers.

The following sites can help you locate interesting employment opportunities in the four corners of the globe:

✔ **Escape Artist** (www.escapeartist.com): I love the name of this site; it totally captures the feeling that a person stuck in a job rut may feel when contemplating a move to another country. If you've ever considered becoming an expatriate and trying your hand at foreign living, this site can help you out with all the logistics.

✔ **Transitions Abroad Magazine** (www.transabroad.com/): Transitions Abroad is a bimonthly print magazine as well as a Web site devoted to divergent study, work, and travel opportunities. The work abroad section contains many useful resources for job hunters, especially those seeking to teach English somewhere in the world.

The primary sections on the GORP site include the following:

- ✔ **Attractions:** Look for information about your kind of vacation by entering the name of a national park, forest, monument, or some other type of interest associated with your intended travels.

- ✔ **Activities:** Search by type of activity (for example, fishing, hiking, or camping).

- ✔ **Locations:** Know where you want to go? Search by destination.

- ✔ **Eclectica:** You find stuff that's hard to categorize such as family, pets, and health matters.

- ✔ **Features:** Search past and present GORP feature articles.

GORP also has links that go to sites offering all sorts of gear to buy and literature to read. You can even buy real gorp (good old raisins and peanuts, the perfect high-energy food).

Resort Sports Network (RSN)

The Resort Sports Network (www.rsn.com), Figure 4-11, got me hooked with its amazing network of Webcams. (You can read more about Webcams in Chapter 11.) This innovative site set up video cameras at resorts all around the world that broadcast to the World Wide Web, so when you want to know the conditions at your favorite ski resort, you can log on and take a look for yourself.

Figure 4-11: The Resort Sports Network home page.

Of course, the RSN site offers more than just Webcams. The site also provides loads of information about mountain resorts — prices, offerings, driving directions, and in some cases, online booking for the resorts.

One caveat: You may find yourself staring at these windows to fabulous resorts while chained to your lonely office desk, wishing you had some vacation time.

Online Virtual Adventures

You can't always travel when you want. For most of you, vacation time and money are just too scarce. A new breed of Web sites has sprung up to address the needs of would-be travelers.

These sites use virtual reality to connect you with virtual adventures that take place all around the world. While these sites won't ever replace actual travel, they can be great for putting off terminal wanderlust.

Using technology, these sites relay the real-world experiences of a team or a traveler to an audience on the World Wide Web. A site may send teams out to explore exciting parts of the world, or it may present an ongoing travelogue that follows, for example, a circumnavigation of the world. (In the past year alone, sites have covered the ascent of Mount Everest, the Whitbred round-the-world sailing race, an expedition to Antarctica, and many, many more adventures.)

Check out the following two categories at Yahoo! for a terrific listing of virtual adventures. (Many of the sites listed here have daily updates with video, audio, and animation. Check back often to see what's being offered.)

 ✔ **Yahoo! Ongoing Travelogues** (`www.yahoo.com/Recreation/Travel/Travelogues/Ongoing_Travelogues/`)

 ✔ **Yahoo! Virtual Field Trips** (`www.yahoo.com/Recreation/Travel/Virtual_Field_Trips/`)

Unfortunately, I can't point you to specific events because their very nature makes them transient and fleeting. However, I can show you a few sites that are examples of virtual travel:

 ✔ **Adventure Everest** (`www.everestonline.com/`): Each year Adventure Everest follows the spring expeditions to the world's tallest peak. Follow the brave souls as they attempt the summit with live audio and video.

✔ **Mungo Park** (www.mungopark.com): The Microsoft virtual expedition site. Though it has been officially canceled by the powers that be, the site's past excursions remain live and waiting for your entrance. Explore many amazing destinations with famous explorers, journalists, artists, actors, musicians, and other celebrities.

✔ **TerraQuest** (www.terraquest.com): TerraQuest was one of the pioneers of the virtual expedition. Though they haven't produced an expedition in a while, the past journeys are still available and make for fun exploration. Journeys include Antarctica, the Galapagos Islands, and climbing the mighty El Capitan in Yosemite.

You gotta plug-in

Many virtual travel sites require you to install software into your browser. The software, called *plug-ins,* are nifty little programs that enhance your browser's capabilities, enabling you to view video clips, sound files, and other forms of multimedia that make a virtual adventure much more tangible. You can usually get this software for free by downloading it from the software company's site.

A site usually tells you if you need a plug-in to view its offerings. If you need a plug-in, the site should offer a link to the place where you can get it.

After you download the plug-in, the software directs you on how to install it, a process that usually requires you to quit your browser application.

The most useful and most common plug-ins for both Apple and PC users include the following:

✔ **QuickTime Virtual Reality (QTVR):** Allows you to view QuickTime files. Download it from Apple at www.apple.com/quicktime/

✔ **RealAudio and RealVideo Player:** Allows you to hear audio files and view video without downloading an entire file. Download them for free at www.real.com/R/HP-1R/www.real.com/products/player/index.html

✔ **Macromedia Shockwave:** Allows you to view movies and games created using Macromedia's Director software. Download it for free from www.macromedia.com/shockwave/download/

Chapter 5

Reading Is Fundamental, Even Online

● ●

In This Chapter

▶ Finding online travel writing

▶ Reading online travel magazines and 'zines

▶ Getting guidance from the travel sections of online newspapers

▶ Reading travelers' diaries and travelogues

▶ Purchasing travel literature online

● ●

Thanks to the Internet, travelers now have access to a wider variety of travel-related writings than ever before. The Internet contains loads of travel reading in all forms, including magazine articles, travelogues, newspaper travel sections, travel literature, and more.

This chapter shows you the many places you can find writings about travel. From an excerpt of the latest Paul Theroux travel book to a newspaper article about discounted airfares, reading about travel is one of the great strengths of the Internet.

Find Me Something to Read

A couple years ago, I decided to quit my job and go on a backpacking journey in Southeast Asia. I knew what to pack (not much) and where to get cheap round-trip airfare (see Chapter 9), but what I really wanted to know was what to expect from a part of the world I knew little about.

So before I left my job, I took advantage of my company's high-speed Internet connection. I stayed late after work, perusing the Internet for writings about Southeast Asia, backpacker culture, and other relevant info. In no time, I was reading tales about trekking in Northern Thailand and getting advice about bus rides in Vietnam. This firsthand info made my job very easy to leave.

Even if you're just taking a car trip to the next state, you can greatly enhance your experience and your travel plans by reading on the Internet.

Looking in the right places

The Internet has many different kinds of travel writing. In order to find the right type of literature to answer your questions, you need to think about what aspect of the travel experience you want to know about. You may be looking for any of the following:

- ✔ **Travel discounts and current travel industry trends:** Because discounts and trends are timely, look for them in online magazines and news sites that have travel sections. (Of course, if it's discounts you want, Chapter 9 of this book gives you some really hot sites to watch.)

- ✔ **Unusual destinations:** For this type of info, check out travelers' online travelogues and diaries. (And Chapter 3 of this book.)

- ✔ **Written entertainment and relief from stagnant life:** Visit an online travel magazine or 'zine (a smaller, less professional magazine) that publishes travel stories.

- ✔ **Where to buy travel books:** The major online bookstores along with smaller bookstores that specialize in travel literature are good places to purchase travel books online. The guidebook sites usually sell their wares online as well, making it even easier to relieve yourself of some cash.

Getting a feel for what's out there

If you're not entirely sure what kind of travel writing you want, or if you just want to see what kind of writing you can find on a certain destination, a broad-sweeping search on a search engine can help.

You can search very generally by entering the name of a destination into Lycos (www.lycos.com) or any of the other search engines. Such a search turns up scores of links; you can spend a lot of time wading through pages of results trying to find some interesting musings. This is a slow method, but you may discover a source of information that you would never have come across otherwise.

If the idea of sorting through endless directory listings sends you to bed with a cool rag on your head, consider consulting the more organized listings in the Yahoo! travel category (www.yahoo.com/Recreation/ Travel). There you find links sorted into the following sections, which facilitate more focused searching:

✔ **Books** (www.yahoo.com/Recreation/Travel/News_and_Media/ Books)

✔ **Magazines** (www.yahoo.com/Recreation/Travel/News_and_Media/ Magazines)

✔ **News and Media** (www.yahoo.com/Recreation/Travel/ News_and_Media)

✔ **Travelogues** (www.yahoo.com/Recreation/Travel/Travelogues)

✔ **Travel Writing** (www.yahoo.com/Arts/Humanities/Literature/ Genres/Nonfiction/Travel_Writing)

Within each of these categories, you find links to various travel publications and directories of publications. Use the short descriptions to guide you to the reading you need.

In addition to the massive Yahoo! listing, I find the following directories highly useful for digging up all sorts of travel writing:

✔ **NetGuide's TravelGuide** (www.netguide.com/Travel/Publications): The Publications and News section at this site contains links to high-quality travel-related publications as well as articles about online travel publications, current noteworthy travel news stories, and travelogues.

✔ **The Electric Book** (www.electricbook.com): You should know about this site even if you don't care about travel writing. The Electric Book catalogs all varieties of online publications: newspapers, magazines, books, and references. The Electric Book organizes links to the various publications into subject categories; the Travel section is very complete.

✔ **Everything's Travel** (members.aol.com/trvlevery/media/ index.htm): This directory of online travel sites features a good Media page. The site sorts the links by genre (newspaper, 'zine, travelogue, and so on).

No Subscriptions Necessary: Online Travel Magazines and 'Zines

The Web is positively brimming with online magazines, many of which contain articles about travel or focus exclusively on travel or a travel-related subject (such as trains or flying). In addition to the written word, magazines also provide great sources of travel photography, a storytelling medium in its own right.

Online magazines have a couple advantages over their print brethren. Most importantly, sites often archive back issues online, allowing you to search for articles that are relevant to the trip you are contemplating. You can also read the vast majority of online magazines free of charge. No more spending your lunch money on *Travel & Leisure* just for that one article about cooking schools in French Polynesia.

Most popular print travel magazines have an online counterpart, and many magazines exist only online. In addition to online magazines, smaller, more narrowly focused publications affectionately called *'zines* (also known as *e-zines* and *webzines*) exist. 'Zines are generally produced by an individual or a small group of people and have a very distinct, idiosyncratic tone to the writing. Some contain lots of artwork and photography, some are just simple text.

Because many different types of people produce travel magazines and 'zines (everyone from your next-door neighbor to multi-national companies), they vary widely in their offerings and quality. At their best, travel publications whet your appetite for a journey with exciting descriptions and images. At worst, you get to read someone's inane babble about what giraffe yawns sound like. In the following sections, I guide you to some travel-related reading that I find consistently informative and entertaining.

Great online travel magazines

The online magazine racks are straining under the weight of the massive number of titles they hold. How's one to separate the worthy from the fluff? For my money (what I am talking about? Online mags are usually free!), a quality magazine must have one or more of the following features (in no particular order):

- ✔ Engaging and frequently updated (at least every couple of months) feature writing — some of your favorite print magazines may update their content more frequently online than they do in print.
- ✔ Quality photography.
- ✔ Archived, searchable articles.
- ✔ Message boards for discussion.
- ✔ Links to other good travel stuff.

For starters, check out a few of my favorite online travel mags, coming right up. After a little reading and exploration, you may discover your own favorites.

Magazine message boards

One of the nicest aspects of an online magazine is that it enables readers to do more than just read. Many online magazines provide forums for their readers to voice their opinions and thoughts about articles by way of message boards. For example, I recently read an article in Wanderlust (www.salonmagazine.com/wlust) about how many Chinese museums are filled with replicas of historical items that are passed off as authentic. In the margin of the story was a link to the Table Talk forum, where readers can interact with the author of the article, an expert on Chinese history. Having traveled through China, I clicked the link and enjoyed reading the postings. From the sound of it, the author found out a few things about China, as well.

Next time you are enjoying your favorite online magazine, check to see if the site offers some sort of forum for discussion. This type of interactivity is a major advantage that online magazines hold over their print cousins. (See Chapter 12 for a full description of online discussion forums.)

Wanderlust

Although it seems like a separate publication, Wanderlust (www.salonmagazine.com/wlust), Figure 5-1, is actually the travel section of Salon Magazine, one of the most lauded magazines on the Web.

Wanderlust offers new articles each week written by professional writers, some of who are well-known travel writers. Wanderlust keeps me interested, week after week, because of its interesting story choices. More than just well-written articles about destinations, Wanderlust publishes stories that expose the wonders of the world we live in. The site archives past articles, and you can search the Wanderlust database to find articles that can sate (or feed) your lust to wander.

You can sign up to receive the Wanderlust e-mail newsletter, which runs down the new articles gracing the pages of the magazine each week. To sign up, click Services (at the bottom of the home page) and then Newsletter Signup. Enter your e-mail address, and you are subscribed.

nationalgeographic.com and National Geographic Traveler

What's that? You've heard of *National Geographic?* Well, that's good — it means you haven't been living in a cave for the past century. The online version of *National Geographic* (www.nationalgeographic.com), Figure 5-2, lives up to the offline version's legendary reputation for amazing photographic essays and that distinctive yellow border.

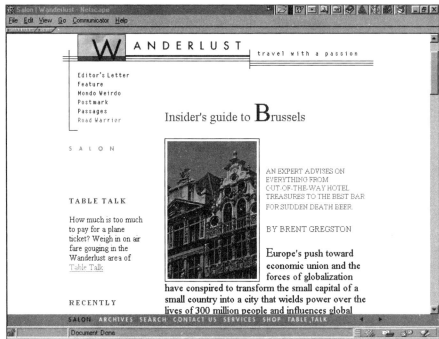

Figure 5-1:
The
Wanderlust
home page.

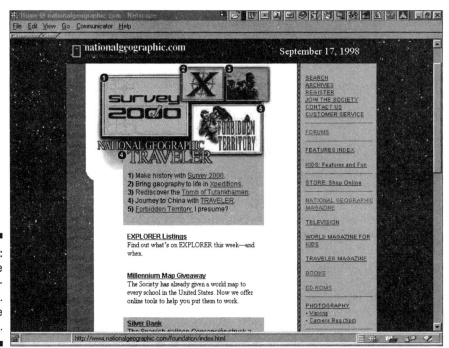

Figure 5-2:
The
national-
geographic.
com home
page.

The National Geographic Society publishes several magazines, CD-ROMs, and books, most of which have sites you can access from the home page:

- ✔ **National Geographic:** The Web site for the beloved magazine.

- ✔ **National Geographic Traveler:** Travel stories with a Nat Geo twist. (Keep reading for a full description.)

- ✔ **World Magazine for Kids:** Nat Geo-type articles geared towards young folks.

- ✔ **Books:** Click the Books link to find out about the books published by National Geographic.

- ✔ **CD-ROM:** Explore the world with National Geo's CD-ROMs.

- ✔ **Television:** Find out the schedule for National Geographic's TV shows.

The National Geographic Magazine photographers and writers chronicle the most fascinating places on the planet, places you may someday want to visit.

While National Geographic covers topics other than destinations, National Geographic Traveler (www.nationalgeographic.com/media/traveler), Figure 5-3, is devoted exclusively to covering interesting locales.

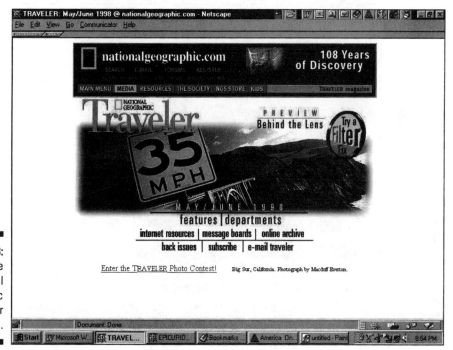

Figure 5-3:
The National Geographic Traveler home page.

Published in print and online six times a year, National Geographic Traveler offers great feature articles, terrific photography, and chat forums for connecting with other travelers. You can search the archived back issues for articles on destinations that interest you.

But wait! There's more at National Geographic Traveler. Click the Resources button on the top navigation bar to access maps, a site index, and links to other Web sites. You can even e-mail the editors with travel and photography related questions, and they'll try to answer them for you.

The Condé Nast Traveler

The Condé Nast Traveler from Epicurious Travel (travel.epicurious. com), Figure 5-4, is also available on conventional newsstands, but I prefer the online version.

First of all, you get much of the offline magazine's content in the section At the Magazine. In addition, you get a great photo gallery of the world's nicest destinations, editor's picks for destinations, a travelers' consumer help desk (complete with an ombudsman for sorting out your disputes with travel companies), and a virtual concierge.

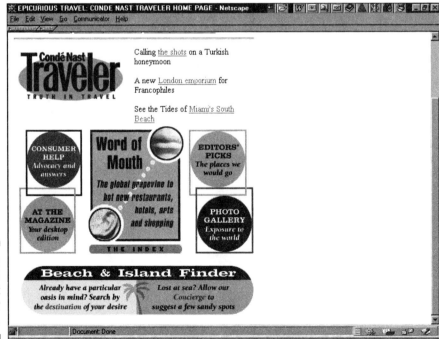

Figure 5-4:
The Condé
Nast
Traveler
home page.

The following three parts make up the Epicurious site:

- ✓ **The Places Section:** Click Places to access a dictionary of places. Enter a destination into the search box to access a concierge feature that allows you to enter criteria about your ideal trip (region, temperature, activities, hotels, cost, and setting, for example), and then returns a list of possible vacations. It actually works, too! You can also access the Fodor's B&B directory.

- ✓ **The Planning Section:** Click Planning to access all the Epicurious planning resources, including a world events calendar, features about travel hot spots, and a planning index.

- ✓ **The Play Section:** Click Play to access interactive forums, brainteasers, and a travelers bookshelf.

You need to have a pretty full wallet to actually partake of many of the trips described in The CN Traveler, but the features at this site offer something to travelers of every budget. (Did I mention the Traveler also offers weather information and a discussion forum?)

Zany 'zines for travelers

Anyone can publish an *e-zine* (a small, focused electronic magazine). All you need is an opinion and a modicum of know-how, and *voilà*, you're a publisher.

A good 'zine should have a few of the following characteristics, in my opinion (though they needn't have any redeemable features, and that's part of the fun):

- ✓ A 'zine should have a definite tone used to express opinions — idiosyncrasies are key!

- ✓ 'Zines should be non-commercial and self-published. Advertisers and multi-national publishers don't have a place in a true 'zine because of the inevitable influence ad dollars have on content.

- ✓ A travel 'zine should be somewhat narrow in focus and speak to a specific audience.

New 'zines are created and others disappear every day. With all the coming and going in the 'zine world, you may find it helpful to consult the following two directories to keep you up on what's currently available (don't worry — there's always an absolute glut of 'zines out there):

✔ **The E-Zine List's Travel Category (**www.meer.net/~johnl/e-zine list/ keywords/travel.html**):** Search the enormous database of e-zines or browse by topic. Each e-zine listing has a description of the publication, the format, and contact information.

✔ **The E-Zines Database Travel Listing (**www.dominis.com/Zines/ ByCategory/Travel/**):** The travel section of this e-zine database contains a long list of online travel publications. Click the title of a publication to read a description of the content, the name of the publisher, the frequency of publication, and other pertinent info.

And what kind of guide would I be if I didn't give you a couple of my favorites? A bad one, that's what kind.

Trippin' Out Magazine

Trippin' Out (www.trippinout.com), Figure 5-5, is for travelers "who can't even afford to look at *Travel & Leisure*." The 'zine is written by college students and recent graduates, giving the content a distinctly young and budget-minded flavor.

A really cool girl named Kelly started Trippin' Out (not that I know her, or anything, but she must be cool to have started such a great 'zine!), and it now provides good overviews of restaurants, bars, clubs, and other attractions in about ten fun American cities, including Madison, WI, New York, NY,

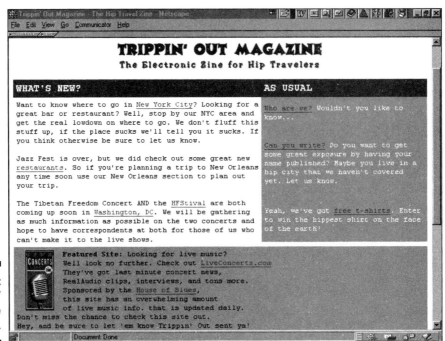

Figure 5-5:
The Trippin'
Out home
page.

Breckenridge, CO, and Baltimore, MD. Click a city (at the bottom of the home page) to read about the clubs, restaurants, bars, and hotels recommended by Trippin' Out.

Travelmag

The British 'zine Travelmag (www.travelmag.co.uk) is published each month (or so) and covers topics that pertain to independent travel. Each issue has feature articles that celebrate the art of independent travel as well as the following regular sections:

- ✔ **Strange news from the world press:** They consistently pick out some bizarre stuff.

- ✔ **Inprint:** Various contributors write about many different aspects of travel writing.

- ✔ **Crime of the Month:** These are some weird, real-life crimes that the Travelmag staff have come across.

- ✔ **Trade News:** The latest travel industry news.

- ✔ **Window on the World:** Readers' photos displayed for all to see.

- ✔ **Health Check:** Keeps tabs on the world's disease epidemics.

Travelmag also has a section of Web links that can come in handy; click Webwide and then select the subject for which you want information. Or if it's a travel deal that you're searching for, select Deals.

Unfortunately, for those of you who don't live in the U.K. or in the U.S., you won't find many bargains. But Travelmag would still love for you to contribute your thoughts or writings.

caffeinated magazine

Do you like café culture? Then you'll love caffeinated magazine (www.caffmag.com/caffmag), a 'zine that lists the best cafés in almost every state in the United States. While it's not a travel 'zine per se, it is useful for those of you who dread leaving your beloved, local café behind when you travel.

Next time you hit the road, check in with caffeinated magazine to find out where you can fill up your tank with a hot cup of java. Choose a state from the list at the left to view the best cafés that state has to offer or click the Cross-Country Map link to pull up a graphical map of the U.S.

Each month, the caffeine lovers who produce this 'zine choose an outstanding café to be The Café of the Month. And surprise — you also get many articles extolling the virtues of caffeinated drinks.

Checking Out Online Newspaper Travel Sections

Most major cities around the world now have an English-language paper that has a travel section. As a result, a little searching should find you an online newspaper that offers travel advice for the region — wherever your travels take you.

Finding and using online newspapers

The following two directories can help you locate an online newspaper for any city in the world which offers one:

- **AJR NewsLink** (`www.newslink.org/news.html`): Find links to nearly every online newspaper in the world, from *The New York Times* to college campus monthlies.

- **Newspapers Online** (`www.newspapers.com/`): Another comprehensive newspaper resource. If it's published online, you can find it in here.

After you find a newspaper that's published in the city or country you're headed to, locating the travel section shouldn't be too difficult — it's the one called Travel!

One of the best aspects of a newspaper's travel section, especially a daily newspaper, is that you know the information you're getting is current. Because newspapers employ large staffs of writers and editors, at least some of the information on the site is updated every day, whereas the print versions usually come out only on Sundays.

In addition, online newspapers almost always archive their past articles into a searchable database, making them a valuable research center for travelers. The articles usually cover topics about regional travel, interesting destinations, and features about what's going on in the travel industry.

Online newspapers often prove to be great sources of information about local events and restaurants. (Turn to Chapter 2 for more information on finding restaurants in your destination city.)

Not just for Sundays: A few great online travel sections

I agree that nothing can replace flipping through the Sunday paper Travel section and looking at the enticing destinations over a cup of coffee. But you can do that only on Sunday — online newspaper travel sections serve as a great travel reference that's always available, all through the week. And you don't get that nasty ink all over your hands and clothes. Here are some of my favorites.

The *Chicago Tribune* Travel Section

The *Chicago Tribune* (cgi.chicago.tribune.com/travel/index.htm), Figure 5-6, does a really nice job of combining its Sunday travel features with other content to create a travel center for its readers.

If you're headed to Chicago (or if you live in Chicago), take a look at the section called Lowest Airfares from Chicago to see a listing of current domestic and international fares from Chicago. Because the site focuses on round trips, you may be able to find the same fare originating from your city to Chicago.

Figure 5-6: The *Chicago Tribune* Travel section home page.

Under Destinations, a map of the world guides you through the *Tribune*'s destination article archive. Click a region of the world to find articles that relate to your trip. And if you're visiting Chicago or the Midwest of the U.S., you may want to check out the section called Midwest that has lots of features about this very, umm, *central* region of the U.S.

The site goes all out for its readers by also providing the following features:

✔ A searchable database of inns and resorts.

✔ A toolbox of travel helpers, including maps, weather information, and a currency converter.

✔ Expert travel advice from travel writers and columnists.

The Washington Post Travel Section

With its magazine-like design and in-depth travel information, *The Washington Post* Travel section (`www.washingtonpost.com/wp-srv/style/travel.htm`), Figure 5-7, is one of my favorite online newspaper travel sections.

For starters, the site offers all the articles from its current and past offline Travel sections (that's quite an archive!). In addition, the *Post* offers up a whole section about traveling in and around Washington D.C. that includes

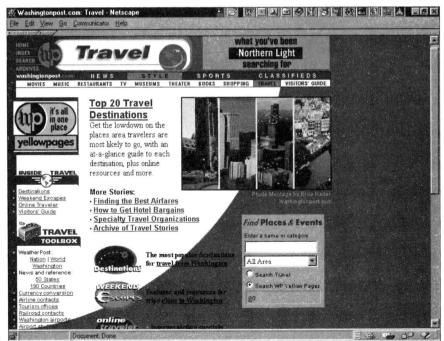

Figure 5-7: *The Washington Post* online travel section.

information on how to get around the metro area, event listings for entertainment and culture, and online tours of the city's many famous (and infamous) sites — on your right is Watergate.

Other useful features of the *Post*'s travel section include the following:

- ✔ In the left-hand column you find the Travel Toolbox. In it you find worldwide weather, fast facts about countries and states, currency conversion, transportation contacts, and info about tourism offices.

- ✔ Use the search box, labeled Find Places and Events, to search the database for past articles and current listings.

- ✔ The Online Traveler section offers readers a look at Internet airfare specials from D.C. area airports and other online travel info.

- ✔ The end of the travel section offers Travel Q&A, Readers Tips, Travel Trivia, and the Story Bank, a feature that shows you recent travel features from the *Post* travel page.

The London Telegraph's Planet

Online travel sections don't only exist in America — here's proof. *The London Telegraph* publishes one of the best I've ever seen called The Planet (www.the-planet.co.uk), Figure 5-8. If your travels take you to the U.K. (or even if they don't) you should pay a visit to this excellent site.

Figure 5-8:
The Planet
home page.

The Planet's feature articles come from the pages of the *Sunday Telegraph* and cover everything from the latest travel news to tales of adventures on the edge of civilization to tips for exploring the far reaches of London.

Search the massive article archives for something that interests you. Or take a guided tour and use some of The Planet's neat technology to go "holiday hunting." Jolly good, old chap.

Read Travelers' Online Travelogues and Diaries

When I head out into the world, I want to know the truth about the destinations, culture, and environment I am going to encounter. I want to know how a place *smells*. The kind of info I can't get from a glossy brochure or a commercial guidebook. You can get this vital information on the Internet in the form of travelogues and diaries. (Chatting with fellow travelers, which you can read about in Chapter 12, provides another great way to get the real skinny on a destination.)

A good travelogue or diary differs from a commercial travel guide in a few important ways:

- ✔ They are generally unedited, first-person accounts.
- ✔ They deal more with emotional reactions and the visceral experience.
- ✔ The writers of travelogues don't care about advertising — they write what they want to say regardless of who it may offend.

Finding online travelogues and travel diaries

When you research your next trip, whether you're planning a roadtrip to Yellowstone National Park or a bicycle tour of Kenya, check to see what other travelers can tell you about similar trips.

Finding travelogues that pertain to your interests is something less than a science, but the following sections offer a few good bets.

Yahoo!

I know I mention Yahoo! a zillion times in this book. Yes, I love Yahoo!
(`www.yahoo.com/Recreation/Travel/Travelogues/`), and I'm not
ashamed to admit it. This directory is the best way to find stuff online. To
find a list of Travelogues and diaries at Yahoo!, in the Travel category
(`www.yahoo.com/Recreation/Travel`), find the Travelogue subcategory
heading.

Yahoo! breaks travelogues down further into the following sub-subcategories:

- **Around the World:** Journals and diaries of folks who have made their
  way around the globe.
- **Aviation:** People who fly and like to write about their flights.
- **Boating:** Epic boat journeys — and even some not-so-epic.
- **Cycling:** Read about people who have peddled all over the place.
- **Families:** More than just trips to Disneyland — but you do find quite a
  few about that very topic.
- **Fishing:** The one that got away.
- **Hiking:** Fascinating tales of blisters and trail walking.
- **Honeymoons:** Those were the good days. . . .
- **Motorcycles:** Thinking about a trip across India on a Harley? I bet
  someone has done it!
- **Ongoing Travelogues:** You can follow a person or group of people on
  some sort of adventure. Following climbers on the Internet as they
  attempt an Everest ascent is a good example.
- **Paddling:** Covers canoe trips from docile creeks to raging rivers.
- **Specific Destinations:** If you're looking for travel tales about a certain
  place, this a good list to check.

The Yahoo! listing also includes a long list of links to sites that contain one
or more travelogues. Read through the descriptions to find stuff that
interests you.

Did you know that you can search Web pages for keywords by using your
browser? This is a good method to quickly scan a long list of link descriptions. Go to Edit on your browser (on both Netscape and Internet Explorer)
and select Find on Page (shortcut: Ctrl+F); then enter the keyword.

The Rec.Travel Library

The Rec.Travel Library (`www.Travel-Library.com/`), Figure 5-9, is one of the oldest travel sites (since 1994!) on the Web and one of my all-time favorites. It contains hundreds and hundreds of personal travelogues organized by destination as well as directories of assorted travel sites.

To find fun reading on your destination, simply click through the appropriate links. For example, if you want to read about the island of Jamaica and its tourist offerings, start by clicking the Caribbean link. The site then presents you with a list of Caribbean islands, and Jamaica has its own listing. On the Jamaica page resides a list of links to assorted travelogues, some recent and some outdated.

The travelogues generally aren't on the Rec.Travel Library server; clicking a link sends you off into the ether, usually to someone's private, slow-loading home page. I know they're slow, but it's worth the wait — many have photos and fascinating accounts of independent travel.

You also get links to sites that provide travel information about your destination. These may or may not be commercial sites, but they're usually good choices.

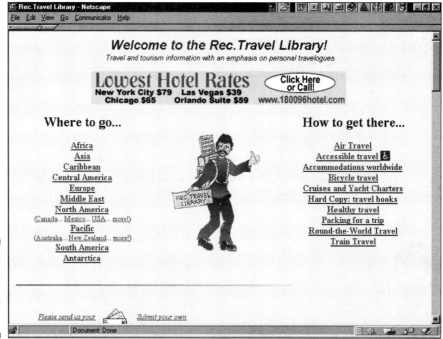

Figure 5-9:
The
Rec.Travel
Library
home page.

Cyber-Adventures.com

Cyber-Adventures.com (`www.cyber-adv.com/`), Figure 5-10, was featured in *The New York Times* a while back, so you know it has to be good. I like this site because it features lots of real travel stories from real travelers — and also because it is updated frequently.

Cyber-Adventures.com arranges its travelogues into the following categories:

- **Choose Your Adventure:** Travel diaries about various topics.

- **Strange (But True) Travel Stories:** Some unusual and weird travel experiences. I should add a few of my own.

- **Weekend Getaways:** Stories about short trips; you can get some good ideas from these.

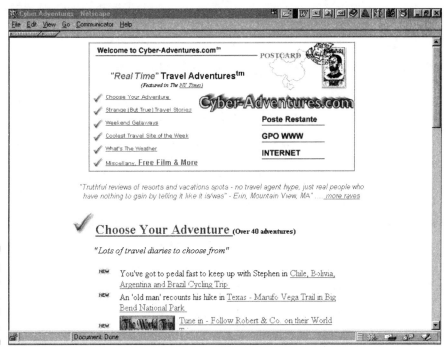

Figure 5-10:
The Cyber-
Adventures.
com home
page.

Publish your own travelogue

If a trip leaves you so inspired that you just have to tell everyone about it, try submitting your story to the Rec.Travel Library or Cyber-Adventures.com. Most sites that collect travelogues accept unsolicited tales, vignettes, musings, and diatribes about travel experiences. Maybe you can start a glamorous new career as travel writer — you don't need a publishing deal or a literary agent to publish your stuff online.

You may even consider devoting a Web page to your travel writing, which you can also do for free and without any specialized

knowledge about putting together Web sites. Many sites on the Web will host a site for you free of charge. These services generally do all the programming for you (if you want) and explain each step of creating your Web site in simple language. Here are a few of the popular Web hosting services (there are many, many more):

✔ Tripod (www.tripod.com)

✔ Geocities (www.geocities.com)

✔ AngelFire (www.angelfire.com)

✔ Homestead (www.homestead.com)

Buying Travel Books Online

If you absolutely must have offline travel reading, try shopping these sites (but don't blame me for the paper cuts):

✔ **The Literate Traveler** (www.literatetraveller.com/): This bookstore based in Beverly Hills, California, specializes in all sorts of travel literature. You can't order books online, but you can print out the order form and fax it in, or use your fax modem to send the fax. Or pick up the phone and your credit card and get the process in motion that way.

✔ **Amazon.com** (www.amazon.com/exec/obidos/cache/browse/travel/): Amazon.com is a mammoth online bookstore where you can find nearly every travel book and magazine published. They even sell audiobooks. Check out the editors' picks, search for a specific title, or just browse the categories. Ordering online is easy and secure; a credit card is required.

✔ **BarnesandNoble.com** (www.barnesandnoble.com/subjects/travel/travel.asp?): The Barnes and Noble travel section lists nearly every title published. Search by title, author, or any other vital statistic, or just browse the categories. Purchase books online via a secure server connection with your credit card.

You can also buy guidebooks online directly from the publishers. Most of the popular series, such as Fodor's, Frommer's, Lonely Planet, and Moon, all peddle their wares at their respective sites.

Part II
Turning Your Computer into a Travel Agent

"OK kids, pick your in-flight snack—cheese sticks or corn nuggets."

In this part . . .

The Internet has revolutionized today's travel experience by enabling travelers to book their own travel arrangements. This part shows you how to buy plane tickets, book hotel rooms, and rent cars without ever talking to a travel agent. I also throw in a chapter about everyone's favorite topic, travel bargains.

Chapter 6

Booking Your Flight Online

• •

In This Chapter

▶ Surveying the online travel-booking landscape

▶ Exploring the "Big Four" agencies

▶ Booking flights from the airline sites

▶ Managing "frequent flyer" awards with Internet resources

▶ Using online resources to make air travel easier

• •

Gone are the days when travel agents had a monopoly on flight information. With the help of the Internet, you now have access to virtually the same airline timetables, ticket prices, routing and seating information, and restrictions details as a professional travel agent. And the best part — you can get all this information for free, any time of day or night, on the World Wide Web.

I designed this chapter to help you make full use of all the online booking options you find on the Internet. This chapter also looks at the Internet resources available to frequent and business travelers for managing their airline awards and smoothing out the bumps involved with hectic business travel. Next time you wake up in the middle of the night and feel the urge to book a flight, tally up your miles, or see if your sister's flight has landed, think of Chapter 6.

Booking with the Big Four Online Travel Agents

Since the advent of the Web, many online travel agencies have set up shop, each vying for a slice of the burgeoning online booking pie. To some degree, the dust has settled, and four full-service online travel agencies have risen to the top to establish themselves as the online booking sites to beat. I call these agencies the "Big Four" — I know, I'm *so* creative.

Each of these four major online travel agencies offers the following features which set them apart from other agencies:

- ✔ **Ease of use:** You shouldn't have to struggle to use a site's features the first time you visit. The Big Four sites are cleanly designed, meaning your eye intuitively moves to the right spot to do what you want to do.

- ✔ **Secure credit card transactions:** You can safely send your credit card and personal information to each of the Big Four sites. (Read the sidebar "Online transaction security" in this chapter for more information on the security issues surrounding business on the Internet.)

- ✔ **Personal profiles:** To aid in the selection of the correct flight, the Big Four online agencies allow you to store a *travel profile*. When you log in, the site knows your preferred airport, preferred airlines, whether you fly mostly for business or pleasure, and how you take your coffee.

- ✔ **Low fare features:** The Big Four constantly develop new ways to keep you informed about low fares. Some have e-mail fare alerts, fare paging services, and many other features.

- ✔ **Access to living travel agents:** While it is their fondest hope that you book all your travel online, the Big Four also employ actual travel agents that are available many hours a day via a toll-free phone number.

Introducing the Big Four

Without further ado, the Big Four travel agency sites include the following:

- ✔ **Expedia** (expedia.msn.com): This site is owned by Microsoft and gets high marks for its ease of use and design.

- ✔ **Internet Travel Network** (www.itn.net): In addition to its own fine site, ITN has carved a niche for itself by becoming the booking site for many of the most popular travel sites on the Web, including CNN and American Express.

- ✔ **Preview Travel** (www.previewtravel.com): America Online users may be familiar with Preview Travel, because it has positioned itself as America Online's travel agency. Preview Travel is also a popular destination for travelers on the Web.

- ✔ **Travelocity** (www.travelocity.com): Travelocity is the descendant of easySabre, the first online booking site (available tpX§ravelers in 1985 on Compuserve!). Travelocity now ranks as one of the best known agencies on the Web.

These four sites have had enormous success in the past few years, and their established relationships with the powers-that-be in the travel industry make these the sites to use for the foreseeable future. Other online booking sites exist, but you can feel confident that when you use one of the Big Four sites, you are dealing with online agents that are highly professional and reputable.

You may be thinking, "I know many other sites where I have seen travel booking advertised." Many sites can access flight information and book travel arrangements. But for the most part, these smaller sites have a partnership with one of the Big Four agencies or another major booking enterprise. So when you access the reservation system at these "other" sites, you usually end up using the same system as the major online agencies.

What you can do

A full-service, online travel agency, such as any of the Big Four, performs many of the roles that you receive from a living agent, as well as a few additional services. They

- ✔ Find and book flights
- ✔ Compare prices, seats, and routings
- ✔ Research destinations
- ✔ Track flights in progress
- ✔ Provide information about discounts and incentives
- ✔ Keep you up on travel news and events

With all these amazing online travel features, it may seem that you never need to speak to another offline travel agent. But ticketing air travel is a complex procedure. Many tickets have complicated restrictions that no piece of software can decipher. Travel agents spend years figuring out how to finesse computer systems and to understand the esoteric ticketing procedures; an astute agent's expertise can't be replaced by any automated system.

Who should use the Big Four

If you are planning an intricate journey with many legs to foreign lands, your needs may be best served by an experienced travel agent, or a combination of online research and live agent interaction. Due to the way the airline industry is currently regulated, online booking is best suited for booking travel within the U.S. and Canada.

While the Big Four have made terrific advances in the past couple years, online travel agents still work best for the following travelers:

- ✔ **Those traveling in the U.S. or Canada:** Due to the nature of the travel industry and the means by which domestic and international air tickets are priced, online travel agents function best for tickets to American and Canadian destinations. You should purchase tickets to exotic and unusual destinations through a specialty travel agent.

- ✔ **Those traveling frequently:** If you travel frequently, booking your own tickets saves you tons of time. Of course, casual travelers should also investigate the Big Four.

- ✔ **Those participating in airline awards programs:** If you covet airline award miles the way some people love to gamble, booking online allows you to make sure that you fly with airlines that participate in your frequent flyer program.

Expedia

Microsoft's online travel agency, Expedia (expedia.msn.com), Figure 6-1, is a late entrant into the cadre of online agency super-sites, but it is certainly one of the finest on the Web.

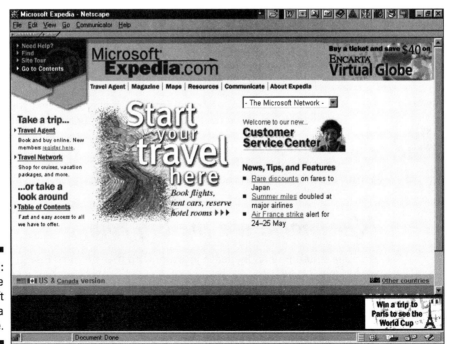

Figure 6-1:
The
Microsoft
Expedia
home page.

Currently, only residents of the U.S. and Canada can use this site; I'm told they are working on versions for the U.K., Germany, and Australia and should have them in place in 1999. Expedia maintains a 24-hour customer service number (1-800-936-4500) for questions, but you must have an itinerary number to use the service.

Expedia distinguishes itself by providing you with a very clean interface, with each screen offering something pleasing to the eye. It does its best to minimize the confusion that can result from a busy design.

You use the menu bar at the top of the page to navigate the site. Click Travel Agent to enter the booking portion of the site. If you need help at any time while using Expedia, click the Need Help? button in the top left corner of every screen.

Registering

If you're a first-time visitor, Expedia requires you to register to use its services. (Don't consider this a point against Expedia; all the online agencies require you to establish a user name and password before accessing the reservation system.) Don't be shy — answer the basic questions – you will use the information if you reserve a flight or book a hotel room.

Aside from the standard questions, Expedia asks you two interesting questions during the registration process:

- **Favorite Destination:** This feature tells Expedia to track the fares to your favorite destination. If you sign up for this feature, the site sends you an e-mail containing the lowest published fare to your destination each week — great for business travelers and long distance relationships. Simply fill in the boxes for the routes you want to know about. The site provides instructions.

- **Travel Promotions:** Clicking the Yes box instructs the site to send you special travel promotions that Expedia and its partners run from time to time. Some of these can save you big time.

On Step 4 of the registration process (the one where you pick your password), you see a box you can check to have your user name and password saved on your computer. If you are like me and have trouble remembering all the passwords, screen names, and secret codes in your life, you may find this feature helpful. If you check the box, the site won't prompt you for this info during future visits.

Using the Expedia Travel Agent

After you register, you can use the Travel Agent portion of the site, shown in Figure 6-2.

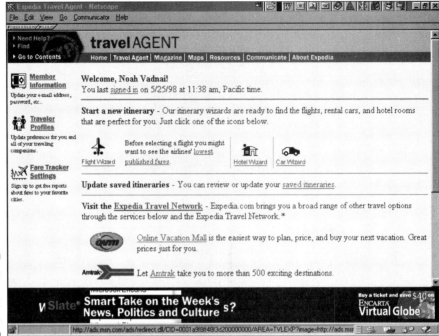

Figure 6-2:
The Expedia
Travel
Agent page.

From the Travel Agent page you can access the reservations systems for flights, hotels, and cars as well as create or edit your traveler profile.

Establishing a profile saves you time when making any sort of reservation with Expedia — I highly recommend doing so if you think you will use Expedia more than once. Your profile contains personal contact info, seat and meal preferences, frequent flyer plans, and car rental plans. You can create profiles for you and everyone you travel with and edit them at any time. Each time you plan an itinerary with Expedia, it accesses your profile, eliminating the need for you to take the time to enter the info. However, you don't need to save a profile to book travel arrangements — but you will then need to enter all your preferences each time.

Also on the Travel Agent page you find fare-tracker settings, a page where you can edit your personal member info, and a link to the Expedia Travel Network. The fare-tracker is a nifty application that you instruct to watch specific routes for fare changes — see Chapter 9 for more on the fare-tracker. Your personal member info is the stuff you entered when you became a member — password, e-mail address, and so on — if you need to change anything, this is the place to do it. The Expedia Travel Network is a collection of links to Expedia's business partners, all travel companies that have trips and travel products to sell you.

Online transaction security

Does the idea of entering your credit card numbers and other sensitive information into a form on a Web page and clicking the Submit button leave you something less than relaxed? Well, relax.

As long as the site you submit your credit card info into has *encryption,* a process that essentially encodes your information into a long code, a miscreant is hard-pressed to decode your credit card number and personal information.

Both the Netscape and Internet Explorer browsers make it easy for you to tell if a site uses encryption:

✔ Look for a chain or padlock in the bottom, left-hand corner on Netscape browser versions 3.0 and 4.0.

✔ Look for a lock in the bottom, right-hand corner of Internet Explorer versions 3.0 and higher.

When the lock is not broken, you know that you are connected to a *secure server,* a piece of hardware that Joe-hacker can rarely break into. Basically, your information is as safe, if not safer, on a secure server than when you give your credit card number over the phone.

Searching for flights with the Flight Wizard

Expedia's computer reservation system is called the Flight Wizard, Figure 6-3, which you get to by clicking Flight Wizard on the Travel Agent page.

The Flight Wizard helps you book a flight by guiding you through a straightforward set of questions. Just follow these steps to get airborne using the Flight Wizard:

1. **Choose whether you are looking for a round-trip, a one-way, or multiple-destination journey by using the tabs above the search boxes.**

2. **Using either the city name (or the airport's three-letter code, if you know it), enter your originating city and the destination.**

3. **Enter the dates you wish to fly, using the standard format (MM/DD/YY).**

   Click View Calendar to check out a calendar for the next few months.

4. **Enter the number of passengers and their classifications.**

   Classifications include adult, senior, child, writer, and so on.

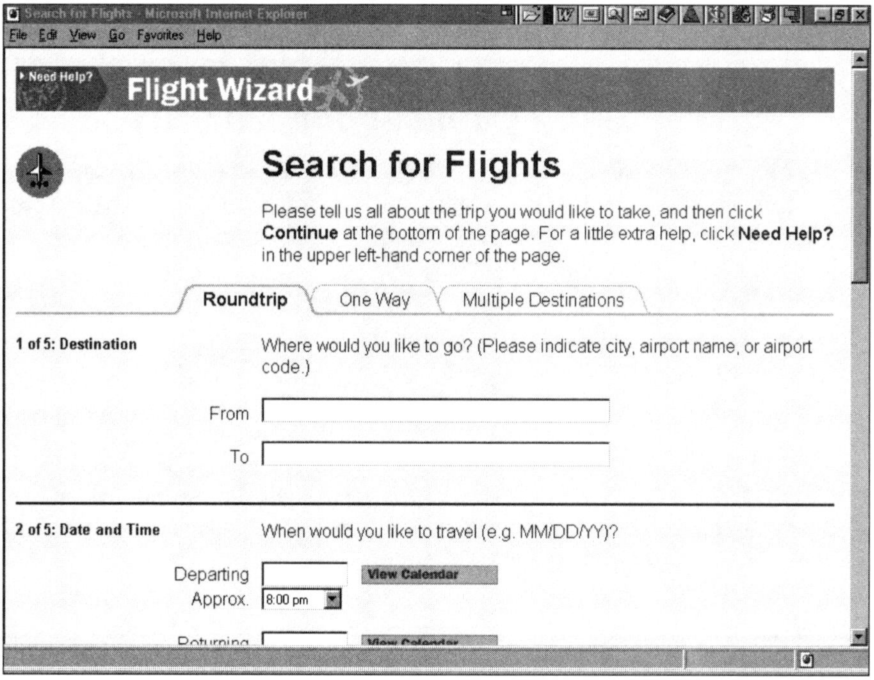

Figure 6-3:
The Expedia
Flight
Wizard.

5. **Choose which ticket class (coach, business, first, and so on), what airlines to search (all or just one specific), and what types of restrictions you want or don't want on the ticket.**

6. **Tell the database how to search.**

   It prioritizes looking either for the best priced tickets or it finds all scheduled flights for the given days.

7. **Click Continue.**

Expedia searches its database for the flights that most closely match your criteria. The site then returns the results of its search on a page that looks something like Figure 6-4.

You can quickly run through the flights, checking on prices (remember whether you selected round-trip, one-way, or multiple-destination trips), times, airlines, and flight equipment. Avoid flights that say batteries not included.

If you see a flight that interests you, you need to check on its availability, routing, and restrictions. Click Choose and Continue on the left side of the screen near the flight price to see this information.

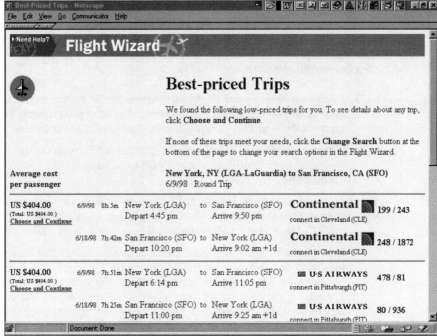

Figure 6-4:
The Expedia
Flight
Wizard
results
page.

The Flight Wizard then offers you the following three choices:

✔ Click Reserve to make a reservation and purchase the ticket. (See the
following section for information on reserving a ticket.)

✔ Click Add to Itinerary to put this flight into an itinerary that you can
change or add to at any time. If you click this button, you are not
reserved on the flight; it just means that you are planning the trip.
Using this feature allows you to book hotels, cars, and other travel
arrangements all at once. Itineraries can be saved for an indefinite
amount of time.

✔ Click Change Search to try for a different permutation of airports,
schedules, or routes.

Before you can reserve or add a flight to your itinerary, you must click the
small box at the bottom of the page signifying you have read and accept the
restrictions that the airline has placed on the flight. If you don't, expect an
armed Expedia agent to arrive at your doorstep within the hour.

Reserving and purchasing tickets

The process for reserving and purchasing your tickets on Expedia is a fairly straightforward, step-by-step process, with good instructions all the way through. If at any time you need help, click the Need Help? button in the top left corner. Here's the way it works.

1. **After you select your flight and agree to the restrictions, Expedia gives you the choice of either reserving and purchasing your ticket immediately or just making a non-confirmed reservation.**

   The non-confirmed reservation holds a seat for you on the flight, but the price is not confirmed until you purchase the ticket with your credit card.

   To purchase the ticket, select Purchase Tickets Now by clicking the box next to that statement and click Continue. To only make a reservation, click the box next to Make Only a Reservation Now and click Continue.

   If you want to purchase your ticket, you can select the traveler profile you wish to have applied to the reservation (refer to the section "Using the Expedia Travel Agent" earlier in this chapter) or go with New Traveler if you have not entered a traveler profile into the system. If you buy multiple tickets, each ticket can have a different profile applied to it.

2. **If you did not use a pre-established profile (New Traveler), you must now take the time to enter the information about the person who will be flying.**

   If you are using established profiles, simply verify that the information is correct. Click Continue to move to the next step when you have completed the traveler info.

3. **Choose or verify your seating preferences by clicking the boxes next to your choice. Click Continue when done.**

4. **Choose to have your ticket issued either as a paperless electronic ticket (see the sidebar "Electronic tickets (e-tickets)" in this chapter) or delivered via U.S. mail to either the credit card holder's address or to an alternate address, which you may specify (the address must be in the United States).**

   Also during this step, you must enter your credit card number and expiration date. If you have stored your credit card number in your traveler profile, you don't need to enter it again. Simply click Purchase and Expedia processes your order — your order is now irrevocably in place.

   The system churns for a moment while it authorizes your card and then presents you with a shiny, new confirmation number. Print out the confirmation for your records. If you decide at any time that you're not sure you want to purchase the ticket, click Cancel and the site saves the itinerary for future use.

   Well done! You bought an airline ticket online.

Electronic tickets (e-tickets)

The issuance of paperless tickets, or e-tickets, has become an extremely common occurrence for air travel in the United States and is becoming common elsewhere. Travelers can now reserve a flight by phone, travel agent, or online and then show up at the airport with valid, government issued identification and collect their boarding pass — all without ever possessing a conventional paper ticket. The whole reservation is held in the computer system; you still get a receipt from the travel agent or airline, either by fax or by mail, but this receipt is not necessary (it *is* helpful) to receive your boarding pass at the airport.

The Internet Travel Network

The Internet Travel Network (`www.itn.net`), Figure 6-5, affectionately called ITN by travelers round the world, provides another fine choice for booking flights (as well as hotels and cars) online. ITN allows you to book flights that originate from any country.

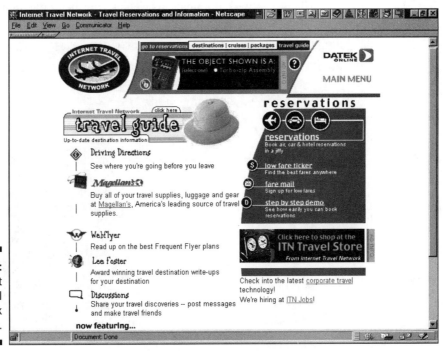

Figure 6-5: The Internet Travel Network home page.

ITN has been in the online travel reservation business for a relatively long time (1995!). Since that time, more than 4 million people have registered with ITN — so rest assured, they have experience. ITN also has a 24-hour customer service center that you can call toll-free (from the U.S. and Canada) at 1-800-253-9822.

In addition, ITN's reservation software is used by many, many of the Web's most popular sites. Almost anytime you come across a site that offers online travel reservations, ITN is usually involved.

From the ITN home page, click the Reservations link on the right side of the page to access the booking system, called the ITN Reservations Center, as shown in Figure 6-6.

If you've never used the ITN system before, you need to establish a user name and a password. Simply enter the name you wish to be called by ITN and a secret word and you are ready to roll. Open sesame!

Creating your traveler profile

I strongly urge you to create a complete traveler profile. Doing so saves you time during future bookings — the system will know your preferences in terms of airlines, seating, and meals, as well as your personal data.

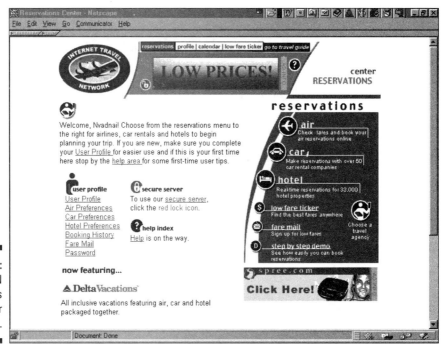

Figure 6-6:
The ITN
Reservations
Center
page.

Special features on Expedia

You want more from Expedia? The following cool features can help you get good deals on flights:

✔ **Fare Tracker:** Keep an eye on the fares on up to three flight routes that interest you. Each week you receive an e-mail showing the best fares available for the given routes. Simply fill out the city pair (departure and destination cities) and then click Subscribe to Fare Tracker. You access the Fare Tracker from the main Travel Agent page.

✔ **Fare Compare:** Use this feature to search the database for the lowest published fares for a flight. But don't get too excited when you find a great price — many of these fares are unavailable. Regardless, this feature helps you benchmark the prices on many different routes. To find the lowest published fares, click the link, Lowest Published Fares, on the main Travel Agent page, next to the Flight Wizard button.

ITN also allows you to save your credit card info in the system, eliminating the need to enter all those numbers time and again. Don't worry — it's safe to give the site your credit card number. (See the "Online transaction security" sidebar in this chapter if you need more convincing.)

Click User Profile to save your vital stats in the system. Set your air travel preferences by clicking, wonder of wonders, Air Preferences. In both cases, the site provides you with a set of questions that helps you provide the necessary information.

Researching and booking a flight with ITN

Going somewhere? I thought so. The ITN Reservations Center page makes booking a flight as easy as the following steps:

1. **Choose the type of travel: round-trip, one-way, or multiple city.**

2. **Enter your originating and destination cities.**

   Use the city codes or city names. You can see a list of city codes by clicking Airport Codes.

3. **Enter the dates you wish to fly.**

4. **Choose the service class.**

   I *always* fly First Class.

5. **Select how you want the results of your search sorted.**

   You can choose from the best prices, fewest number of connections, and so on.

6. **Choose how many flights you want displayed in the results and which airlines you want to search.**

   The default setting is *All*.

7. **Click Check Flight Availability.**

   Sit back and relax! In a few moments, the site returns a page displaying the flights it finds for you (Figure 6-7).

The Internet Travel Network's results page can be a bit confusing. The page displays each leg of your flight separately, and you must select each leg separately as well. Click the box next to the leg that you wish to select in the flight results list. (A flight leg refers to a trip that goes from one city to another. A round-trip flight is made up of two flight legs. A multiple destination journey has more than two flight legs.)

If you are purchasing a round-trip ticket, you can't get a price quote until you select both legs of the flight. Remember, if you select the first leg of a trip (New York to San Francisco, for example) on United Airlines, and the second leg (San Francisco to New York, for example) on American Airlines, the price could be a lot higher than the sum of the prices of the two legs. To get the cheapest ticket, always compose a round-trip using the same airline, if possible.

Figure 6-7:
The ITN
Flight
Availability
page.

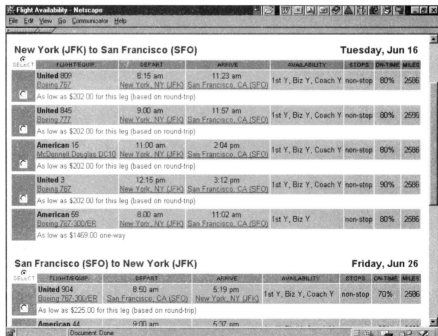

The ITN results show you flight numbers, plane types, times, seat-class availability, routing, distance, and on-time percentages. If any of the flights interest you, you can select the flights by following these steps:

1. **Click the small radio boxes (the little circles that you can fill in with a click of the mouse) on the far left of the page next to the flights that interest you.**

2. **Click Price Selected Itinerary.**

   ITN's computer system checks to see if it can find flights that do the same route at a lower price, perhaps at a different time or different airport. If ITN finds other, less expensive options, it displays them for you.

3. **With all the information in hand, you can select the flight you want by clicking the arrow on the left of the itinerary.**

   The site takes you to a Reservation Request Form page. If you filled out a traveler profile (refer to "Creating your traveler profile" earlier in this chapter), most of this page is filled out already. Be sure to read all the information about ticket delivery and billing addresses carefully.

4. **To finish the reservation, click the I'll Wait While You Book These Travel Arrangements button at the bottom of the page.**

   If you do not yet have a travel profile, fill out all the boxes with your personal info and a valid credit card number and then click the I'll Wait . . . button.

   Your tickets are now reserved. The site displays a confirmation of the reservation that you should print and retain for your records.

 But wait! I want to show you a great feature of this site. ITN allows you to pick your seat using an animated graphic. Click Choose Your Seats and another browser window automatically opens, which you can see in Figure 6-8. The new window loads slowly showing you a graphic of the plane, but if you're finicky about where you sit on the plane, it's worth the wait.

After the graphic appears on your screen, click a green seat. (Green seats represent available seats. X's represent unavailable seats.) You may choose a seat for each flight you have reserved. Highlight the flight number in the box in the upper-left corner to choose which flight you are selecting seats for.

If you are confused and need help, click the Help button. Otherwise, when you have selected seats for all your flights, click the Reserve button. Your seats are selected and you are returned to the Reservation/Booking Request Form.

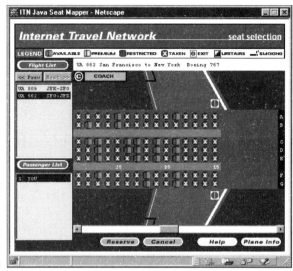

Figure 6-8:
The ITN
Java Seat
Mapper.

Ticket delivery

The ticketing process is complete, but where are your tickets?

You can choose to have electronic tickets, meaning that the tickets are stored in the airlines' computer system and you retrieve them when you arrive at the airport. This is quickly becoming the most popular means of ticketing all flights within the U.S. and around the world — it's totally safe and reliable. Just remember to bring the credit card you purchased the ticket with and a government issued, photo identification.

ITN can also mail you the tickets by Federal Express. The site only offers this option on international tickets where no e-ticket is available; you must pay the FedEx shipping fee.

Does the ITN booking process still seem a bit frightful? Click the Step by Step Demo button on the home page to get a handle on it.

Preview Travel

Preview Travel (www.previewtravel.com), Figure 6-9, has been in the online booking game for some time now. Found both on the Web and on America Online, Preview sells many, many tickets each week on the Internet.

Special features on ITN

For your discount pleasure, ITN offers the following features, which you can access from the ITN home page:

✔ **Low Fare Ticker:** Opens a small browser window where low fares from your selected home airport continuously scroll by. Keep the window open while you work; you may wind up somewhere you only dreamed about.

✔ **Fare Mail:** Go to the Fare Mail page to sign up to receive e-mail updates of the fares to destinations of your choosing. You can set Fare Mail to mail you as often as you'd like. I get mine every day so that I feel popular.

Preview Travel puts an emphasis on user-friendliness — that is, the site goes out of its way to make it easy to buy all kinds of travel products online. Preview has also made many partnerships within the online and traditional travel industry, so you are bound to see special travel promotions advertised on the site.

Figure 6-9: The Preview Travel home page.

Currently, you can't book flights on Preview Travel that originate outside the U.S. (Puerto Rico included) and Canada. Preview Travel has no 24-hour customer service phone number, but it does have an e-mail help service.

To enter the reservation system, click the graphic that looks like a bellhop (it's labeled Reservations, in case you are unsure!). The site prompts new users to set up an account before using the reservation system. Choose a user ID and a password, preferably something you'll remember.

After you establish your user ID, Preview asks you to create a traveler profile — a very useful and timesaving step. In addition to your name, address, e-mail address, and most frequently used airport, you should also set up your travel preferences (seating, meals, frequent flyer info, and so on). Having a profile saved in the system saves you time when you make future reservations. Don't worry — Preview won't send you any mail or give your name to solicitors.

Preview walks you through this registration and profile process; after each step, click the Continue button at the bottom of the page. At any time during your use of Preview Travel, you can click the Customer Service button at the bottom of each screen to access some help options.

Planning and purchasing a plane ticket with Preview Travel entails a seven-step process. The menu bar at the top of each Airline Reservation page tells you what step you are currently on and how many you have left to go. Remember to breathe, remain calm, and hit the Continue button as you follow these steps:

1. **Plan your air travel.**

   Choose what type of itinerary you need: one way, round-trip, or multi-leg (more than two stops) and how many people are traveling on the itinerary.

2. **Search for flights.**

   After you click the Continue button at the end of Step 1, you see the screen shown in Figure 6-10. This is the big step. Tell the site where you want to go and when you want to go there (and return) as well as which airlines you prefer (if any) and how you want your flights displayed (by best price, by time, or by airline). (Don't you just hate parentheses?)

   You can also choose to have the database return only unrestricted flights. But be warned — these flights are generally very expensive.

3. **Choose your flight.**

   Now you can start getting excited. Your plans are coming together; you just need to choose the flights that best suit you in terms of price, time, and airline.

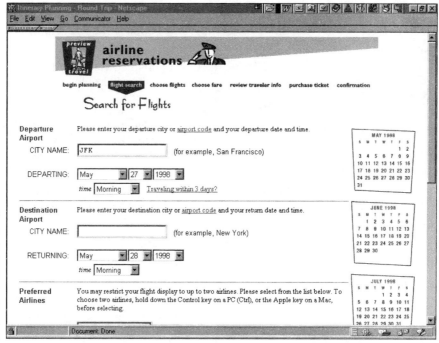

Figure 6-10:
The
Preview
Travel
Search for
Flights
page.

The site displays its results for each leg; a round-trip consists of two legs. You must select a flight for each leg.

One-way tickets are the most expensive class of ticket. Buying two one-way tickets on different airlines is the most expensive way to get there and back. Try to fly the same airline for both legs.

Preview has a nifty feature that displays how many tickets are left in each section of the plane, located at the far right of each flight listing. To select a flight, click the box at the left of the listing. You must also select which class of ticket (coach, business, or first class) you wish to purchase during this step from the colored box after each flight leg.

4. Choose the flight with the best fare.

After you choose the flights for each leg of the journey, Preview calculates the fare and runs through its database to see if it can find any less expensive combinations that might serve you just as well.

Select the flight that you desire by clicking Choose This Fare.

5. Review your traveler info.

You see the profile information that Preview has in the system for you; you can make changes or just continue. Not a very exciting step, is it?

6. Specify your delivery options.

Wow, you are really getting close. Choose the delivery option — either e-ticket or first class U.S. Mail.

If you choose to have the ticket delivered via mail, the ticket can only go to the billing address of the credit card holder. Choose wisely.

7. Purchase your ticket.

When you see the screen shown in Figure 6-11, the moment of truth has arrived. Do you really want this ticket? Do you really want to visit the in-laws in Fort Lauderdale for your vacation? Speak now or, well, you know the rest.

If you decide to take the plunge and purchase your ticket, enter your credit card information and click the Purchase Ticket button. Otherwise, the site discards your itinerary and you must start anew.

8. Print out your confirmation information.

Okay, I lied. There are eight steps. But this one is just for your records to show that you actually bought an airline ticket online.

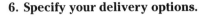

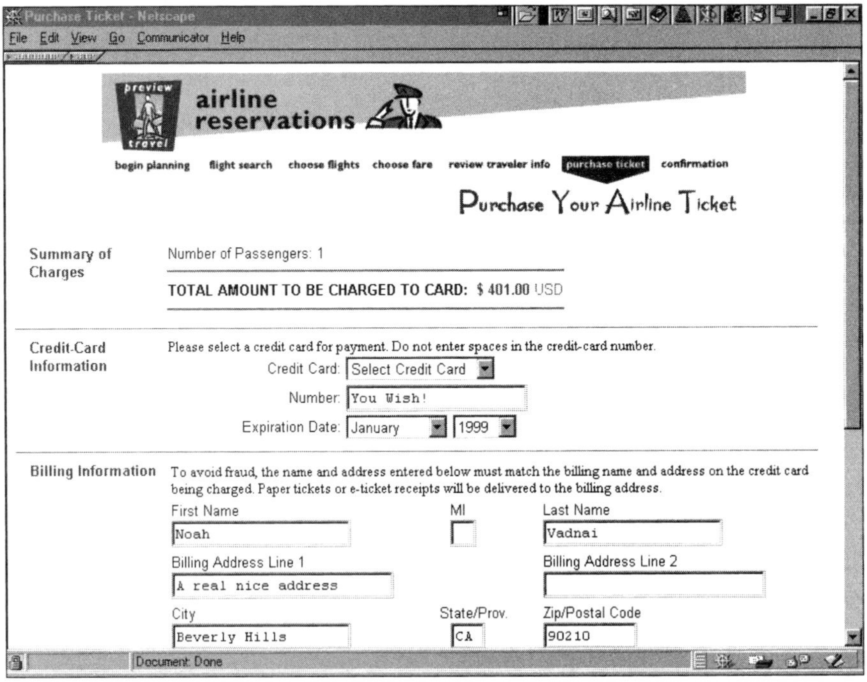

Figure 6-11:
The
Preview
Travel
Purchase
Your Airline
Ticket page.

The Preview FareFinder

Unless you purchase tickets regularly, it can be tough to stay abreast of the current fares for a flight. Preview offers a feature that can help you with this tedious chore; select your departure city and the Preview FareFinder shows you the latest fares in the Preview Travel database. All fares are for available flights; some have restrictions.

The FareFinder's results are hit or miss. Sometimes, the fares are genuinely good deals. But more frequently, I get fares I know to be higher than what a good discount retail travel agent can get for me.

Despite its shortcomings, the FareFinder can prove a valuable tool to have at your disposal to familiarize yourself with the fares on an unfamiliar route.

Travelocity

You may be acquainted with Travelocity's parent company, The Sabre Group. Sabre was the first computer reservation system to offer its services to the general public, way back in 1985, on the Compuserve service. The original reservation system, easySabre, still exists on Compuserve and on the Web (www.easysabre.com) but it functions as a very stripped down, no frills online reservation system. Now anyone can search Sabre's enormous database of fares to check and reserve flights on the Internet at the Sabre Web site, Travelocity (www.travelocity.com).

Travelocity's database of fares is one of the largest and busiest, performing millions of reservations requests each day; unfortunately, the site's popularity sometimes makes Travelocity very busy and slow to use.

You can book flights that originate from any country with Travelocity. In terms of customer service, there's no 24-hour phone service, just an e-mail submittal form.

To enter Travelocity's reservation system, click the Travel Reservations button. Then click the Flights button to select air travel as the type of reservation you wish to make. The site takes you to the Flights Menu page, a display of all the air travel related features offered by Travelocity.

If you've never used Travelocity before, the system prompts you to create a traveler profile. This profile, containing your travel preferences and vital statistics, is saved in the system and accessed every time you make a reservation, saving you time and effort in the booking process.

To get started, you have to tell the Flights Menu how you want to search. You have the following choices:

- **Three Best Itineraries:** Instructs the database to find the three lowest priced flights that meet your travel needs.
- **Flights & Prices:** Pulls out all the flights that meet your criteria, regardless of price.

Pick which method suits your needs and follow these steps (they are the same for both methods) to get where you want to be:

1. **Make a flight request.**

   How many people are you traveling with? Which airlines do you want to travel on? You must answer these questions as well as instruct Travelocity how to search for lower-priced alternative flights and which fare types you want (with restrictions, first class, business, and so on).

   Then fill out the form telling the system where you want to go and when. Check the box to select a round-trip flight and enter the return date. For multi-leg journeys, use each search box as a trip segment. Then click the Submit button to move to the next step.

2. **Review the flights and prices and make a selection.**

   If you use the Three Best Itineraries feature, you see three tempting prices for your selected trip. If you search using Flights & Prices, the system displays all the flights that satisfy your request regardless of price.

   In any case, select the flights that are best for you by clicking the Buy it Now! button or the Hold for 24 Hours button.

3. **Check the price and rules.**

   Check the price and applicable restrictions by looking closely at the quoted prices and then clicking the links in the Fare Rules box.

   The fare rules are restrictions placed on the tickets that you want to purchase. Read the rules carefully — a legend helps you decipher the abbreviations. Click the Legend link at the top of the page to access the list. When you are satisfied with your ticket and its restrictions and price, click Continue.

4. **Choose your preferred delivery method.**

   You can choose to have your tickets sent to you by FedEx or issued from a participating Sabre travel agent. Search the directory for a local Sabre agent if you don't know of one.

5. **Specify your passenger info.**

   The system now asks which profile you want used to complete your ticketing, assuming you created more than one profile.

6. **Give your credit card information.**

   Time to pay the ferryman. Give up your credit card number or cancel the order.

7. **Add a car or hotel reservation to your itinerary or tell Travelocity to get lost.**

   Want to reserve a place to sleep? How about a car to get around in? Travelocity is more than happy to make the reservation for you, and asks if it can have the pleasure of doing so. If you choose to add a hotel or car reservation, you are taken through another search and reservation process. Otherwise, proceed to the final step.

8. **Review your reservation.**

   Travelocity presents your reservation info for your confirmation. Have a great trip!

Extra special flight features on Travelocity

I highly recommend that you visit the Flights Menu and take a look at the following features listed below the 3 Best Itineraries and Flights & Prices options (the site tells you how to sign up for each feature):

✔ **Departure/Arrival Times:** Want to know when a specific flight to a specific city arrives and departs? Simply enter the info into the form and you have access to the current info for nearly every airline, even if you don't know the flight number.

✔ **Flight Paging:** This is truly neat. If you have an alphanumeric pager, Travelocity can alert you when flights are delayed or canceled by paging you. The pager also displays gate and baggage claim info. I must get a pager!

✔ **Flight Timetable:** Ever tried to decipher the airline schedule book? It is no fun. But this feature is — just enter your query into the search form and click Submit. Now you can easily know the schedules for almost every airline.

✔ **Fare Information:** Enter the appropriate airports and find out the current published fares between two points.

✔ **Fare Watcher E-mail:** Enter up to five pairs of cities you wish to have Travelocity monitor for fare information. The program notifies you via your e-mail account when the fares change by more than $25. You can also visit your personal fare watcher page at any time to see the fares between your selected city pairs.

Buying Directly from the Source: Airline Sites That Sell

The Internet has not only revolutionized the way travelers purchase tickets, it has also completely changed the way tickets are sold. By using their Web sites as virtual ticket counters, airlines can now sell tickets directly to their customers, eliminating all the commission-demanding intermediaries.

For you, the savvy Information Age traveler, knowing about the airlines that sell tickets online can be very lucrative and pleasant for the following reasons (especially if you travel frequently for business or use airline award programs to collect free travel):

- ✔ Many airlines offer incentives (award miles and travel bonuses) to encourage you to buy tickets online.
- ✔ The airline sites often offer exclusive travel discounts for online customers only.
- ✔ You get to fly on airlines you know and like.
- ✔ Some airline sites allow you to book other airlines' flights.

However, you should also keep in mind that airlines are somewhat constrained in terms of the discounts they can offer on airfares. On international routes, airlines must adhere to a system of published fares and therefore are usually unable to offer the discounts that travel agents make available to their customers.

Fly the friendly Web

For the most part, only North American airlines offer online booking. (Lufthansa and Virgin Atlantic are exceptions.) You can currently reserve and purchase tickets online from the following airlines:

- ✔ Alaska Airlines (www.alaska-air.com)
- ✔ Air Canada (www.aircanada.ca)
- ✔ American Airlines (www.aa.com)
- ✔ America West Airlines (www.americawest.com)
- ✔ Continental Airlines (www.flycontinental.com)
- ✔ Delta Airlines (www.delta-air.com)

- ✔ **Lufthansa** (`www.lufthansa-USA.com`)
- ✔ **Northwest Airlines** (`www.nwa.com`)
- ✔ **Transworld Airlines** (`www.twa.com`)
- ✔ **United Airlines** (`www.ual.com`)
- ✔ **Virgin Atlantic** (`www.fly.virgin.com`)

Using individual airline sites

Each airline's booking system has its own features and gizmos, but all require you to create some sort of a profile, including a user name and password.

All the airline booking sites utilize secure server technology to ensure your personal information doesn't fall into the wrong hands. (See the sidebar "Online transaction security" in this chapter for more information about secure server technology.)

Many of the airline booking sites use the same computer reservation systems as the online travel agencies (the airlines own stakes in these systems), just with a different interface. (American Airlines, for example, uses the same system as Travelocity.) If you are new to online booking, these sites generally make it very it easy on you by walking you through the process step by step.

As an example, take a look at the American Airlines (`www.aa.com`) booking process for a new user. In order to use its online booking, American Airlines, like many other airlines, requires you to join its frequent flyer awards program (they try to make sure you have an incentive to keep flying American). If you are already a member of the AAdvantage program, you need your AAdvantage number and your PIN to log in on the American Airlines home page. If you're not a member, they are happy to enroll you online; just supply the basic info the site requires and you get an ID number, user name, and password to add to your collection. Also, you can elect to have the site store your AAdvantage Number in the system by clicking the check box below the login boxes, on the left side of the home page.

American then asks you to supply your travel preferences so that it can create a travel profile for you. Contained in your profile are the standard preferences: billing address, phone numbers, seating, meals, and credit card number (if you wish). Next, the site presents you with a travel planning page.

From this page, you can make the following choices related to your reservation. Each is explained with easy-to-follow instructions on the site:

- ✔ **Make Reservations:** Use the American Airlines booking system to reserve and purchase AA flights. The system works in a similar manner to Travelocity (see "Travelocity" in this chapter).

- ✔ **Book NetSAAver Fares:** This is the good stuff. As detailed in Chapter 9 of this book, American Airlines sends out a listing of discounted fares each Wednesday. Book these fares directly by using this feature — it's the best way to insure you get the coveted discount seats. This is the only place you book these special, last minute fares online. Your other option is to call AA to book a NetSAAver Fare, but remember, these fares are only available for a few days each week — roughly, from Wednesday to Saturday.

- ✔ **Check Flight Schedules, Gates, and Times:** Use this feature to check the entire AA flight schedule and to check arrival times and airport gates.

- ✔ **Fare Quotes:** Use these feature to quickly check the AA fares for a given flight route.

- ✔ **Current Reservations:** Modify your existing AA reservations or use awards to upgrade your service.

- ✔ **AAdvantage Locator Map:** Find the nearest AA ticket office or partner hotels and restaurants.

- ✔ **Refund Information:** Learn how to collect on unused AA tickets.

American Airlines was one of the first airlines to realize the possibilities the Internet presents to travelers, and thus it has had the most time to refine its site. Not all the airline sites are as slick and easy to use. But they'll get there.

Managing Your Airline Awards with Online Resources

Maybe you've seen them at the airport. The harried business travelers with their garment bags in tow and wallets brimming not with family photos, but rather with a multitude of airline frequent flyer program membership cards. Or maybe you *are* one of these hapless souls, haggling with the airline representatives over upgrade certificates that have somehow disappeared.

Well, the Internet can't keep you from losing your certificates, but it does contain resources that can help in all aspects of the frequent flyer gauntlet, including helping you:

✔ Manage your hard-earned miles

✔ Compare frequent flyer programs

✔ Buy and sell miles and awards and earn more miles

✔ Find other obsessed frequent flyers and get some advice that won't cost you any mileage

The CD-ROM that comes with this book also offers two award tracking programs that you may wish to try. Turn to Appendix B to read more about these programs.

Required reading for frequent flyers

Those of you who are really into the frequent flyer game probably already know about *InsideFlyer* magazine. Started by the world's most knowledge-able frequent flyer, Randy Petersen, *InsideFlyer,* the print magazine, has an online version called WebFlyer (www.webflyer.com), Figure 6-12, where all the info is free of charge.

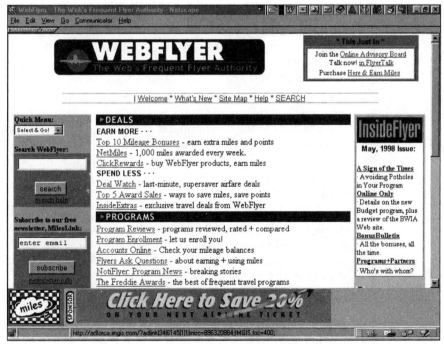

Figure 6-12: The WebFlyer home page.

The future of online booking

Just when you master using online travel agencies, everything is bound to change. But luckily, the changes that the future holds for online booking, and electronic commerce in general, should make the process of finding and buying goods and services on the Internet easier.

Intelligent agents, or *bots,* are pieces of software that scour the Web for whatever it is you're looking for. Though this technology is still in the formative stages, TheTrip.com (www.thetrip.com), a well-known site for business travelers, released Intellitrip in early 1998. Intellitrip is an intelligent agent that searches numerous computer reservation systems all at once, essentially eliminating the need to search several sites to get a good deal. And it works!

However, even though the technology works, Intellitrip requires its developers to enter business partnerships with the major online travel agencies. The online agencies initially gave Intellitrip the go ahead, but soon became disenchanted with the implications of the business partnership. Without permission to search the major computer reservations systems, Intellitrip is of little worth. But stay tuned — the future is bright for *bots.*

In terms of frequent flyer info, WebFlyer has it all, including the following:

- **The Deals Section:** Check in on the Top 10 Mileage Bonuses of the month and other ways to earn more miles. Also take a look at the five best ways to save miles and save points, plus lots of other timely and ingenious advice.

- **The Programs Section:** Get the lowdown on all the frequent flyer programs and then enroll in the ones that interest you. This section also has links to the most popular programs' sites so that you can check your balances easily and quickly.

- **The Travel Section:** Wait, isn't this all about travel? Check for award blackout dates (the scariest phrase to a frequent flyer) or just track a flight.

- **The Interactive Section:** Do you wish that you knew someone who shares your love of awards programs? Click FlyerTalk to interact with other frequent flyers in a threaded bulletin board area. You can read the questions travelers have asked the frequent flyer guru, Randy Petersen, or pose your own tough question.

- **Extras:** Still want some more? How about some comic relief? Or political issues that face frequent flyers? The site also offers frequent flyer screensavers and horoscopes. "You will receive many free miles from a man in Milwaukee. . . . "

Show me the miles! Managing your miles

Most frequent travelers belong to several awards programs. It quickly gets very confusing keeping track of all the mileage and points. Luckily, the digital age has (somewhat of) a solution.

A site called Biztravel.com is one of the best sites for business travelers on the Web. Here, business travelers can book flights, hotels, rental cars, get info about destinations, and keep track of their awards miles in the section called bizMiles (bizmiles.biztravel.com), shown in Figure 6-13.

The first time you visit bizMiles, you need to register by filling out the online form that asks for your name, address, your award program membership numbers, passwords, PINs, and the number of miles you have.

To add awards programs to your listing, click Add/Update Programs and write your membership info into the corresponding program forms. It's pretty much as simple as that.

bizMiles then contacts the award programs' databases and accesses your account info. You can access all your award info in one discreet package.

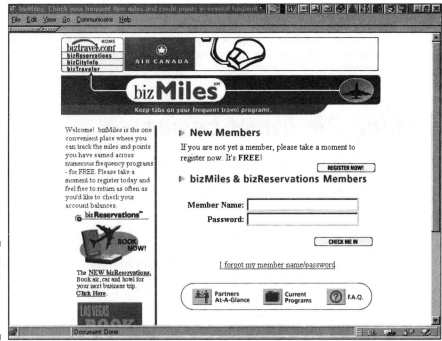

Figure 6-13: bizMiles on the BizTravel.com site.

Unfortunately, I have found the bizMiles program to be fairly buggy. It often seems to have problems accessing my awards program information and apologizes profusely. Still, Biztravel.com is a reputable company, and they have assured me that the problems will be fixed.

In the meantime, you should try using MaxMiles, a cool piece of software for managing travel awards. To get you started, I include a copy of MaxMiles on the CD-ROM that comes with this book.

Buying and selling awards and miles

While it's not illegal by U.S. or Canadian laws, the sale and transfer of award coupons, miles, and points is strictly prohibited by every travel supplier that offers an awards program.

But this is not to say that coupon brokers don't exist on the Web. They most certainly do, but they get busted quite often (the airlines sue them and in the process get their customer logs and then freeze the accounts of the participants) and to point you to the ones that I currently know about would be an exercise in futility, as they probably won't exist when this book is published. And, I really don't think it's worth the risk of losing your hard earned miles.

If you want to take the risk of using a coupon broker, you can search for them in Yahoo! by using the phrase *frequent flyer awards.* For more information on coupon brokers, consult the WebFlyer site and search for *coupon brokers.*

Making Air Travel Easier

Unfortunately, frustration is an inseparable aspect of air travel. If you've ever arrived at the airport in New York to pick up a friend or family member only to find that the flight has yet to even leave Houston, you know what I'm talking about.

You can turn to the Internet to help you alleviate much of the stress involved with air travel, both for the traveler and the person who must pick up the traveler at the airport. Even if that means finding a bar near the airport to cool your heels while you wait.

Tracking flights in progress

Before you head out to the airport to catch a flight or pick up a sister, consult the World Wide Web to make sure the flight is on time.

TheTrip.com (www.thetrip.com), a great site for business travelers, offers a terrific graphical flight tracking application that you can use free of charge. (You can go directly to FlightTracker, at flight.thetrip.com/flightstatus/.) The FlightTracker tracks flights in real-time; the application gets live information from the Federal Aviation Administration so you can be confident you are getting correct info.

To track a flight you need to know the airline and the flight number. Armed with your flight information, you can choose from two different tracking options:

- ✔ **Original FlightTracker:** If you're in a rush or have a very slow connection rate, choose this option, which is just a text display, no graphics. You can search by airline and flight number or by destination and time. You get the flight's vital statistics: takeoff time, landing time, altitude, speed, and distance to airport. You can track a random flight if you've got a little extra time on your hands.

- ✔ **Graphical FlightTracker:** Enter the airline and flight number and then the program displays a map of the country below the flight and graphical representation of the airplane and its route. You can actually watch the flight's progress. The site also tells you the plane's air speed, altitude, heading, and, of course, the updated arrival time. A very Zen experience to watch flights on your computer. Just don't lose track of time while watching your loved ones' flights and forget to go to the airport.

Know your airports

Frequent travelers' brains contain maps of many of the airports they use. But in an unfamiliar airport, you can waste valuable time searching for the baggage claim, ticket counters, ground transportation, and adjacent hotels.

Before your next trip, you can get the lowdown on airports all over the world by consulting the following Web sites:

- ✔ **QuickAID (**www.quickaid.com**):** QuickAID offers listings for almost all the world's airports. Click the Airport Directory link to find your airport of interest. Each airport listing has info on ground transportation, hotel information, airlines, a terminal map, and an Airport Yellow Pages (a directory of airport information).

✔ **TheTrip.com's Airport Strategies (**www.thetrip.com/strategies/airport/**):** Want to know the most important factor in saving time at the airport? Or how about three things to check when using curbside check-in? The advice offered at this site can save you something more important than time: your mind. TheTrip.com also has guides to airports on the site.

✔ **Yahoo! Directory Listing of Worldwide Airports (**www.yahoo.com/Business_and_Economy/Companies/Travel/Airports/**):** Check out the official site for almost any airport worldwide with this comprehensive alphabetical list of airport sites. Click Directories to find even more airports. Who knew the airport in Lukou had a Web site?

Finding airline information, Web sites, and toll-free phone numbers

Maybe you just want to give an airline a call or check out an airline Web site. A quick way to contact almost any airline in the world is located on a Princeton University server. Airline Toll-Free Numbers and Web sites (www.princeton.edu/Main/air800.html) is a plain text, alphabetical list of airline toll-free phone numbers and links to airline Web sites.

Or maybe you want to get a handle on the tremendous amount of airline and aviation information available online. Airline Information On-line on the Internet (iecc.com/airline/) is one of the best directories to the vastness of airline info on the Internet. It's updated frequently by John Levine, one of the authors of *The Internet for Dummies,* 5th Edition who is extremely knowledgeable about the subject of air travel.

Chapter 7
Finding a Place to Sleep

• •

In This Chapter
▶ Finding online hotel directories and hotel chain sites
▶ Locating Bed & Breakfast inns, hostels, and homestays
▶ Booking hotel rooms online
▶ Exchanging your home for someone else's

• •

*T*he Internet is a great way for a traveler to find a place to sleep. Whether you want to stay in a hotel in Hot Springs, a Bed & Breakfast (B&B) in Bedford, or a pensione in Penang, online resources can help you find a place to get a good night's rest.

Not only can you a find accommodations anywhere in the world on the Internet, you can now directly reserve and pay for rooms in many hotels and other forms of lodging by using sites on the Web.

This chapter discusses how to find and reserve all sorts of accommodations anywhere in the world. No Vacancy signs may be a thing of the past for you.

Deciding Where to Stay

Finding a good place to spend the night can make all the difference when you're on the road. The Internet can help you find a bed for the night, and with multimedia technology, many hotel sites enable you to take an online tour of the facilities. Unfortunately, you still can't check the firmness of the mattress — maybe in the new millennium.

Limiting what you're searching for

When you begin your online search for a place to stay, you need to know what type of accommodation you're looking for. Accommodations generally fall into the following categories:

- **Worldwide hotel and motel chains:** You have probably stayed in a Sheraton, Holiday Inn, or a Motel 6 at some point in your life, or at least driven by one on the highway. These types of accommodations are huge companies, with a standard of service the world over. All of the major chains now have sophisticated Web sites where travelers can find locations and prices, view different properties, and make reservations.

- **Unique hotels, small hotel chains, and motels:** Most cities have lodgings that are not part of a worldwide hotel chain. More and more independent hotels and motels are creating Web pages to connect with travelers and allow them to make reservations.

- **Bed & Breakfasts (B&Bs), inns, and pensiones:** Small, family-run lodgings are fun and intimate places to stay. Even though these establishments are small, many directories exist on the Web containing information on this type of lodging. (Since B&Bs and inns generally don't have an advertising budget, the Net is the perfect place for them to market their business.) Most smaller lodgings don't yet have the capability to do reservations online, but the Internet is the best way to find a great inn because of the great depth of information that online directories have.

- **Hostels and guest houses:** By using the Internet, budget travelers can find affordable accommodations, including hostels and guest houses, anywhere in the world. Many Web sites devote themselves to hosteling and lodging for budget travelers. (See Chapter 9 for more on budget accommodations.)

After you decide what type of accommodation best suits you, you can set about finding it on the Internet.

Finding accommodation directories

It's easy to be overwhelmed by the amount of accommodation information on the Internet. Don't believe me? Fine, just try a search using the keyword Hotels on any search engine and see what happens.

Don't despair, excellent directories of accommodations exist to help you focus your search for a place to sleep. Some directories list major hotel chains (called *first-tier properties* in the industry). Some directories concentrate on B&Bs, and some directories feature listings for geographic regions. And some directories offer a hodge-podge of just about every combination of listings. The key to using online accommodation directories is finding the directory that best suits your needs. (If you haven't decided what kind of lodgings you're looking for, read the section, "Limiting what you're searching for," earlier in this chapter.)

You can start your search for the perfect accommodation directory with a directory of directories. The Yahoo! directory of accommodation listings (www.yahoo.com/Business_and_Economy/Companies/Travel/Lodging/ Hotels/Directories/) provides links to about 80 directories, listed alphabetically with short descriptions.

Look for directories that focus on specific geographic regions — otherwise you end up spending a lot of time pouring over hotels in places you don't have any desire to visit.

You can also use the site's search capabilities to find accommodation sites and directories. One way to narrow your search is to search all of Yahoo! by entering a keyword framed by quotation marks. For example, if you want to find hotels in Sweden, perform a search with the phrase "Sweden hotels," which produces a list of sites that have something to do with hotels in Sweden. The other method is to use the pull-down menu (located next to the search box, at the top of the page) while you are looking at the directory of hotel listings. This search method enables you to search the current page of Yahoo! results for specific keywords.

Both methods work well, especially when you are looking for hotels in unusual or out of the way places. This practice works equally well in other search engines.

Gimme shelter: Great online accommodation directories

In addition to finding an accommodation directory that has listings specifi-cally for your destination, several general, extremely comprehensive, directories have risen to the top. Bookmark the following sites so you can research lodging opportunities quickly when you travel.

TravelWeb

TravelWeb (www.travelweb.com), Figure 7-1, is one of the largest accommo-dation databases in the world. The database connects to a sophisticated computer reservation system, called Pegasus, that allows you to check room availability and make reservations in thousands of hotels all over the world.

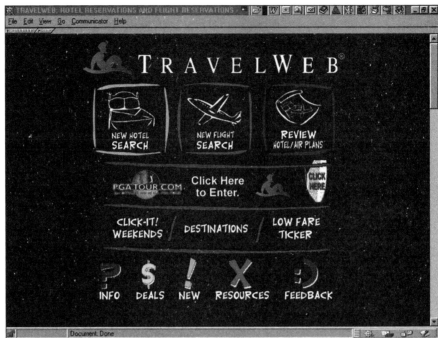

Figure 7-1:
The
TravelWeb
home page.

Pay a visit to TravelWeb when you want to stay in a top-tier property, that is, a Hilton, Hyatt, or other big, fat hotel chain. TravelWeb also lists independent hotels (hotels that are not part of a large chain) among its 17,000 or so hotel listings; these independent hotels generally provide a comparable level of service to the big-name hotels.

Searching the TravelWeb database is easy. Just follow these steps:

1. **Click the New Hotel Search button on the home page.**

2. **Enter your search criteria into the short form or click Browse by Hotel Chain or Browse Independent Hotels.**

   If you choose to use the short form, select the location and click Search. To see a listing with specific characteristics, select a hotel chain, price range, and desired amenities. One important criteria: Choose whether you want all hotels or only those that you can reserve online.

   If you click Browse by Hotel Chain, choose from the list of hotel chains that appears and then check to see what properties exist in each city. The system works the same way if you click Browse Independent Hotels, except that the list consists of links to non-chain hotels.

The search results give you the name of the hotel, the city where it's located, and whether the hotel can be booked online, along with other information about the hotel. If the hotel makes a photo available, TravelWeb also posts the picture so you can check out the boudoir.

TravelWeb's greatest selling point is its ability to provide real-time availability and reservation information, meaning, you see the rooms that are available at that moment in time, helping you better assess your options. After you find a hotel you want to stay in, you can go ahead and make your reservation online.

The booking process is quite simple. Just follow these steps:

1. **Click the Book It! button.**
2. **Check the availability by filling in the dates you want to stay and your bedding preferences (king size or peasant size).**
3. **Enter any travel awards program info.**
4. **Click the Check Availability button.**

   The system churns for a moment and then returns the availability.

5. **Select the room and rate you desire and then enter your credit card info to reserve.**

   The transaction is conducted over a secure server, so your credit card information is safe.

   Be sure to read the restrictions and cancellation policy. As with any agreement that involves money, you should know what you're getting into.

   It's a good idea to print out your confirmation page — that way you have a record of the transaction in case there are any questions. You're all set. Sleep well.

TravelWeb is an extremely useful resource for people who travel on business and people who just travel a lot. The site loads quickly, even on slow connections, so you can zip through the reservation process when you really need to get some sleep.

All Hotels on the Web

The name All Hotels on the Web (www.all-hotels.com), Figure 7-2, makes quite a claim for a Web page. In actuality, the site has a ton of listings (more than 10,000), and is a very good way to find many different types of hotels in any part of the world. But no single site could ever catalog all the hotel listings on the Web.

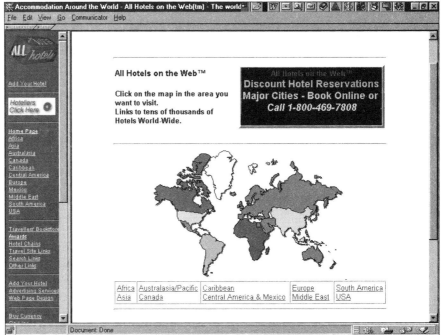

Figure 7-2:
The All
Hotels on
the Web
home page.

After you arrive at the site, you can click the appropriate location on the world map or use the navigation links on the left-hand side of the home page to locate hotels the world over.

All Hotels on the Web is just a directory of hotels that have a Web presence; you won't find direct booking or availability here. All the links lead to actual hotel pages or, in some cases, other hotel directories.

The real strength of All Hotels on the Web is that it lists not only the hotel mega-chains, but also a nice selection of independent accommodations. The listings for most of the hotels have little in the way of description, but the links are organized by location, making them easy to browse. The North American listings come the closest to substantiating the claim of All Hotels on the Web.

Hotels and Travel on the Net

Hotels and Travel on the Net (www.hotelstravel.com/), Figure 7-3, truly is a mammoth directory of accommodation information. Boasting more than 100,000 links to hotels and accommodation directories in over 120 countries, this directory would be a bit overwhelming if the information in it weren't so well organized.

Figure 7-3:
The Hotels
and Travel
on the Net
home page.

Click the Hotels/Travel Information link to access a geographic directory of
links to countries listed by continent. Select your destination country and
continue to drill down until you reach the locale you plan to visit.

The country pages contain links to regional and countrywide directories
(listings dedicated to specific geographic areas) as well as links to actual
hotel pages.

In addition to its extensive accommodation directory, Hotels and Travel on
the Net also offers a bunch of links to other useful travel resources, such as
destination guides, hotel chain sites, official airline sites, and more.

Places To Stay

Places To Stay (www.placestostay.com), Figure 7-4, is a unique, online
accommodation directory and reservation system. Not only can you search
for hotels, B&Bs, and resorts worldwide, but Places To Stay also allows you
to make reservations at all the accommodations listed in the database.
Places To Stay uses a snazzy new computer reservation system called
WorldRes (the owner of Places To Stay) that earns a living by enrolling small
hotel chains and inns and allowing travelers to make reservations online.

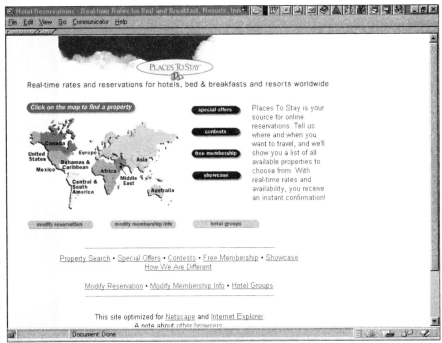

Figure 7-4:
The Places
To Stay
home page.

You can search the database by clicking the map of the world and finding the country, state, or province where you want to stay. You can book all the properties online, and most have photos. The online reservation procedure goes something like this:

1. **Fill out a membership form and select a username and password.**

2. **After you find a place where you want to make a reservation, click the accommodation's name.**

3. **Click the Click Here for Rates and Availability button.**

   This button may be hard to find amidst all the information about the property. But keep looking. It's there.

4. **Enter your arrival date and the number of rooms and nights you wish to stay. Click Check Availability.**

5. **Select the type of room you want and the number of adults and children that will be staying. Click Make Reservation.**

6. **Confirm your personal information and then enter a credit card number. Click Make Reservation. The reservation process is now complete.**

This database is constantly expanding and is well worth bookmarking. (See Chapter 15 to hear more about bookmarking.)

Online hotel information in all shapes and sizes

You can find accommodation information all over the Internet, not just on sites devoted to hotels and lodging. Try a few of the following types of sites for a different perspective on the lodging issue:

✔ **Online travel agencies:** Great places to research accommodations. You can search for availability and make reservations at this type of site. 1travel.com (www.1travel.com) is a great example of an online travel agency where you can find and reserve lodgings in a hurry. (Chapter 6 discusses the prominent online travel agencies.)

✔ **Official state and country tourism sites:** These sites exist to encourage tourism, so you won't find it surprising that they often have an extensive database of hotels and other lodging. Check out The Irish Tourist Board (www.ireland.travel.ie/) to see a good example of this kind of site.

✔ **Destination travel sites:** These sites, dedicated to travel in a specific place, have info on where to stay at the destination. France.com (www.france.com/) provides a wonderful example of what you can find at these kinds of sites. (Many of the sites in Chapter 1 offer accommodation information.)

✔ **Online travel guides:** These guides usually offer suggestions for good hotels and other accommodations. The Insiders Guides (www.insiders.com) is one such guide.

When you conduct a search for a room, don't shy away from using multiple types of sources, especially if you are looking for a place with a little more pizzazz than your average Motel 6.

Having No Reservations about Online Hotel Reservations

Booking a hotel room online is, by and large, an option only at the big hotel chains. This situation is rapidly changing, with systems like the one Places To Stay deploys (see the section, "Places To Stay" earlier in this chapter). But mostly, it's the global hotel chains that have the sophisticated computer reservation systems in place, similar to those the airlines use (often, the same systems) to manage their reservations. (See Chapter 6 for more information on booking airline reservations online.)

The first few times you book a hotel room online, you may wonder if you're really saving any time. But after you go through it once or twice, you'll find that booking a hotel room online is a simple and quick procedure.

Using online travel agencies to book accommodations

All the major online travel agencies, such as Travelocity (www.travelocity.com), offer online hotel reservations for the big hotel chains. The advantage of using an online travel agency to make a hotel reservation at a specific hotel company site is that you can access many different hotel chains through an online agency (see Figure 7-5). Booking a room at one of these sites is a simple, step-by-step process, similar to the process I outline in the section "TravelWeb" earlier in this chapter.

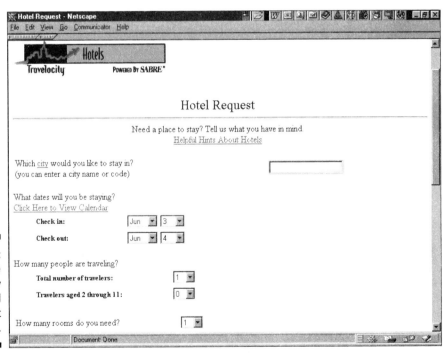

Figure 7-5:
The Travelocity hotel request page.

Most of the online agencies' hotel searches/reservation processes go something like this:

1. **Click Hotel Reservations from the site's home page.**

2. **Enter the name of the city where you want to stay.**

   If you want to stay near the airport in your destination city, you usually can specify that option, sometimes by entering the airport's three letter code.

3. **Enter the dates you want to stay.**

4. **Enter the number of travelers.**

   Most sites then allow you to narrow your search by setting preferences for room amenities, favorite hotel chains, and price ranges.

5. **Select a property from the list of hotels and then select the type of room you desire.**

6. **Confirm your personal information.**

7. **Enter your credit card information and complete your reservation.**

The results of a hotel search at an online travel agency provide you with prices, availability, hotel info, and (sometimes) photos of the property. Some of these reports even tell you what kind of chocolate you can expect to find on your pillow.

Booking from the hotel chain sites

Every major hotel chain has a Web site and most allow travelers to explore the hotel properties and make room reservations online. These sites are usually very well designed, enticing you with slick photography, detailed descriptions, and graphics, such as on Holiday Inn's online reservation page (www.holiday-inn.com), Figure 7-6.

If you have a favorite hotel chain, you may feel most comfortable using its Web site instead of an online travel agency, anyway. But the real advantage offered by hotel chain sites is that you find out about special promotions and bargains — information that an online travel agency may not have.

You can make online reservations at the following Web sites. My list by no means presents a complete list of hotel sites that allow you to book rooms online; I include many of the most popular hotel chains:

- ✔ **Best Western** (www.bestwestern.com)
- ✔ **Hilton** (www.hilton.com)
- ✔ **Holiday Inn** (www.holiday-inn.com)

Figure 7-6:
The Holiday
Inn online
reservation
page.

- ✔ **Hyatt Hotels** (www.hyatt.com)
- ✔ **Marriott** (www.marriott.com)
- ✔ **Ramada** (www.ramada.com)
- ✔ **Sheraton** (www.sheraton.com)

The hotel sites walk you through the process of checking on the availability of rooms and reserving a room. The hotel listings contain all the specifics about the hotel and the room. Some sites even have pictures of the different room configurations; all have toll-free phone numbers if you decide that you really want to talk to a living person about your reservation.

Even if you're really tired and can't wait to fall into bed, the online reservation process at the major hotel sites is a snap. The hotels want to encourage you to stay with them by making it easy to reserve rooms; you usually find very easy-to-follow instructions at each site.

To show you how easy it is to reserve a room at one of the major hotel chain sites, I want to walk you through making a reservation at a typical chain site — the Marriott Hotel's reservations desk.

Suppose that you and your family are heading to New York City for a weekend next month. You've always wanted to stay in the Marriott Marquis in Times Square. So you go to the Marriott Web site (`www.marriott.com`) and start the reservation process by clicking Reservations on the home page. After that, it's all booking history:

1. **Select New York from the destination list on the right-hand side of the screen and click it.**

   The next screen asks for your arrival and departure dates and any award program membership information. After you enter this information, click ? (the question mark symbol).

2. **The availability screen appears showing the types of rooms available; click Select Rate to choose a room.**

3. **Enter your personal and credit card information, and your room is reserved.**

You and the family are all set.

Other online accommodation booking options

During your surfing, you may come across other sites that claim to provide online booking for accommodations. In general, these sites have business deals with either online travel agencies or the actual computer reservation systems. What some of these other sites mean by online reservations, however, is that you can send an e-mail from the site to an administrator or a travel agent who then takes care of the reservation.

 These travel sites may come in handy for researching accommodation options, but securing reservations via e-mail is awkward, at best. You're better off getting the accommodation's phone number and calling directly to ensure that you're not getting duped by an unsavory business operation. As in all fields of commerce, the travel industry has some incidence of fraud and deceit — cautious vigilance is always the best policy.

Finding Unique Accommodations Online

A big chain hotel, such as a Holiday Inn, may be fine for an overnight layover by the airport or a hectic business trip. But you may prefer to stay someplace a little less basic. A small, family-run inn or B&B fits the bill much better than a hotel chain if you're looking for someplace that can be a destination in itself.

The Internet is positively loaded with directories and sites that can help you find the perfect B&B, inn, hostel, or even a homestay. This section focuses on directories that deal exclusively with accommodations that are not part of global corporations.

Locating inns and B&Bs online

B&B and inn hopping has become an extremely popular type of vacationing in recent years, a fact that becomes apparent when you start looking around the Internet for B&B information. You find tons of listings for these smaller businesses. B&Bs and other small accommodations generally operate on shoestring budgets — they have no money for advertising. But having a listing in a directory is a cost-effective means for a small inn to connect with potential guests, which is why you find so many B&B listings and directories on the Internet.

To help you sift through the offerings, try any of the sites listed in this section.

The Professional Association of Innkeepers International

The Professional Association of Innkeepers International (PAII) Web site (www.paii.org) maintains a large directory of B&Bs that's useful for travelers as well as professional innkeepers. To be listed in the site's database, a B&B must be a member in good standing with the PAII, ensuring good reputations among the listed B&Bs.

PAII has a host of resources geared towards innkeepers. The part of the site that's of interest to travelers is called the InnPlace (www.innplace.com). You can search the entire directory by keyword or browse by location.

The directory includes inns in all 50 states of the U.S., as well as inns in several other countries. The listings are comprehensive, providing inn-depth (sorry) information about the property's offerings and location. Most listings also offer photos.

The PAII site also lists notable B&B directories on a page of its site (www.paii.org/directories.html). These directories are a good bet for finding high-quality inns the world over.

The Bed & Breakfast Channel

The Bed & Breakfast Channel Web site (www.bbchannel.com), is an enormous database (more than 20,000 listings) of inns around the world. The site has a slick design that makes it easy-to-use, and it is updated frequently with new listings and refinements. The Bed & Breakfast Channel is the premier online guide to B&Bs and inns.

Use the site's straightforward search engine to find listings for inns all over the world:

1. **Find the search box near the bottom of the home page.**

2. **Input the city, state, and country for which you want to find inns.**

3. **Click Submit. The listings offer detailed information and many include color photos.**

You can also use the Amenity Search if you want your accommodation to have a particular feature. Want an oceanside inn? Or maybe you want a fireplace in the room. Click Amenity Search (below the home page search box) and select as many or as few features as you desire. The database then pulls out the inns that comply with your search.

Yahoo! directory of B&B directories

The Yahoo! directory of B&B directories (www.yahoo.com/ Business_and_Economy/Companies/Travel/Lodging/ Bed_and_Breakfasts/Directories/) is a good way to get a handle on the throngs of inn information on the Web. The 80 or so directories listed in Yahoo! are by no means the complete collection of inn directories, but because of its depth and ubiquity (every Webmaster wants their site listed on Yahoo!), Yahoo! is certainly a good place to start a search, especially if you're looking for a directory that services a specific region.

Use your browser's capability to search for keywords within a Web page to find sites that match your interest. You can find this search function under the Edit menu on both Netscape and Internet Explorer. The Yahoo! site also furnishes a function that allows you to search within a specific category. You activate this function by using the pull-down menu next to the search box. Invaluable!

Getting Bed & Breakfast advice from wired travelers

In addition to plying directory after directory of B&B listings, you can enlist other travelers in your search for the perfect inn.

Chapter 13 of this book deals extensively with using newsgroups, but I want to mention a newsgroup that is dedicated to discussing B&B's all over the world. However, if the urge strikes you, feel free to skip to Chapter 13 and read all about newsgroups.

You can post questions and requests for information to
`rec.travel.bed+breakfast` when you want to find a B&B in some region
of the world or tell others about a great experience you had at an inn. The
group is very active with B&B connoisseurs exchanging information.

Searching for hostels

If you travel on a tight budget, the Internet has some great resources for
finding inexpensive lodging in the form of hostels, guest houses, pensions,
and homestays.

The Yahoo! general lodging directory (`www.yahoo.com/
Business_and_Economy/Companies/Travel/Lodging/`) features catego-
ries for hostels, homestays, farmstays, and campgrounds. Searching on
those keywords in other search engines also yields sites that can aid in your
search for affordable digs.

You can also go straight to any of the sites listed in this section to start your
search for accommodations that won't break your budget. (See Chapter 9
for more on budget traveling.)

The Internet Guide to Hostelling

The word *hostel* technically refers to a supervised residence, but it has
taken on a broader definition in the lexicon of budget travelers, referring in
general to any low-budget accommodation. Some hostels are dormitory
style (featuring several beds in one room) and some have private rooms.
Some require that guests take on a chore. The unifying factor is that all are
cheap. (See Chapter 9 for more on budget traveling.)

The Internet Guide to Hostelling (`www.hostels.com/`) is the foremost
directory of inexpensive hostels on the Web. You can use the Worldwide
Hostel Guide section to search for hostels and guest houses by region. The
listings contain the contact info (address, phone number, e-mail, and so on)
and prices for each hostel. Some also include links to Web pages for individual businesses.

Hostelling International

Hostelling International (`www.hiayh.org/`) is a not-for-profit organization,
and, in its own words, "dedicated to making travel possible for those on a
budget through its low-cost, self-service network of accommodations."

Becoming a member of Hostelling International enables you to stay at 5,000
hostels in 71 countries and pay a lower nightly rate than non-members.
Membership also grants you access to the International Booking Network,
which currently allows advance bookings (by phone or in person) for
hostels in more than 200 locations.

The Hostelling International page has a searchable directory of member hostels. The search is straightforward: click Hostels, and then select U.S. hostels or international. The listings are organized by country or state, and the site gives you the requested listings alphabetically. Currently, it isn't possible to make hostel reservations online. But you can find detailed information on the HI-AYH Web site about how to make reservations by phone, fax, or mail.

Homestays and other interesting lodging options

When you stay in a big hotel, you can go through a whole trip without ever meeting any local people, which, if you ask me, is a pretty weird way to visit a place. At the other extreme are homestays, where you find a family or individual that opens up their home to travelers and you have a chance to interact on an intimate level (doing dishes together, arguing with in-laws — that sort of stuff). While this type of accommodation does not appeal to everyone, the Internet is a good means of finding homestay experiences if that's what you desire.

Though my word processor doesn't recognize the word, *homestay* has been in Webster's dictionary since 1956 and thus is a recognized term the world over, and the one you should use when you conduct a Web search for this type of lodging. I recommend pairing the word homestay with the country you want to visit (for example, **Homestay + Spain**). Using these words should turn up resources to aid you in your quest.

The homestay theme has been expanded to *farmstays* (you can probably guess what it means). You can even find a category on Yahoo! for this type of experience (`www.yahoo.com/Business_and_Economy/Companies/Travel/Lodging/Farmstays/`). **Just be ready to milk some cows and get up with the roosters.**

There's No Place Like Someone Else's Home: Home Swaps

Every time I look at the sites on the Web promoting home exchange, I wish I had a home to exchange. Somehow, I just don't think anyone would want to swap his or her home for my tiny Manhattan apartment.

In any case, when you think about taking an extended vacation or sabbatical leave, or really, any extended time away from home, you may want to consider entering into an arrangement where you swap homes. Yes, I mean with a perfect stranger. Sound risky? Well, it really isn't. But do everything in your power to learn about the people you are swapping with — a reputable home swap service should have a screening process.

The Web has a slew of sites devoted to helping people find other people looking to do a little home switcheroo. These sites also typically explain the logistics involved with such an arrangement.

Home exchange sites on the Web

Yahoo! has a category for home exchange containing about 40 sites, including sites about exchanging condominiums, RVs, yachts, houses, apartments, and almost anything else people live in. At most sites, you can search for people offering to swap or you can list your own property and wait for responses.

Noteworthy home swap sites

You can find a lot of home exchange info on the Web, but the following are sites I know are reputable and of high quality:

- ✔ **Holi-Swaps (**`www.holi-swaps.com`**):** You can list your home or vacation property at this site for about $30 per year, and you can view other members' offers for free. If you see a place that strikes your fancy, contact the owner by e-mail and conduct the negotiations on your own.

- ✔ **HomeExchange.com (**`www.homeexchange.com`**):** HomeExchange.com currently charges $30 per year to list a property. You can search the site's listings by country free of charge. The site also offers listings for long-term exchanges (more than just a few week holiday).

- ✔ **Stay4Free (**`www.stay4free.com`**):** Great name, right? This free accommodation network breaks its listings down into four main categories: Business (for business travelers looking to exchange), Exchange (vacationers looking to exchange), Gay (homosexual home exchanges), and Backpackers (exchanges geared toward independent, budget travelers). (See Chapter 9 for more on budget traveling.) Select your category, become a member (for free) and then search away.

One last piece of advice: When you swap your house, always remember to hide your embarrassing stuff. You don't want to come home to find that your collection of porcelain donkeys has been unearthed.

Chapter 8

Hitting the Roads and Rails

. . . .

. . . .

*Y*ou can easily rent cars, book train tickets on railroads around the world, and find out about fantastic rail journeys, all from the comfort of your computer.

Chapter 8 contains loads of advice about how to best utilize the online resources available to people who want to travel on wheels. After reading this chapter, you may even decide to forgo air travel altogether!

Renting the Wheels Online

Because the big car rental companies all use computer reservation systems, you can tap into their reservation services from any computer connected to the Internet. You can use these services at primarily two types of sites on the World Wide Web:

> ✔ **Car rental company sites:** These official company sites range in sophistication, but most of the larger companies offer their customers some type of online reservation option.
>
> ✔ **Online travel agencies:** The big online agencies are more than happy to arrange a rental car for you either at the airport or anywhere else rental companies have offices. Most agencies search many rental companies at the same time and return the best priced rental cars.

Either way, the process is simple and highly enjoyable. Okay, maybe I exaggerate a bit — you probably won't find yourself booking cars in your spare time just for fun. But reserving a car online is easy and saves you the aggravation of waiting on hold for a rental company's customer service agent. Renting a car online also allows you the luxury of seeing all the available models of cars in the company's fleet. Check it out.

Renting from official car rental company sites

The big car rental companies would like nothing better than for you to use their sites to rent cars every time you need one. But don't do it to please the companies; rent your cars on the Internet because it's easy to use, the service is always available from anywhere with a phone line, and it costs nothing. You can also find out about special promotions and other rental deals.

You incur no cost by checking availability or reserving cars using the online reservation system.

Personally, I prefer checking availability and reserving a car online to waiting on the phone while a rental agent does essentially the same procedure. Doing the process yourself ensures that you're getting exactly what you want; most rental sites have photos and descriptions of all the cars in their fleet. Booking online allows you to check out your other options if your desired vehicle isn't available at a certain location, and makes it easy to comparison shop among several rental companies. And, perhaps best of all, you can print out your reservation confirmation, so when you arrive at the pickup point and your car isn't available, you have proof of your reservation. Grrrr.

All the rental car company sites' online reservation systems operate in a similar manner. Renting a car at any of the major car sites resembles the following process for renting at the Hertz Rent A Car site (www.hertz.com), one of the biggest car and truck rental companies in the world:

1. **From the Hertz home page, click Rates & Reservations.**

2. **Choose a reservation option.**

   If you participate in any of Hertz' frequent customer programs, choose the link that corresponds to your membership. Otherwise, enter through the general option.

3. **Using the reservation query form, input the dates and times you want to rent a car and your country of residence, the rental location, and your airline info (if applicable).**

   Refer to Figure 8-1 to view this query page.

   The system asks you which city in the country you've chosen to rent the car from. It then asks where in the city you wish to pick the car up (if Hertz maintains more than one office in that city).

4. **Confirm that the location info is correct and then choose, using the pull-down menu, which class of car you want and type in any additional vehicle requirements.**

   This page shows you the availability for your request and the fare information. Check to see that all the information looks good.

5. **Click Submit to continue on to the next page to reserve the vehicle.**

6. **Make sure the next screen is in secure server mode by checking for the lock in the bottom-left corner (Netscape) or bottom-right corner (Internet Explorer) and then enter your credit card info to confirm the reservation.**

   The site sends you to a confirmation page to let you know that you're ready to rumble.

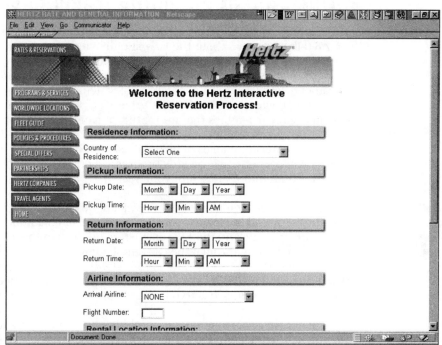

Figure 8-1:
The Hertz
Rent A Car
reservation
query page.

Always print out the confirmation page and bring it with you when you pick up the vehicle — if something goes wrong with your reservation, you have proof of your reservation.

If you have any trouble with a company's online reservation system, every rental company has a toll-free phone number listed on its Web site that you can use to rent a car the old fashioned way.

Most of the big, global car rental companies maintain sites online at the following addresses:

- ✔ **Alamo** (www.goalamo.com)
- ✔ **Avis** (www.avis.com)
- ✔ **Budget** (www.budgetrentacar.com)
- ✔ **Dollar** (www.dollarcar.com)
- ✔ **Hertz** (www.hertz.com)
- ✔ **National** (www.nationalcar.com)
- ✔ **Thrifty** (www.thrifty.com)

Renting cars at an online travel agency

All the big online agencies offer car rental services to their customers. (Chapter 6 tells you more about the largest online agencies.) Online travel agencies offer one huge advantage over renting from the car companies themselves (see the preceding section): the agencies can search for rental options among several car rental companies, which allows you to find exactly what you want, and for the best price. The process for renting a car through an agency resembles that for renting at a car rental company site (see the preceding section), except that you can choose to have the agency search all the rental companies in its database, or search just a few of your favorites. If you participate in awards programs, you can enter this and all corporate account information into your search.

Most online agencies require travelers to pick up the rental car at the airport, whereas the car rental company may offer a more convenient location in the city. If you prefer to pick up the car somewhere other than the airport, you may need to go directly through the car rental company.

Check out these online travel agencies that have car rental services to discover what each agency has to offer:

- ✔ **Biztravel.com** (www.biztravel.com): Biztravel.com makes it a little complex to rent a car only, without a flight or room included — the site is designed to rent cars as part of a travel package. So if you're not arriving at an airport, I recommend using another online agency.

However, because Biztravel.com is a popular site, and useful for travel packages, I decided to include it in this list. Click bizReservations and then Plan a New Trip. You must then name your trip — I named mine Steve. On the next page select Car where it says "For this destination I need:" Biztravel.com generally links car rental to flight times, but if you just want to rent a car, click Car & Hotel Rental. Finally, the site presents you with a form to enter your rental dates, and you can take it from there.

✔ **Expedia (**`expedia.msn.com`**):** Expedia is a full service, online travel agency. To rent a car, choose Car Wizard (the adorable name assigned to the car rental portion of the site) from the Travel Agent main page, which takes you to the Search for a Car page (see Figure 8-2). The site's Wizard then gives you step-by-step instructions, querying you when it needs information from you. Simple as that!

✔ **Internet Travel Network (**`www.itn.net`**):** Click Reservations and then select Car Rental from the menu on the right. Select Car from the reservations menu and enter the days, times, and preferred car rental companies. Click Check Car Availability and you're on your way to driving away. Choose a car from the results list, enter your credit card information, and your car is reserved.

✔ **Preview Travel (**`www.previewtravel.com`**):** Using the reservations portion of the site, select Cars to access the car rental form. Preview Travel then walks you through the car search and reservation process, which consists of six easy steps: car search, rental location choice, car choice, car info review, reserve your car, and finally, the confirmation.

✔ **TheTrip.com (**`www.thetrip.com`**):** Select Ground Transportation and then click Book Online Now. If the rest of the process looks familiar, that's because it is! TheTrip.com uses Internet Travel Network's reservation system to book cars. See above for details.

✔ **Travelocity (**`www.travelocity.com`**):** Select cars from the Travel Reservations menu and you're on your way. Enter the location where you want to rent a car, the dates, times, and type of vehicle — then click Submit. Next, choose a car from the list and reserve it. Add your credit card information and the car is as good as yours.

Planning a Road Trip with the Information Super-Highway

Due to the legendary highway Route 66 and Jack Kerouac's book *On the Road,* most people associate road trips with America. However, road trips are a great way to see any part of the world. But I know that most of you don't have an Internet connection in your car, so it's well worth spending some time exploring the online resources geared toward road trip research before you head out on the highway.

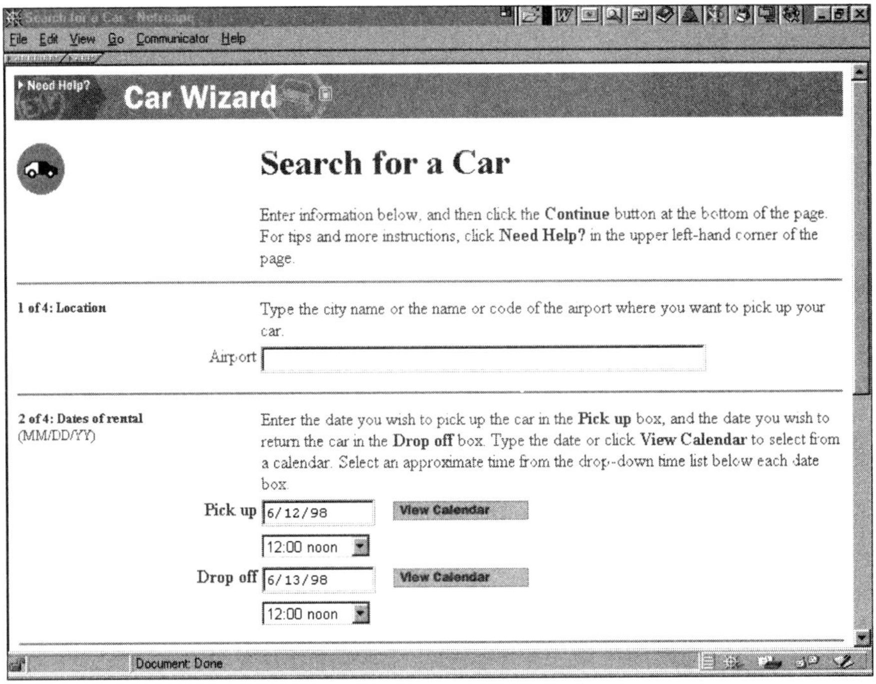

Figure 8-2:
The Expedia
Search for
a Car page
of the Car
Wizard.

Getting down to the route of the matter

Chapter 11 tells you how to find the best way between two points, but the Internet gives you access to much more information about roads that can really help you make the driving part of your road trip special. Using the Internet's search engines allows you to pull up all kinds of Web pages that can tell you about what you'll be seeing out your car windows, including pages on scenic roads and points of interest.

To search for information about your route with one of the search engines, use the name of your destination coupled with the word roads (for example, Oregon + roads). This method returns many pages, but usually you can quickly glean from the short descriptions whether the site is worth your time. If you search for route information in Oregon on Yahoo! (www.yahoo.com), for example, you go through the following process:

1. **On the Yahoo! home page, click Travel and then Automotive.**

   The Automotive section has subdirectories within it.

2. **Click Highways and Roads to find road listings broken down by state.**

   You can also try the Scenic Roads and Byways listing to see if your region has a listing. Another good method is to use the limited Yahoo! category search (the pull-down menu next to the search box) to search for the keyword Oregon.

3. **Under Highways and Roads, scroll through the alphabetical, state-by-state listings to find Oregon.**

   The entry in this listing for Oregon is Oregon Highways and Routes (`www.hooked.net/users/mwiley/Oregon_Highways/index.html`) and sounds promising. I also found a good Oregon roads site under the Scenic Roads and Byways category — 101 - Oregon's Coast Highway (`www.oregon1.org/coast/`).

Using the Web to avoid traffic

Being stuck in traffic is one of the worst feelings in the world. People deal with it in different ways: my father curses and attempts alternate routes, while my friend Tom rolls down the windows and turns the music up. You could choose to deal with traffic by using the Web to make sure that you avoid troublesome jams. Before you leave on your road trip, look for a Web site where you can check the current traffic and road conditions before you exit the driveway.

Yahoo! has a category called Traffic and Road Conditions (`www.yahoo.com/Business_and_Economy/Transportation/Traffic_and_Road_ Conditions/`) that lists traffic sites for many American metropolitan regions. Find your region in the alphabetical listing.

The following sites can also help you steer clear of traffic:

- ✔ **The Definitive Table of Real Time Traffic** (`www.itsonline.com/rttable.html`): This simple list of sites provides real-time (constantly updated) traffic information for a number of metropolitan regions around the world.

- ✔ **Rand McNally Online: Road Construction** (`www.randmcnally.com/construction/index.htm`): Find out about ongoing road construction operations in the U.S. and Canada and adjust your route accordingly.

- ✔ **RWA Direct** (`rwa.metronetworks.com/RWADirect.HTML`): Get traffic, weather, and road conditions for anywhere in the U.S. at this nifty site. Select the state and then peruse the detailed listings provided by state government agencies.

- ✔ **SmarTraveler** (`www.smartraveler.com`): This site currently provides real-time traffic info for four American cities, with many more planned in the near future. The traffic and road condition info is updated every few minutes and is accessible through a map of the selected city's roadways.

Finding roadside attractions

The best thing about a road trip is stopping often to eat and check out stuff along the way. Americans have elevated roadside businesses to an art form, and because Americans produce a great many Web sites, you find a whole crop of road trip Web sites to point you to the best diners, truck stops, and monuments. Did I neglect to mention toilet seat museums? And road trip information is by no means limited to America or American sites — the Net is a great way to research a road trip anywhere roads exist.

Yahoo! offers a section called Roadside Attractions (`www.yahoo.com/Recreation/Travel/Automotive/Roadside_Attractions/`) composed of sites that are directories of stuff you find on the side of the road and sites that are all about one particular attraction. You have to check out the world's largest ball of twine at The Blue Skyways Page (`skyways.lib.ks.us /kansas/towns/Cawker/twine.html`).

Roadside America

Roadside America (`www.roadsideamerica.com`), Figure 8-3, is one of my favorite sites on the Web. You needn't be planning a road trip to appreciate this chronicle of amazing Americana.

Figure 8-3: The Roadside America home page.

Use the Electric Map to find attractions in any state you pass through or "probe the lobes" of the Travel Brain if you are feeling a bit low on cognitive power and need to be guided around the site.

Or just dive in and click around to find some of the oddest human constructions this side of the World's Largest Catsup Bottle. A few of my favorites include the beer can house in Houston, Texas, the Muffler Man mystery (www.roadsideamerica.com/muffler/index.html), and, of course, the toilet seat artist (www.roadsideamerica.com/attract/CABORtoilet.html).

EatHere.com

Roadside eateries range from the delectable to the disastrous, but they are a must for any self-respecting road tripper. EatHere.com (www.eathere.com), Figure 8-4, celebrates roadside food as a distinctly American genre of gastronomy.

Visit EatHere.com to locate classic diners, barbecue joints, truckstops, and loads of other purveyors of tasty roadside goodies. You can search the site either by type of food and restaurant or by keyword. Each eatery listed in EatHere.com has driving directions, background information about the establishment, food reviews, and other fun information. Some entries even have menus. Check out Pot Roast News for the latest on what's going on around the U.S. in terms of roadside feeding.

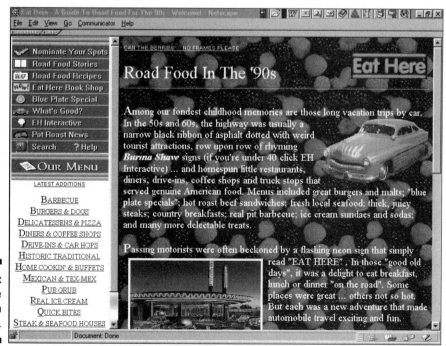

Figure 8-4:
The
EatHere.com
home page.

Route 66

You can't talk about a road trip without mentioning the Mother Road, Route 66, which is represented on the Internet by a site called, astoundingly, Route 66 (`route66.netvision.be`), Figure 8-5. Stretching from Chicago to Los Angeles, Route 66 is often eulogized in song and literature as the quintessential American roadway. A Route 66 cult of sorts has embedded itself in the world's consciousness (the site is produced by a Belgian) and this Web site is a great place to research the mythic road. Regardless of whether you plan to drive any or all of Route 66, the site is a terrific place to gain an appreciation of American road tripping. If you've read *On the Road* by Jack Kerouac, you'll see what I mean.

You use the left-hand links to navigate through the history, events, descriptions, and numerous other categories of information all about Route 66. The site also offers an excellent slide show and many links to other Route 66 info.

Online resources for recreational vehicle enthusiasts

Recreation vehicle (RV) enthusiasts resemble upscale nomads, cruising the roads of the world in style. Those of you who spend your vacation time

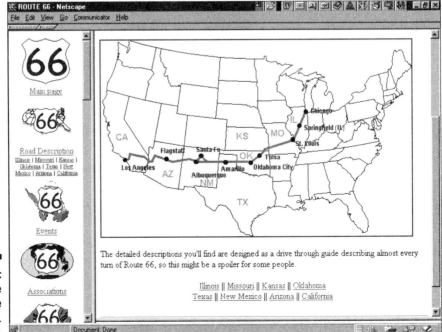

Figure 8-5:
The Route 66 home page.

in a house on wheels have loads of helpful information waiting for you on the Internet.

The Yahoo! category for RVs (www.yahoo.com/Recreation/Travel/ Automotive/Recreational_Vehicles/) provides a great place to start when you want to find info about renting, buying, or driving an RV. Yahoo! breaks its RV category down into the following subcategories:

- ✔ **Airstreams:** Info about the classiest brand of recreational vehicle.
- ✔ **Companies:** Loads of information about the companies that make RVs and RV products.
- ✔ **Events and Shows:** In the market for a new vehicle? Attend an RV show and comparison shop.
- ✔ **Magazines:** Read up on your hobby.
- ✔ **Organizations:** Join up with other RVers and meet folks who share your passion for the open road.
- ✔ **RV Parks:** RVs are self-sufficient up to a point . . . sometimes you just need to plug in and relax a little. For this, you need to find an RV park, which you can find in this category.
- ✔ **RV Tours:** Want to go on a planned itinerary with a rented RV? This is the place to find a tour.
- ✔ **Usenet:** Talk to other RV aficionados and get questions answered — or just converse about whatever interests you in a Usenet newsgroup devoted to RV topics. (I tell you more about newsgroups in Chapter 12.)

In addition to using Yahoo!, when you find a good RV site, be sure to check whether the site provides links to other RV resources — one of the best methods for finding quality sites.

Internet Training: Riding the Rails

A train trip affords you with a generally inexpensive and safe means of travel. Many trains have dining cars, beds, and first class service. You may find nothing more relaxing than falling asleep to the sound of a chugging locomotive in the gentle swaying of a rail car berth. Use the Internet to acquire all sorts of railroad information, including fares and schedules, booking information, routes, and unique train travel opportunities.

Whither and whence the trains cometh

In areas where train travel is very popular, you may find yourself faced with the task of sifting through hundreds of thousands of train listings *per day*. (For example, an estimated 300,000 train movements take place a day in Europe alone.) Deciphering a schedule, or even acquiring the correct timetable, can be a serious task. The Web is definitely the best way to find out when your train is coming and where it's going, for almost any country in the world.

RailServe

When you want to find out about a specific train route or train info about a region, instead of conducting an involved Web search, I recommend first checking with RailServe (`www.railserve.com`), Figure 8-6. RailServe is a mammoth directory aimed at railroad enthusiasts, containing thousands of links to sites about every aspect of trains — from model trains to train travel.

For travelers, RailServe offers several very useful categories. Click Switchyard to view site categories. You then see categories called Passenger and Urban Transit; you find six categories in all, each corresponding to a different continent and containing links to all sorts of sites about train travel in that region. The site organizes the links alphabetically and even includes

Figure 8-6:
The
RailServe
home page.

short descriptions for each. Some links lead to official, state-run railroad sites, others to independent sites. A bit of surfing should turn up the schedule and route info you're searching for, whether it's subway, transcontinental sleeper train, or a Lionel train set.

Check out how to find the schedules for a fictional train trip in Holland (keeping in mind that it takes a bit of patience to find railroad info):

1. **From the home page, under Switchyard, click Passenger and Urban Transit - Europe.**

2. **Find the link, by perusing the list, for Dutch railway information. You find three listings — I choose the ones that are in English, as I don't speak Dutch.**

3. **The link takes you to a new site, with lots of Dutch train info. After a moment of looking around, I find a link for Dutch train schedules.**

Mercurio — The European Railway Server

The European Railway Server (`mercurio.iet.unipi.it/home.html`), Figure 8-7, has much the same purpose as RailServe (see the preceding section), but Mercurio focuses only on Europe's rails.

Mercurio is a notoriously slow-loading site. Be patient!

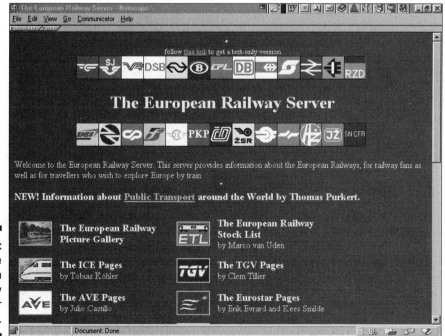

Figure 8-7: The European Railway Server home page.

Because such a high percentage of the world's railroads are located in Europe, you'll value having Mercurio amongst your travel bookmarks, especially if you plan to travel in Europe. You find the most useful link for travelers on Mercurio at the bottom of the left-hand list of links; Links to European National Railways and Timetables (`mercurio.iet.unipi.it/misc/timetabl.html`) contains links to every major European rail line, grouped into the following three categories:

✔ **European National Railway Servers:** Click the country's rail logo to access the official railroad server. These servers contain a variety of information about a nation's railroads: from technical data (of no interest to travelers) to timetables and prices. Many of these links are the same as the category below, European Railway Timetables.

✔ **European Railway Timetables:** These links go to pages containing official timetables for most major European railroads, usually provided on the official national railway servers. You may notice that many of the links are the same as the above category, European National Railway Servers, though many go directly to the timetable page on the official railway server.

✔ **The Best Unofficial European Rail Sites:** Visit this page to find links to unofficial sites that are good for researching rail journeys and getting an unofficial perspective. Many of these pages are not written in the native language of the country they describe.

Amtrak

Train travel, unfortunately, isn't as easy or popular in the United States as it is in other parts of the world. If you want to travel by train in America, the only option is to ride Amtrak (`www.amtrak.com`), Figure 8-8, or a commuter railroad. Amtrak has service between most major cities, but it is often slow and expensive. The Amtrak site, however, is easy to use to find routes and schedules. In addition, the site allows you to make online reservations.

To check schedules and routes for Amtrak trains, click Schedules on the home page. You then have the following five options, depending on your level of Amtrak knowledge, to check train schedules between cities:

✔ Simply enter your starting point and destination and the system shows you a list of departure times. You can allow for two connections.

✔ If you know the Amtrak city codes, enter them into the two boxes and click Let's Go!

✔ Enter the train number if you really know what you're doing.

✔ All Amtrak trains have names. If you know the name of the train that travels your route, you can search for schedules by selecting the name from a pull-down menu.

✔ Use the Amtrak reservation system to find and book your train route. The site tells you what to do step-by-step.

Figure 8-8:
The Amtrak
home page.

Another cool feature of the Amtrak site is the Travel Planner. If you're contemplating a trip to a certain region of the U.S. and you're curious about Amtrak's offerings, consult the Travel Planner for a full run down of what to expect from the train routes in the region.

Use the options on the site's home page to examine all the particulars of a train and route. For example, The City of New Orleans is one of Amtrak's best known trains and contains sleeper cars, sightseeing cars (glass roofs), and operates between Chicago and New Orleans.

Finding interesting and exotic rail journeys online

Does the idea of train travel conjure up images of ornate, Victorian rail cars speeding through an alien landscape? Well, those type of trips still exist (along with many, less ornate ones), and after a little research on the Internet, you can find yourself rolling across Asia aboard the Orient Express or in a darkened trainyard, waiting for a freight to leave for Tulsa.

Unless you know exactly what you're looking for (name of the train or railroad and the contact info), general searches for train travel in a search engine are likely to be time-consuming and somewhat fruitless. When looking for ideas for an interesting rail journey, your best bet is to spend some time surfing train directory-type sites on the Web; hopping from site to site using links usually proves an effective way to gather information about any topic. A few good starting points make the surfing much more productive. Use links to jump from site to site or read articles about interesting journeys, and then conduct further searches using the names of railways. Check out the following sites for starters:

- **RailServe** (www.railserve.com): Click Switchyard to view tons of links for all sorts of train-related sites in the sections entitled Passenger and Urban Transit. In addition to the links contained in these sections, check the advertisements and links to site sponsors on the site. Some of these are travel agencies that specialize in train tours.

- **The Rail Travel Center** (www.railtvl.com/): This site serves as a tour operator that specializes in train tours around the world. Check out its current tour offerings.

- **The World By Rail — Tripp Explorer** (www.trippexplorer.com): Check out this tour operator that runs some terrific sounding tours, including the South American Explorer, Turkish Explorer, and Alpine Europe.

- **The Cyberspace World Railroad's Lounge Car** (www.mcs.com/~dsdawdy/Parlor/parlor.html): Here you can read first person accounts of interesting journeys people have taken by rail.

- **Trans-Siberian Railroad Page** (www.xs4all.nl/~hgj/): This site details the classic rail journey, akin to the Orient Express. Tons of info about this amazing journey and over 70 links about the trip.

- **North Bank Fred's Freighthopping Site** (www.snowcrest.net/bndlstif/index.html): You can find all the info you need to *ride* freight trains all around North America, including trainyard descriptions and train schedules.

Purchasing a Eurail Pass on the Web

The Eurail system enables travelers to purchase one rail ticket and travel around 17 European countries by train, regardless of railroad. Of course, some restrictions apply to traveling times and routes, and many different varieties of tickets exist. You can get the complete Eurail picture, and even purchase your ticket online, by visiting a few choice Web sites outlined in this section.

Finding Eurail sites

Searching the Internet is easy when you have a unique keyword to search for, such as, hmmm, let me think — Eurail! Nothing else in the world can be confused with the word Eurail, except maybe the Ural Mountains, so go ahead and enter the word into any search engine and just watch the results pour in. Of course, any search finds some chaff, but for the most part, these search results offer lots of valuable info for a potential Eurail traveler.

The term Eurail has become somewhat of a generic term for any European rail ticket that allows unlimited rail travel, within one country or covering a region. Most European countries now offer variations of the Eurail-type inclusive ticket. Some tickets are just for regional travel, some for travel in a few countries, and the mother of all passes, the Eurailpass, allows you to travel almost everywhere in Europe. So when you find sites that talk about Eurail passes, make sure to find out exactly what the site is talking about.

Visiting sites about Eurail tickets

Rail Pass Express (www.eurail.com) is one of the largest outlets of European rail passes in the U.S. (though people from any country can purchase tickets here, provided they have a credit card) and is a great place to gain an understanding of the many types of passes available. Eurail is not actually a company, but rather an unincorporated association of European railway representatives. Rail Pass Express and other companies, such as Rail Europe (www.raileurope.com), are private companies that have agreements with various European rail companies and associations to distribute rail passes in the U.S. and around the world.

Go directly to the European Rail Passes section to check out the different pass varieties and prices. When you see a pass that interests you, click its name to get more detailed information.

If the whole Eurail travel experience seems a bit daunting, the site offers a bunch of good guide information to get you started. For example, you can click Trippin' with the Fergusons to order the best-selling offline guidebooks, or you can scroll down towards the bottom of the home page and click Traveling Europe by Eurail to access a bunch of articles covering the site's most frequently asked questions.

After you have your destinations figured out and have decided on the type of ticket that's right for you, you can purchase your ticket online by clicking Ordering. The process is easy — it uses grocery store metaphors (shopping carts, check out, and so on) to help you navigate through the choices:

1. **From the menu, select the type of rail pass that fits your needs and click it.**

2. **Select the pass you desire and the class ticket by entering the amount of passes you want into the quantity box.**

3. **Click the Add Items to Cart button (as in shopping cart).**

4. **After you order your passes, click the Checkout button.**

   The site asks you to fill in your shipping address and other personal info.

5. **Supply your credit card info and your passes are on the way.**

   Your order is placed over a secure server, so don't fret about your vacation fund being hijacked by cyber-wrongdoers.

Chapter 9

Using the Internet to Find Bargains

In This Chapter

▶ Making the discounts come to you

▶ Finding airfare bargains online

▶ Using the Internet to find discount hotel rooms

▶ Participating in online travel auctions

▶ Getting great deals on vacations and cruises

*L*et me guess. The first thing you did after picking up this book was flip right to Chapter 9. I don't blame you — *everyone* loves to find travel deals, no matter what kind of budget they have.

Much has been said both on- and offline about how you can use the Internet to find low airfares, discount cruises, and other deals on travel products. As with acquiring any coveted item, you need to do a bit of work and have a modicum of knowledge (not to mention a healthy portion of patience) to obtain travel deals online.

This chapter explains how to tap into the constant flow of online discount travel offerings. After you read this chapter, you can make your e-mail inbox full to the brim with timely, discounted travel offerings. You'll also know how to electronically monitor the changes in a specific airfare's price, purchase travel products by bidding on them at an online auction, and understand the benefits of being a little patient. But enough with being patient, read on to find out how you can snag those travel discounts.

Getting Travel Discounts by E-Mail

With the rapid growth in popularity of the Internet, airlines, cruise lines, hotels, and other travel-product suppliers quickly realized that they could use the Internet to sell their unused inventory at the last minute via e-mail.

Instead of having planes fly half full, for example, the airlines much prefer to sell their empty seats at cut prices. To fill those empty seats, most airlines gladly send out a free, weekly e-mail newsletter containing deals on flights.

Other suppliers offer such newsletters that focus on hotels, vacation packages, and other products. These discounted fares come directly from the travel suppliers — airlines, hotels, and tour operators — so you won't find the deals listed at discount travel Web sites.

However, the only way to take advantage of these bargains is if you are flexible with your schedule and willing to fly at the last minute. For the most part, these deals only become available about a week prior to the departure dates.

You *need* to subscribe to these newsletters in order to get your foot in the online travel discount door.

Subscribing to airline discount e-mail newsletters

If you travel frequently, or if you are flexible with your travel arrangements, airline newsletters are the best way to keep tabs on the latest and lowest airfares to a variety of locations. Receiving these newsletters can also boost your ego — you can brag to your friends about all the e-mail you get from people that want you to travel with them. The fares detailed in discount newsletters can cut more than 40 percent off the published airline ticket prices and regular vacation package prices.

Most of the major North American airlines offer some sort of weekly electronic mailing about discount fares that you can sign up for free of charge. The deals you find in these newsletters are almost always for the travel during the upcoming weekend. Some deals allow you to depart on Thursday, but most are for Friday departure with a Saturday night stay required.

To make getting these newsletters even easier, most of the major airlines use the same process to sign you up. Regardless of the airline, the sign-up process goes something like this:

1. **Visit the airline's official Web site.**

   You can find every airline's Web address by visiting a site called Airline Toll-Free Numbers and Websites (`www.princeton.edu/Main/air800.html`).

2. **Find the link on the airline site's home page that leads to the newsletter subscription and discount information.**

   A few of the better known programs are American Airlines' NetSAAver fares, Continental Airlines' CO.O.L. Travel Specials, and Northwest Airlines' CyberSavers.

3. **Input your e-mail address, name, and perhaps some additional information into the form on the airline site.**

Most airlines ask you for your home airport and then tailor your e-mail newsletter to reflect the available discounted fares that depart from your city. Some airlines, such as TWA, allow you to specify the routes that most interest you and then mail you fares each week for just those routes.

4. Click a button to submit your newsletter request.

After you submit the info, you will usually receive a confirmation e-mail to let you know that you're signed up and then begin receiving the newsletter on the next date of publication.

If you find that the discount e-mails just wind up as unread clutter in your mailbox, you can easily unsubscribe. Most newsletters include instructions at the end of each mailing on how to unsubscribe. Usually, you just send an e-mail to a certain address with the word UNSUBSCRIBE in the body of the message.

The following list tells you all about the most popular airline e-mail newsletters and the features each offers, the days of the week each is published, and the Web addresses for the subscription forms:

- ✓ **American Airlines NetSAAvers** (`www.aa.com`): Each Wednesday, American Airlines, a pioneer of travel services on the Web, publishes its NetSAAver fares, which tell you the available discounts for travel in the United States for the upcoming weekend. To sign up for or to check the latest specials, click Specials at the top of the home page and then click Subscribe to NetSAAver Fares.

  You should also consider subscribing to NetSAAver Fares International to receive listings of international airfares and other international promotions, which the airline publishes each Monday. You find the subscription info on the same page as the domestic NetSAAver.

- ✓ **America West Airlines** (`www.americawest.com/eto/surfngo.asp`): America West does not have a newsletter, but from Wednesday to Friday each week, it publishes its Surf N Go Specials on its Web site at this address. The discounts apply to air travel during the upcoming weekend.

- ✓ **Continental Airlines CO.O.L. Travel Specials** (`www.flycontinental.com/cool/cool.asp`): Subscribe to the Continental Online Travel Specials (feel free to use the snazzy CO.O.L acronym) to receive discount airfare listings for all over North America. The site also publishes a newsletter for international flights every other Friday. You can register for both newsletters at the same time, on the same Web page, by checking the appropriate newsletter boxes with your mouse.

- ✓ **Northwest Airlines' CyberSavers** (`www.nwa.com/travel/cyber/cyber.html`): Wednesday is the day to check your e-mail for Cyber-Savers to all the cities to which Northwest flies. On the registration page (see Figure 9-1), you can select to receive domestic, international, and vacation package deals in your newsletter. Also, be sure to specify your home airport so that the site can customize your newsletter for you.

✔ **Trans World Airlines** (`www.twa.com/hot_deals/index.html`)**:** TWA lists its specials on its Web site each Tuesday. In addition, you can sign up to receive a customized newsletter each Tuesday for selected routes. You can also receive a newsletter containing prices for all available routes by selecting Anywhere to Anywhere as the departure city and arrival city in the selection box.

If you have access to multiple airports in your city, select each airport as a departure point and then select Anywhere as the destination for each. This way, you're bound to know about all the low fare opportunities.

✔ **US Airways E-Savers** (`www.usairways.com/travel/fares/esavers.htm`)**:** Sign up to receive delightfully low fares to destinations all over North America (including Canada and much of the Caribbean) each Wednesday from US Airways. You can specify departure cities to limit the amount of information the newsletter sends you, or you can select All Cities to receive the full listing.

If you notice, most of the newsletter mailings go out on Wednesday. This is not just the airlines' favorite day of the week; the airlines can't judge until the middle of the week how much inventory they have remaining, and thus know which tickets they should sell at cut rates.

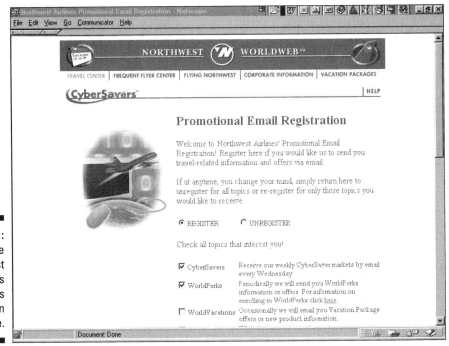

Figure 9-1: The Northwest Airlines CyberSavers registration page.

You must purchase any discounted fare you read about in an airline newsletter directly from the airline by either calling the reservation phone number or using the airline's Web-based reservation system. (Chapter 6 tells you all about reserving tickets online.) Act fast because these last-minute deals always get gobbled up very quickly.

Tapping into weekly newsletter compilations

In addition to the weekly newsletters published by airlines, many Web sites and services produce weekly mailings that can save you loads of money on your travel arrangements. Some of these newsletters aggregate the contents of various airline newsletters, alleviating the hassle of pouring over numerous newsletters. Others contain listings of noteworthy vacation packages, fare wars, and low cost tour operators.

Arthur Frommer's Vacations for Real People daily magazine

Arthur Frommer is one of the world's foremost authorities on all things travel related. For decades, travelers have relied upon Frommer's guidebooks and advice to lead them around the world. Mr. Frommer has a serious philosophy regarding travel: He sincerely believes (as do I) that interesting travel opportunities are accessible for everyone, not just the lucky few who can afford the gilded vacations pictured in the pages of *Travel & Leisure*. And he proves his beliefs each day by publishing an amazing magazine/newsletter of affordable travel opportunities, entitled Vacations for Real People, Figure 9-2.

The daily magazine is free for the asking. Just visit the Frommer's site (www.frommers.com) and click Subscribe near the top of the page in the right corner. Or you can read the latest magazine each day on the site itself. When you subscribe, you must specify in which format you want to receive the mailing. You have the following choices:

- **America Online Version:** This is recommended only for AOL account holders.

- **HTML Version:** I highly recommend this version, unless you have very old e-mail software. Most current mail readers allow for HTML mail, meaning your mail page looks like a Web page — full color with embedded links. Clicking a link in the HTML version opens your browser and leads you to a page on the Frommer's site.

- **Plain Text Version:** If you have a very slow connection or an arcane mail reader, choose plain text. I pity you. You are stuck with a very dull-looking newsletter — but it still presents the information just fine.

Figure 9-2 :
A typical
page from
Arthur
Frommer's
Vacations
for Real
People daily
magazine.

The site archives all past newsletters, making it possible for you to use the site's search function to find information on a particular topic or destination. In addition, much of the Frommer's site, Arthur Frommer's Outspoken Encyclopedia of Travel, is devoted to budget travel. Conducting a search using the Frommer site covers both the daily newsletter archive and all the other facets of the Encyclopedia — a search is bound to turn up some pointed bits of information.

Mr. Frommer and his writers pull no punches with their advice; if a deal stinks, you'll know it, or if something really hot happens, like a fare war, you can be sure they'll write about it.

Best Fares Magazine Online

Best Fares Magazine (`www.bestfares.com`), Figure 9-3, profiles the latest developments in the travel industry, including hot airfare deals.

Best Fares can be a frustrating site to navigate; it has tons of info organized somewhat haphazardly, it's a bit slow to load, and much of the info is restricted to paid subscribers. To access the subscriber information, you need a password, so don't even try if you haven't paid your money. Nonetheless, you can find quite a bit of worthwhile travel advice and news here, even if you choose not to subscribe. (However, if you decide that you want a subscription, click the Subscribe Here box on the left side of the home page. The cost is about $60 per year, and you can subscribe using the online form, by conventional mail, or by phone.)

Bargain hunters should definitely check out the Air Travel Bargains section (located in the right column of the Best Fares home page). You can choose from U.S. and Canada (domestic), International, Low-Cost Airlines, Senior Fares, and College & Youth Deals. The listings for guests (non-subscribers) is tantalizing; you see an enormous list of timely, somewhat cryptic headlines about sale fares and discount news. You may be able to glean enough info from the headline to track down a cheap flight. For example, a recent headline read "Travel Update: Kiwi Expands Service To Puerto Rico From Orlando & Newark." Now I know Kiwi has great deals and I live near Newark Airport, so if I'm headed to Puerto Rico, I know to check them out. A frequent traveler will definitely want to subscribe and have access to the full story.

Keep 'em coming: More discount newsletter compilations

More and more travel sites are offering e-mail newsletters. While you definitely want to be careful about the number of newsletter compilations you have flowing into your inbox each day, you may find the following sites helpful in capturing the elusive airfare discount:

✔ **Best Fares Magazine's Hot Deals by E-mail** (www.bestfares.com/e-deals/e-deal.htm): A must for any budget-conscious traveler. The leading budget travel magazine sends out this newsletter on a semi-regular, weekly basis. Hot Deals can be a terrific source of discount travel information.

- ✔ **The Air Travel Update:** This weekly newsletter compiles deals and bargains from all over the Internet. To subscribe, send an e-mail to `majordomo@listserv.prodigy.com` with the phrase "subscribe airtravel" in the body of the e-mail (no quotation marks). (By the way, this newsletter comes highly recommended by John Levine, author of *The Internet For Dummies,* published by IDG Books Worldwide, Inc., and an extremely knowledgeable online travel planner in his own right. Check out his Web site, Airline Information on the Internet, at `www.iecc.com/airline`.)

- ✔ **WebFlyer's Deal Watch** (`www.webflyer.com/@deal/@deal.htm`): This isn't a newsletter, but rather a compilation of many airlines' weekly deals. Check in each week to search for domestic and international flights, hotel deals, and car rental promotions.

- ✔ **TravelHUB's Travel Specials Newsletter** (`www.travelhub.com/club.html`): TravelHUB acts as a venue for travel agents to showcase their hot travel deals. You can get the newsletter either multiple times daily or in digest form once a day. I strongly advise the digest format because of the high frequency of the mailings. It can be overwhelming to have three or four mailings each day.

- ✔ **Epicurious Travel Detours Newsletter** (`travel.epicurious.com/travel/d_play/07_detours/detour.cfm`): Sign up for this free newsletter containing deals on airfares and interesting vacations.

- ✔ **Smarter Living Travel Specials Newsletter** (`www.smarterliving.com/weekend_travel.htm`): Smarter Living apparently equates intelligence with bargain hunting skills — each Wednesday it sends out a newsletter summarizing the airfare bargains for many airlines. Enter your e-mail address to subscribe to the newsletter.

- ✔ **Fare Wars Mailing List** (`www.travelersnet.com/gr/listinfo.html`): Keep abreast of the latest airline fare skirmishes by subscribing to this mailing list. As soon as airlines lower their fares, you'll know about it.

- ✔ **The Hotel Reservations Network** (`www.180096hotel.com/html/hotdeals/joinlist.html`): Hotel Reservation Network is one of the best places on the Web to find cheap hotel rooms in good hotels. Sign up to receive periodic mailings about discount accommodations.

Subscribing to discount cruise newsletters

Your e-mail address is one of the best tools you can use for keeping abreast of the latest cruise discounts. The following newsletters are sent out regularly and detail all sorts of bargains, news, and happenings that affect the cruise industry:

- ✔ **1travel's Weekly Cruise Deals** (`www.1travel.com/cruise.htm`): A weekly mailing that, in its own words, "offer savings up to an amazing 70% discount." Sounds pretty hot, right? To subscribe, click the Best Cruise Deals Weekly Mailing graphic on the upper-left side of the home page and then enter your e-mail address.

- **The Cruise News Daily (**`www.reply.net/clients/cruise/cnd.html`**):** Published each day, this newsletter details the latest developments in the cruise industry, including new routes, new ships, and cruise promotions. To subscribe, follow the link on the main page entitled "E-Mail Subscription to Cruise News Daily (free)" and then enter your e-mail address.

- **The Cruise Outlet's Latest Specials (**`www.thecruiseoutlet.com/specials.cfm`**):** These come out each week. Send your e-mail address to this discount cruise agency (`naba@ix.netcom.com`) and they'll clue you in on all their weekly specials.

- **Cruisin Specials Weekly (**`www.asource.com/cruisin/specials.html?`**):** Another compilation of weekly cruise deals. Enter your e-mail address into the box at the bottom of the page, and then click Submit.

Beware the fantastic deal

Some dishonest parties take advantage of travelers' desires to get great deals by luring them into scams with really great deals. Just as in conventional commerce, the online marketplace has its share of schemers and fraudulent businesses. You may run into a simple scheme just to get your e-mail address so that you get added to an advertising mailing list or something more insidious, such as a ploy to get your credit card number.

To avoid these schemes, ask yourself these questions when you see a deal that seems too good to be true:

- Who maintains the Web site? Is it a well-known travel supplier? Do they belong to any of the travel industry trade organizations (the ASTA, CLIA, and so on); reputable vendors will always proudly display these memberships. Do the site sponsors offer contact information, such as a mailing or e-mail address?

- Why are they offering a discount on the product? Nobody gives away something for nothing. It's not good business. Think about how the vendor's business works. An airline, for example, has incentive to sell unfilled seats on its airplanes, but a private travel agency doesn't gain by selling vacation packages at prices far below market value.

- Is this an advertisement or an available product that is for sale? Occasionally I come across amazingly low airfares at discount travel sites. But upon closer inspection, I find that these fares have no availability. In fact, I have never been able to book one of these juicy fares, which leads me to believe that if it was ever available, only one or two seats are for sale at that price, and the vice-president's nephew got those. I guess the idea is to lure you in with the great deal in the hopes that you'll settle for a more expensive fare.

Unsubscribe!

Some sites make it hard to stop getting a newsletter after you sign up. They keep sending you their newsletter, and sometimes awful, promotional e-mail, every day long after you stopped reading the stuff.

Reputable sites make it easy to unsubscribe (a postmodern word if ever there was one) by entering your e-mail address and clicking the button for Unsubscribe.

As you cruise around the Internet, you're bound to turn up more sites that beckon you to subscribe to their newsletter. Choose wisely: Make sure the content on the site looks solid and up-to-date. Sticking to the newsletters I recommend in this chapter should keep you in safe waters.

Finding Airfare Bargains on the Web

That's a pretty juicy heading, but before you salivate all over your keyboard, you should know no sure-fire method exists to get an airfare bargain every time you wish to fly for every route you wish to fly. You can, however, consistently find tasty fares if you know how and where to look, but you may have to be flexible with your times and destinations. The following methods can help you find that elusive travel bargain you're pining for.

Using discount online travel agencies

In addition to the "Big Four" online travel agencies I discussed in Chapter 6, you can find online travel agencies that specialize in selling discounted airline tickets (and sometimes also cruises, vacation packages, and other travel products).

Before you scan to find the URLs to these sites, let me warn you — just because someone says there's gold in them hills, doesn't mean there is. Often, the flights you find at these sites are unavailable or have many restrictions. But you can also find terrific low fares and great vacation deals. Just remember to read any and all fine print.

1travel.com

1travel.com (www.1travel.com), Figure 9-4, specializes in all kinds of discount travel products. You can get great prices on flights, hotels, resorts, cruises, and vacation packages by checking in on this unique site.

Figure 9-4:
The
1travel.com
home page.

1travel.com gets many of its flight prices from consolidators, making it possible for you to save big bucks by searching the 1travel.com database. While 1travel.com may not have as many flights in its database as its bigger online competitors, its prices are sometimes better, especially on international flights. (I recently found a round-trip from New York to London for $502 on a major airline.) To search the database, follow these steps:

1. **Click Lowest Airfares (the cute, little airplane illustration) or use the pull-down menu to select the type of flight you want to research and then click Submit.**

2. **Enter your route info, including the pertinent cities, dates, and times you want.**

3. **Click Show Me the Available Flights to put the wheels in motion.**

Unfortunately, the 1travel database doesn't immediately show you prices: You first must select the flights and then the system displays prices. But sometimes the extra work pays off — for example, I found a round-trip New York to San Francisco fare for $401, which I consider a fairly good deal.

1travel.com provides a Fare Beater feature (select Fare Beater by checking the box at the bottom of the page and clicking Show Me the Prices) that automatically searches for better priced flights on similar days and routes, ostensibly eliminating the need to try tons of permutations. I still recommend trying different combinations of airports, times, and dates yourself. Due to the enormous number of permutations, a computer system may not search every combination.

LowestFare.com

LowestFare.com (www.lowestfare.com), Figure 9-5, offers lots of money-saving travel options. You can search for cheap flights through its computer reservation system, peruse the Hot Deals section for last minute bargain getaways, and find low-priced cruises. Although the site offers information on all kinds of travel deals, LowestFare.com's focus is clearly on discount airfares. Follow these steps to find travel bargains though the site's reservation system, called Quick Rez:

1. **Choose a user name and password and then enter the route you wish to fly.**

   The system returns a list of fares, listed from cheapest to most expensive. Fares listed in bold lettering are exclusive prices for LowestFare.com. However, just because a fare is listed, does not mean that the flight is available.

2. **Click Check Flights to see if a flight is available and to view the exact routing.**

3. **Make sure that restrictions don't stop you from using the flight by clicking Fare Rules.**

When I checked out the site, I found some very low fares (a round-trip, New York to San Francisco, for $218), some of which were unavailable, but I was generally impressed with the prices the system turned up.

As for vacations and cruises, LowestFare.com constantly updates its offerings. Check often. If you see a trip or cruise that interests you, click Book It! and fill out the form that appears. A representative then contacts you and you can purchase the trip over the phone.

Tracking fares on the Internet

Given that airfares change often, you want to know when the fare changes in price so you can scoop up a good fare or know to wait on it. Before the invention of the *fare tracker,* monitoring fares meant checking in constantly with different airlines. The fare tracker, a very helpful piece of software available for free at many Web sites, does this monitoring for you.

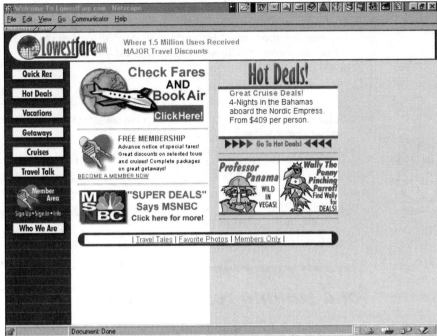

Figure 9-5:
The
Lowest-
Fare.com
home page.

The process is very simple: You enter your desired flight route into the fare tracker. Every time the flight's price changes, you receive an e-mail. This method works great for someone with more time than money — when the flight is cheap, you travel!

Some sites let you track multiple flights, some just one. I recommend the following fare trackers because they are very easy to use:

- ✔ **Expedia's Fare Tracker:** Allows you to track up to three flights at once. You must have an account on Expedia to use the fare tracker — signing up for an account is free. Access the Fare Tracker by clicking the Fare Tracker logo on the left side of the Travel Agent page (you must be signed-in to use the Fare Tracker).

- ✔ **Internet Travel Network's Fare Mail:** Lets you choose up to five destinations and the prices you're willing to pay for the routes. You can instruct the program to contact you only when the fare drops and specify how often you want to be notified. To sign up for Fare Mail, click Fare Mail on the right side of the ITN home page.

- ✔ **1travel.com's Savings Alert:** Tracks airfare deals from many sources and doesn't require you to enter a full route, just up to five departure cities from which to track deals. Configure the Savings Alert by clicking Savings Alert on the right side of the home page.

✔ **TheTrip.com's Deals 2-U:** Enables you to receive updates on up to ten flight routes. The system only updates you when someone offers a deal, so your mailbox won't be unduly cluttered. To sign up for Deals 2-U, select Low Fare Notification from the pull-down menu on the home page.

✔ **Travelocity's Fare Watcher E-mail:** Notifies you every time the fare changes by more than $25 on up to five flight routes. Simply enter the departure and arrival cities. Sign up by clicking the Fare Watcher link on the lower left side of the home page.

If you know that you need to fly somewhere well in the future (a month or two), keep an eye on the fare for a bit — just don't wait too long or you won't need a fare tracker to tell you its expensive. Tracking fares on the Internet makes it possible to recognize a good fare by giving you a frame of reference about the current prices for given routes.

Airtech.com: Getting rock-bottom prices (and staying really flexible)

I want to tell you about a Web site that can get the cheapest airfares you've ever heard of, *if* you can be flexible with the exact days you fly. Aside from backpackers and other connoisseurs of budget travel, not many people know about this gem.

Airtech.com (www.airtech.com/), Figure 9-6, specializes on getting flights on major carriers between the following regions:

✔ The United States to Europe

✔ Europe to the United States

✔ The United States to Mexico and the Caribbean

✔ San Francisco, Los Angeles, and Phoenix to Hawaii

✔ Hawaii to San Francisco, Los Angeles, and Phoenix

Here's the catch: You must provide Airtech.com with a window of time (usually about five days) during which you can travel (you may also need to be flexible with your departure, and sometimes arrival points). If you can deal with not knowing an exact departure date, Airtech.com will get you on a flight — for the cheapest possible fare. Also keep in mind that most of the prices quoted by Airtech.com apply only to one-way trips (except where noted otherwise).

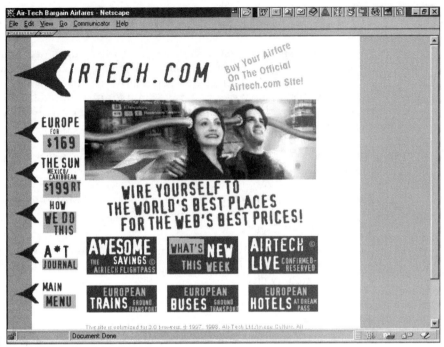

Figure 9-6:
The
Airtech.com
home page.

For these routes, you can use Airtech.com to obtain unbelievably cheap flights by following these steps:

1. **Click AirTech FlightPass to make a flight request.**

2. **Click the route you wish to fly.**

   Your choices are limited to the routes I mention earlier in this section.

3. **From the pull down menu, choose your departure city.**

4. **Choose, from the menu, your preferred destination.**

   The site displays the one-way price for the options you request.

5. **Select how many tickets you wish to purchase.**

6. **Click Purchase Now.**

   The site asks you to select your travel window, meaning a four day period during which you are willing to depart.

7. **Enter your travel dates and contact information.**

8. **Provide your credit card info (the site offers a secure connection) and you are on your way to getting the cheapest ticket of your life.**

While you're at the site, check its other offerings for cheap hotels and other flight plans.

Resting Assured: Discount Hotel Rooms

Paying exorbitant rates just to have a place to sleep does take some of the fun out of traveling. But on the other hand, staying in a sketchy motel can leave you something less than well-rested. The Internet offers a great solution to this quandary — you can search for discounted hotel rooms and also, in most cases, see a picture of the hotel, which really helps you steer clear of the more sketchy establishments.

You have a couple of options when it comes to finding a discounted hotel room on the Web:

- ✔ **Visit the official hotel sites.** You can often find promotions and special rates at an official hotel site. Before a trip, check with a few of your favorite hotels' sites.

- ✔ **Check a directory of hotel discounts.** Some Web sites pull together the best hotel rates in the U.S. and compile them into a database so you can search by city.

Deals from the source: Official hotel sites

Every night, thousands and thousands of hotel beds go to sleep all by themselves, completely untouched, the sheets neatly made, and the bedtime mint uneaten. The hotels chains hate this. So they make deals on available rooms, beckoning potential guests to come and stay the night with the lonely beds.

The hotel chains create special discount pages to encourage sleepers to take advantage of their deals. For example, the following sites show just how far the major hotel chains are willing to go to get you into their beds:

- ✔ **Hilton Special Offers** (`www.hilton.com/specials/index.html`): Tells you all about travel packages, special offers, and Hilton Value Rates at hotels across the globe.

- ✔ **Holiday Inn Promotions** (`www.holiday-inn.com/Promo.html`): Get the lowdown on the latest Holiday Inn promotions.

- ✔ **Hyatt Hot Deals** (`www.hyatt.com/hotdeals/index.html`): Find special offers round the world, last-minute deals, and other promotions.

- ✔ **Marriott Hotel Fridays Promotion** (`marriotthotels.com/friday/`): Get 10 to 20 percent off at participating Marriott hotels each week.

- ✔ **Sheraton Hot Deals** (`www.sheraton.com/hot_deals/index.html`): Check in to see what's being offered for Sheraton guests.

This is just a partial list; check with your favorite hotel's Web site before you make a reservation to see if you can save some money. You're sure to make some lonesome bed very happy.

Hotel Reservations Network

Hotel Reservations Network (HRN) (`www.180096hotel.com`), Figure 9-7, has made a name for itself by doing one thing and doing it very, very well: providing rooms in great hotels in selected cities across the U.S. at low rates.

HRN's rates are amazingly low — sometimes up to 65 percent off the standard rate. They also can get rooms when a hotel tells you that it is sold out; HRN buys up blocks of hotels rooms at a wholesale price and then passes the savings on to you. It's awful nice of them. Just follow these steps to find out what HRN has to offer:

1. **Select the appropriate city from the list.**

2. **Enter the dates you want to stay.**

3. **Click Display Rates.**

   The search yields a list of hotels, with star ratings and nightly rates. You can get more info about a specific hotel and a map by clicking the corresponding buttons.

Figure 9-7:
The Hotel
Reservations
Network
home page.

4. **Book the hotel online after you make a selection by inputting your personal and credit card information.**

   You can also call the toll free number (it's part of the site's address) and speak to a representative seven days a week.

Not too difficult, huh? If you have any problem, the site posts a toll-free number all over the place, and you are encouraged to dial.

If you do a lot of traveling, sign up for the Hot Deals newsletter. Enter your e-mail address into the box on the home page, and you receive the newsletter of hotel deals the next time the site publishes it.

Click-It! Weekends

Waiting till the last minute to plan a trip has definite advantages in terms of its effect on your wallet. Click-It! Weekends (www.travelweb.com/ TravelWeb/clickit.html), Figure 9-8, is a last-minute hotel room clearance service of TravelWeb, one of the premiere online hotel reservation systems.

Click-It! Weekends provides a reliable way to get cheap hotel rooms in top notch properties (mostly the big, global hotel chains — Hilton, Sheraton, and so on) around the world. Combine it with a last minute, discount flight and you've got yourself a cheap weekend getaway. The site works like this:

1. **A thrifty traveler, such as yourself, needs a place to stay for the coming weekend (Friday to Sunday).**

2. **On Monday (the site is updated each Monday) you point your browser to** www.travelweb.com/TravelWeb/clickit.html.

   You can look at the site on any day, but the deals get scooped up quickly, so I recommend looking as soon as you can.

3. **Click Locations (listings for hotels around the world) or Hotels and search the database to find discounted rates at a variety of major hotel chains.**

4. **Check availability by clicking the hotel link, selecting the arrival date and preferred bed size, and clicking Check Availability!**

   The site presents you with the available rates.

5. **Select the rate that best suits you and book the room online with a credit card.**

Figure 9-8:
The Click-It!
Weekends
home page.

Going, Going, You're Gone! Online Travel Auctions

At an offline auction, bidders offer a sum for a service or product. A fast-talking auctioneer attempts to get the highest possible price from the bidders. The auction ends when the highest bidder purchases the product for the said amount and smiles ruefully at his losing counterparts.

Well, it's now possible to bid on travel products, such as plane tickets, cruises, and vacation packages, and get low prices by way of an *online* auction. The principle is the same as a real world auction, only the bidding takes place over the Internet, and you can't hear the auctioneer spurting out prices.

Traditional-style online auctions

Admittedly, online auctions for travel products have yet to become popular; only very few sites attempt to sell travel through a bidding method. But a few places on the Web consistently auction off all sorts of quality travel products — participants often get very good deals. It doesn't cost anything to participate in an online auction. On the downside, it can be difficult to plan a vacation when you're unsure if your bid will be accepted.

Bid4Travel

The online auction site Bid4Travel (www.bid4travel.com), Figure 9-9, specializes in travel. You can bid on everything from airline tickets, car rental, and cruises to vacation packages and other travel products at the site.

In order to bid on stuff, you must first register (for free). The registration process is not complicated, it just has a few steps:

1. **Click the Register button and fill out your personal information, e-mail address, and establish a user name and password.**

    Pretty standard stuff. You must wait for the system to mail you a confirmation number. It should only take a few minutes (if that).

2. **Check your e-mail and retrieve the confirmation number.**

3. **Click the Confirm button; enter your user name, password, and confirmation number (from the e-mail) in the space provided.**

Okay, now you're registered — want to start bidding? Just follow these steps:

1. **Click Auction Categories to see what's available for bid.**

2. **Click the category you're interested in to see the specific items.**

Figure 9-9:
The
Bid4Travel
home page.

3. **If you see something that interests you, click the item number to see the full description, photos, starting bid price, auction closing date, and bid submittal form.**

4. **Using the pull down menu, select the amount you are willing to pay for the item.**

5. **Enter your user name and password and hit Preview Bid.**

The moment of truth. While you are not technically bound to purchase a product if your bid is selected, the product supplier may be able to take legal action against you if you decided not to purchase the item, so you should be sure about the bids you make.

6. **If you're sure about your bid, hit Place Bid.**

The waiting begins. . . . After the specified closing date of the auction, you'll be notified by e-mail if your bid was accepted. Exciting, isn't it?

You can sign up to be notified by e-mail of the latest Bid4Travel's offerings and even enter a desired travel product into the Wish List. Maybe someone will hear your plea.

Cathay Pacific's auction

From time to time, Cathay Pacific, one of my favorite airlines, holds an auction for its cyber-savvy customers at www.cathay-usa.com/auction. It's a very straightforward type of auction: The airline puts up for bid various flights and packages of which it has a backlog of inventory and then customers do battle for the bargains using a conventional bidding process. You enter an amount you are willing to pay for whatever is on the auction block. If no one bids higher than you, the merchandise is yours.

I can't tell you when the next auction will be held, but I can tell you that if you plan on traveling to Asia, it's definitely worth your while to pay a visit to the Cathay site and check to see if an auction is coming up soon.

A new-wave of auctions: Priceline.com

Priceline.com (www.priceline.com) has a terrific (and patented) concept. I wish I had thought of it. Anytime you are thinking of making an air journey that departs from the U.S., you can submit a price that you wish to pay for the flight to Priceline.com. Within an hour, you will be contacted via e-mail and told whether the service was able to fulfill your request (24 hours for international flights).

However, you should understand that Priceline is not hurriedly shopping your proposed fare around to every airline on the planet (that would be amazing if they could do that in an hour), rather, the service has negotiated fares with many airlines for many routes in advance.

I don't know Priceline's threshold for accepting a proposed fare, but you can be sure they are not going to lose money. If your fare request is less than their negotiated fare, you're out of luck. But if it is equal or greater, then Priceline stands to make a profit and will gladly issue you a ticket.

The bottom line: You must know the going rates for the fares you request. Spend time researching fares on the Web and check up with travel agents.

To submit a request, follow this quite simple, and quite long (in terms of steps, not time), process:

1. **Click Ticket Request on the bottom navigation bar.**

2. **Enter your departure city (which must be in the U.S.) and your destination and then hit Next.**

3. **Enter the dates you wish to travel.**

   Dates can be up to six months in the future.

4. **Enter the number of tickets you wish to purchase.**

5. **Enter the amount you wish to pay for a flight.**

   Priceline recommends that you spend some time researching your fare using online travel agencies or by any other means so you know a ballpark figure of the going rate. Here's the kicker: you're only allowed to request a quote once per flight. If you're denied because your price was unreasonably low, you're out of luck. So make it count. I recommend checking the latest cyber-saver fare for the route and attempt to get a fare close to that amount.

6. **Select the airports you wish to travel through.**

7. **Enter the amount of stops/connections you are willing to make on your flight.**

8. **Submit your name, delivery method, and contact information.**

9. **Initial the agreement stating the amount you wish to pay and the routing.**

10. **Submit your billing information.**

    A major credit card is required to make a fare request.

11. **Confirm the price you wish to pay for the trip.**

    Make sure you ask a reasonable price; there are no second tries. Furthermore, make sure you want to go: If the site accepts your price, you've bought the non-refundable ticket.

12. **Enter your credit card number.**

    That's it. Good luck. Within an hour you'll know if the airline gods smiled upon your case. Perhaps you should make a small offering at your local airport or light a candle.

I've personally never used Priceline.com to obtain a plane ticket, but I've heard both good and bad. The problem, as you may have guessed, is that most people enter prices that are lower than Priceline's best fare and the request is denied. On the other hand, I have a friend who got a great price on a ticket from Chicago to New York and swears by her experience. I know *I'm* going try it next time I need to fly somewhere on the cheap (which is always).

Getting Great Deals on Vacations and Cruises

Finding travel deals (online or otherwise) is almost like a full-time occupation. Deals don't just appear on your doorstep; you have to do the research, make the phone calls, and ply the Internet if you really want to save money on a trip.

Getting discounted vacation packages

The following two sites provide excellent examples of services that scour the world for vacation deals. The staffs at Frommer's and Epicurious Travel know their stuff. Check the directory section of this book for more sites that can help you find deals on vacation packages.

Arthur Frommer's Outspoken Encyclopedia of Travel

I also speak about Arthur Frommer's site earlier in this chapter, but it's so good, that I want to tell you more. In addition to subscribing to the newsletter, budget travelers should check in on Arthur Frommer's Outspoken Encyclopedia of Travel (www.frommers.com) often.

Whether you're looking for inexpensive vacation packages, cruises, or discount tour operators, Frommer's can usually lend a hand. Try searching the archives of the newsletter by clicking the Archives button near the top right of the page. This allows you to scan the headlines of the last week's newsletters. Also try the search function of the site to search for keywords that apply to the trip you're planning.

Also of great value is the Budget Travel section (www.frommers.com/budget) where Frommer's lays his hard-won budget travel advice on you. Find out how to save money when you go for currency exchange, about entertainment books, and about the cheapest place on earth (I'm not telling!) by navigating through the three sub-sections in Budget Travel.

Epicurious Travel

Each week, Epicurious Travel (`travel.epicurious.com/travel/c_planning/planning.html`) highlights a vacation deal of the week that is almost guaranteed to make your mouth water and your feet itch (in a good way).

If the current trip o' the week doesn't strike your fancy, no worries, because the site offers an archived listing of past deals that are still current and available. Click the Other Current Deals button to view a list of hot vacation deals.

Or maybe the deal makes you think of a friend? Click the E-mail this Deal to a Friend button to send it to a deserving compatriot. My address is `nvadnai@hotmail.com`: I love tropical climates; keep me in mind if you see a good deal.

Cruisin' the Internet for discounts

The Internet is brimming with information about cruises. Many sites claim to offer the best discounts, but you must be ever-wary of bogus and inflated claims. Look to see if the agency or service belongs to any of the well-known travel trade organizations, such as Cruise Lines International Association (CLIA) or the American Society of Travel Agents (ASTA). Sites that belong to these organizations generally are proud to display the logos at their sites.

Looking on the search engines

For starters, you can search the Web for travel agencies, cruise wholesalers, and other purveyors of cruise packages by entering the phrase "discount cruises" into a search engine. Or you can check out the following categories available at some of the larger search engines:

- **Yahoo!** (`www.yahoo.com/Business_and_Economy/Companies/Travel/Cruises/`): A mammoth cruise category that is sure to yield some valuable information for intrepid cruisers.

- **Infoseek** (`www.infoseek.com/Topic/Travel/Cruises`): Highlights quality sites and breaks cruises down into subcategories.

- **Lycos** (`www.lycos.com/wguide/network/net_969263.html`): Allows you to surf through the listings and easily return to the list.

- **Excite** (`city.net/features/interests/cruises`): Offers updated cruise and vacation news headlines and lots of links to cruise through.

Frommer's Best Current Cruise Bargains

Frommer's has the market cornered on discount travel information; why should cruises be any different? Frommer's Best Current Cruise Bargains (www.frommers.com/hottest/cruise), a section of the Outspoken Encyclopedia, contains current listings of many diverse types of cruises. Each of the 100 or so listings has a short description of the cruise including ports of call, prices, dates, and advice provided by the Frommer's staff of travel experts. Frommer's also includes a link to opinionated reviews of many of the ships offering discount cabins.

If you see a cruise that whets your appetite for shuffleboard and buffets, click the link at the end of the individual listing to fill out a booking form. Frommer's then forwards your info to the cruise discounter. An agent then calls you to complete your reservation.

Cruise.com

Cruise.com (www.cruise.com) is the Web site of a cruise discounter; this is just one of hundreds of online cruise discount agencies. You can probably do equally well at many other sites, but I like Cruise.com because of the straightforward service it provides. It doesn't bombard you with flashing offers and gimmicks.

Click Cruise Values and then choose a region to see the offerings with prices, cabin types, and amount of discount off the cruise line's asking price. For the really low priced cruises, click Hot Cruise Deals. If you see something you like, click the Request-A-Quote button to submit a form. A consultant follows up with a call to help you book the trip.

1travel.com

The offerings at 1travel.com (www.1travel.com) are terrific. Click Discount Cruises on the home page, and you see a list of available cruises offered by a variety of operators that specialize in discount cruises.

The short descriptions on this page allow you to quickly compare offerings. Clicking a cruise listing either brings you to the cruise operator's site or a page on the 1travel site where you can get the full skinny on the trip as well as the booking procedure (usually carried out by phone).

Flipping through online classified ads

Online classified ads are another great means of tracking down individuals and organizations that have cruises to sell on the cheap. In fact, online classified ads are good places to look for all sorts of travel deals. You never know what you'll find. Maybe you can find a person to go on the trip with you in the personals next to the cruise listings in these classifieds:

✔ **Yahoo! Classifieds (**`classifieds.yahoo.com/tickets.html`**):** From Yahoo!'s home page, click Classifieds near the top of the page and then click Tickets. You must then select which city's listings you wish to search. I suggest searching departure cities for cruises, including Miami, New York, and Los Angeles.

The listings generally contain a short description and the contact info for the supplier, including e-mail addresses.

As always, make sure the person you're dealing with is reputable by asking the right questions: Do you work for a travel agency? If so, do you have references? Never give out your credit card number until you know that a deal is legitimate.

✔ **Classifieds2000 (**`www.classifieds2000.com`**):** Classifieds2000 is an enormous database of classified ads for everything from real estate to pets. To see the travel and cruise listings, click Everything Else (I guess that means miscellaneous) and then click Travel. Select the type of travel classified you wish to look at and the price range, and then hit Search.

The resulting page of listings just shows the cruise route, price, and contact phone number. Click the individual listings to access a description and seller info, as well as a form to contact the seller by e-mail.

The Travel
Planning Online
For Dummies
Internet Directory

The 5th Wave   By Rich Tennant

When I reserved this thing online, I thought a dromedary was the name of a late model Chevy station wagon. Now, which one of your agents do I see to get a refund?

In this part . . .

The *Travel Planning Online For Dummies Internet Directory* provides a guide to some of the best travel sites on the World Wide Web. I organize the listing into categories so that you can use this directory to quickly find the right site to research transportation options, destinations, accommodations, and specific types of travel.

The Travel Planning Online For Dummies Internet Directory

How do you find the good stuff in a place as enormous as the Internet? Someone shows you, that's how!

Some of the travel sites in this directory have been around since the dawn of the WWW; others are new on the scene. Regardless of their age, the sites that follow all have made a commitment to innovation on the Internet and to providing accurate, high-quality travel information.

I cover some of the sites listed here in the main body of the book. When that's the case, I give a short description and identify the chapter in which you can find a comprehensive review of the site.

Micons

As you look through the directory, you see icons that point out features of the sites. Here's what the icons denote:

You can use your credit card to purchase travel products.

This site requires a registration process (username and password).

$ You must pay for some services at this site.

Accommodations Directories

Whether you want a four-star hotel or a $2 hostel, the Web has the resources to help you find a place to rest your weary head. Take the guesswork out of finding good hotels and inns — check out the following hotel guides and directories before you leave home.

All the Hotels on the Web

www.all-hotels.com

Worldwide hotel database: This site sets a high standard for itself with its name — maybe a bit too high. Even so, you can find a hotel in almost any country in the world. All the Hotels on the Web doesn't offer online reservations, but offers links and more links to hotel Web sites, organized by city and country.

Inns & Outs

www.innsandouts.com

Massive B&B database: If you're looking for a B&B, look here first. The Inns & Outs site is actually a launching pad to four other B&B sites. The Bed and Breakfast Channel (www.bbchannel.com) is the best one for travelers, offering listings of tens of thousands of inns around the globe. Inns and Outs also links you to the Bed & Breakfast Club (www.bbclub.com), which offers participating members discounts on inn stays. This site links to two other sites that target innkeepers.

The Innsite

www.innsite.com

B&B directory: Tired of sterile hotel rooms? Find B&Bs and inns worldwide by searching with the powerful InnCrawler search engine, an amalgamation of many of the online B&B directories. An InnCrawler search plows through more than 12,000 indexed pages of small inns and B&Bs.

International Youth Hostel Federation

www.iyhf.org

Hostels around the world: With more than 4,500 hostels in more than 60 countries, the International Youth Hostel Federation is the largest association of hostels in the world. Use the site to locate inexpensive accommodations and place reservations. Members can now use the online reservation service to reserve beds in many hostels. The info on the site explains how to become an IYHF member.

The Internet Guide to Hosteling

www.hostels.com

Budget accommodations worldwide: For budget travelers, hostels provide an indispensable advantage of traveling on the cheap. The Internet Guide to Hosteling is an ever-expanding resource that locates affordable international accommodations. And if you're new to hosteling, the page also answers frequently asked questions.

Leisure Planet

www.leisureplanet.com

Online hotel booking with property images: Leisure Planet is a full-service, online travel agency that puts an emphasis on worldwide hotel bookings. The Leisure Planet hotel database contains listings for over 50,000 accommodations, almost all of which you can book online. And best of all, most listings have photos illustrating the hotel exteriors, room interiors, and other amenities.

TravelWeb

www.travelweb.com

Online reservations for most major hotel chains: TravelWeb, the preeminent online reservation system for hotels, does let you make other types of travel reservations (such as air and car travel), but clearly focuses on accommodations. All the big name hotel chains appear on the system, and you can reserve and pay for rooms throughout the world by using your credit card. (See Chapter 7 for a complete rundown of TravelWeb's features.)

WorldHotel

www.worldhotel.com

200,000 hotels in one database: Enter the city, state, or country where you want to stay and WorldHotel delivers. The majority of listings provide fairly basic info, such as addresses and contact info, but some listings have photos and links to further information. Use the Chain Search button on the home page to view listings for major hotel chains.

Other Sites to Check Out

Bed and Breakfast Channel
www.bbchannel.com

Central Reservation Services
www.reservation-services.com

CNN Hotels
cnnhotels.com

Holi-Swaps
www.holi-swaps.com

HomeExchange.com
www.homeexchange.com

Hostelling International
www.hiayh.org/

The Hotel Guide
www.hotelguide.com

Hotel Reservations Network
www.180096hotel.com/html/hotdeals/joinlist.html

Hotels and Travel on the Net
www.hotelstravel.com/

Places to Stay
www.placestostay.com

Stay4Free
www.stay4free.com

Traveler Net
www.traveler.net/beds/index.html

Active Vacations

These sites help you experience the world, whether you want to camp, hike, ski, or travel the globe in an ecologically responsible way. You can research almost any adventure or activity on the Internet.

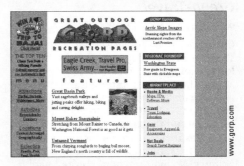

Eco Travels in Latin America

www2.planeta.com/mader

Ecotourism in Latin and South America: The Americas, with their vast (and endangered) rain forests and natural wonders, is one of the premier destinations for nature lovers and ecotourists. This site acts as a traveler's resource center for ecotourism in the region, providing background info, scholarly reports, and links to ecofriendly sites.

GoSki

www.goski.com

Tons of ski resorts worldwide: GoSki focuses on the maxim, "It's snowing somewhere, right now." As such, it boasts more than 2,000 resorts in its database.

D-6 Active Vacations

Get a ski report, find out about lodging, or plan your trip with one of its featured tour companies.

Great Outdoor Recreation Pages (GORP)

www.gorp.com

The complete resource for the outdoor enthusiast: Before you go outside, go online. GORP devotes literally thousands of pages to exploration of the great outdoors. If you do it outside, from camping to spelunking, GORP has info for you. Many outdoorsy companies use GORP to host their sites, as well as publish information about tours, destinations, gear, and more.

Green-Travel

www.green-travel.com

Comprehensive ecotourism info: Green-Travel is probably best known for its long-running mailing list, moderated by Marcus Endicott, an Internet and ecotourism luminary. But it also performs splendidly as a directory to ecofriendly resources on the Internet. The site organizes its links, which focus on destinations, by continent and then by country. No matter where you're headed, you most likely can find a link to eco-information about it at this site.

High Adventure Travel

www.highadv.com

Around the world airfares and adventures: If you're considering a round-the-world, multi-leg, adventure journey, you can use this experienced agency's site to get a frame of reference for prices. Of course, they're glad to book the trip for you, as well.

iSki

www.iski.com

Complete ski vacation resource: Although the site doesn't offer a whole lot of new

information during the summer (when there's no snow), iSki is a terrific way to research a ski vacation. More than 800 resorts are listed in the database, each including mountain stats, lodging info, transportation, lift ticket prices, and lots more. iSki also provides up-to-date ski reports, rundowns of the latest gear, and snow country news reports. Join the Mountain Club to receive discounts on ski products.

Mountain Travel — Sobek

www.mtsobek.com

Acclaimed adventure tour operator: Looking to break out of your boring, sit-at-the-beach vacation rut? Mountain Travel — Sobek can help. This forward-thinking company has been marketing their fantastic adventure excursions on the Internet for years. Use the site to find out about some great trips.

Outside Online

outside.starwave.com

Great outdoor vacation ideas: The Internet counterpart of *Outside* magazine provides terrific outdoor advice, opinions, and ideas. Consult the Going Places section for destination reviews, adventure advice, and expedition updates. The site also features current news that affects active travelers and vivid photography sure to get your heart pumping.

ParkNet — U.S. National Park Service

www.nps.gov

U.S. National Park news and info: Before you head to Yellowstone with a carload of kiddies, consult the NPS site. Click Visit Your Parks to access information about every park in the National Park system, including maps, operating hours, entrance fees, and campground reservations. And for individuals seeking information about the many diverse features of America's national parks, the site also offers loads of historical and background info.

Specialty Travel Index

www.spectrav.com

Find tour operators and outfitters: The Specialty Travel Index enables you to search four different ways for adventure travel and special interest vacations around the world. Search by your interest or activity, by geographic region, by tour operator, or by keyword. More than 600 operators are cataloged at the site, which is updated monthly.

Other Sites to Check Out

Backpackers.com
backpackers.com

Fly Fishing Travel Online
flyfishto.com

Golf Travel Online
gto.com

GolfWeb Travel
www.golfweb.com/travel

Mountain Travel Online
mountainto.com

Ski Travel Online
skito.com

Resorts Sports Network
www.rsn.com

Airlines

More and more airlines offer online reservations directly via the Web. The following carriers all let travelers book tickets, check schedules, find out about promotions, and check awards program mileage at their sites. Each site here also allows online purchasing and requires registration.

Air Canada

www.aircanada.ca

Alaska Air

www.alaska-air.com

American Airlines

www.aa.com

America West Airlines

www.americawest.com/

British Airways

www.british-airways.com

Cathay Pacific

www.cathay-usa.com

Continental

www.flycontinental.com

Delta

www.delta-air.com

Lufthansa

www.lufthansa-USA.com

Northwest

www.nwa.com

Singapore Airlines

singaporeair.com

TWA

www.twa.com

United

www.ual.com

US Airways
www.usairways.com

Virgin Atlantic
www.fly.virgin.com

Other Sites to Check Out

Airline information on-line on the Internet
iecc.com/airline/

Airline Toll-Free Numbers and Websites
www.princeton.edu/Main/air800.html

Inside Flyer
www.insideflyer.com

QuickAID
www.quickaid.com

TheTrip.com
www.thetrip.com

Business Travel

Business travel has its own set of unique concerns that the following sites address. These sites are especially good for business travelers who make their own travel arrangements, as well as those who participate in travel award programs.

American Express Business Services

www.americanexpress.com/
travelservices

International travel services: Membership may have its privileges, but you no longer have to be a member to reap the benefits

of American Express worldwide travel centers. Anyone can take advantage of the many travel resources at the American Express Web site. Especially helpful is the worldwide AmEx office locator, which comes in handy when you run out of traveler's checks.

Business Traveler Online Magazine

www.btonline.com

Better than any in-flight magazine: This site is the online counterpart to the well-respected *Business Travel Magazine.* Check in monthly for well-written feature articles about the issues that face business travelers, including info about destinations, news, and travel data (weather, international holidays, and so on). Search the archives of the site when you need to know about a business travel topic.

Biztravel.com

www.biztravel.com

Full-service, online travel agency for business travelers: Biztravel.com strives to alleviate much of the hassle associated with business travel. The site enables you to make air, hotel, and car reservations, check on the weather and culture at the destination, and keep track of frequent-traveler award plan points. Biztravel.com adds innovations constantly to make business trips less taxing.

ExpoGuide

www.expoguide.com

Trade show and conference info: Looking for the perfect venue to sell your product? ExpoGuide lists thousands of trade shows, conferences, and exhibitions around the globe. Search the massive database alphabetically, by date, by location, or by keyword. You can also add your organization's event to the listings, free of charge.

Foreign Entry Requirements

travel.state.gov/foreignentryreqs.html

Official entry requirements for getting into countries from A to Z: Bet you don't know what you need, in terms of official documents, to enter Bangladesh. It's a notarized note from your mom! Jokes aside, this U.S. State Department site has country-by-country listings of the requirements for U.S. citizens traveling on business or pleasure.

TheTrip.com

www.thetrip.com

Full-service, online travel agency for business travelers: TheTrip.com is the first site to devote itself exclusively to the business traveler, and bills itself as "worth your trust." It covers all aspects of a business traveler's experience, from hotel reviews from Frommer's Guides to graphical flight trackers so you don't spend time waiting for a flight to arrive. TheTrip.com helps make business travel less taxing.

WebFlyer

www.webflyer.com

Everything you ever wanted to know about frequent flying awards: Randy Petersen, the most famous frequent flyer of all time, produces WebFlyer, the preeminent site for people who fly frequently. WebFlyer is jammed with info and applications for managing your awards. Did you know there's even a political action center for frequent flyers (a group that lobbies for frequent flyers rights)?

Other Sites to Check Out

On the Go Software
   www.onthegosoftware.com

Trade Show Central
   www.tscentral.com

Cruises

These sites help you choose the right cruise for you and find good deals on cruise vacations. After you look at a few of these sites, you'll be singing the theme to the Love Boat — and soon I'll be loading another site! Remember to check the online travel agents section for cruise info as well.

Carnival Cruise Lines

www.carnival.com

Fun ship cruises: Explore the many Carnival cruises to the Caribbean, Alaska, or Mexico. This Web site can help you find a travel agent near you if you want to investigate booking a Carnival cruise.

Cruise News

www.cruise-news.com

The latest cruise industry news: You may find it surprising just how much news the cruise industry produces. Cruise lines routinely introduce new boats, new ports of call, and discount prices. Check in with Cruise News for the latest news, as well as for ship statistics and reviews.

CruiseOpinion

www.cruiseopinion.com

The skinny on big boats: Finding the right cruise is no easy task. You need advice,

D-10 Cruises

and not from someone who sells cruises for a living. CruiseOpinion is a collection of commentary posted by fellow cruisers about specific boats, cruises, and routes. And when you return from your cruise, don't forget to post your thoughts for others to read.

Cunard Line

www.cunardline.com

The line of the Queen Elizabeth 2: Cunard isn't the biggest fleet, but experienced cruisers give it high marks. Explore the options online.

Fielding's Cruise Finder

www.fieldingtravel.com/cf/index.htm

The authority on cruise ratings: Fielding Guides have been helping people choose waterborne vacations for more than 18 years. Use the online version to quickly compare boats and cruise offerings. The database enables you to search for cruises by region, boat, ratings, amenities, and more.

Get Cruising

www.getcruising.com

Cruise ship comparisons: Use the Easy 3 Step Cruise Selector to match your cruise interests and desires with the right cruise for you. The site also includes plenty of other resources to comparison-shop for cruises.

Holland America Line Westours

www.hollandamerica.com

A high value cruise line: Holland America earns high marks for its reasonably priced cruises. Check out the different packages online.

Mining Company Guide to Cruises

cruises.miningco.com

Clearinghouse of cruise links and info: Find out about every aspect of cruising at this comprehensive, up-to-date cruise directory. Cruise expert Linda Coffman has hit on every conceivable question you could ask about the world of big boats on the high seas. You can even enter a chat: Wednesdays at 9:00 p.m. EST.

Norwegian Cruise Line

www.ncl.com

A really pretty cruise site: Norwegian Cruise Line's site has cutting edge design and provides a great way to find out about the line's offerings. Especially useful is the page detailing the current specials and promotions for NCL packages.

Royal Caribbean Cruise Lines

www.rccl.com

A great cruise line with a nice Web site: Royal Caribbean is one of the most popular cruise lines in the world. Check out its cruises (not all of them cruise the Caribbean) at the nicely designed Web site.

Windjammer Barefoot Cruises

www.asource.com/windjammer

Cruises of a different ilk: If you dream of sailing away on a big schooner, Windjammer can help make it come true. Check out the fleet of sailboats and the ports of call. You can also request a quote online — and yes, shoes *are* optional.

Other Sites to Check Out

1travel.com Best Cruise Deals
www.onetravel.com/1travel/cruisemailing/index.cfm

Arthur Frommer's The Nation's Best Current Cruise Bargains
www.frommers.com/hottest/cruise

Cruise News Daily
www.reply.net/clients/cruise/cnd.html

The Cruise Outlet
www.thecruiseoutlet.com/specials.cfm

The Cruise Page
www.cruisepage.com

Cruise Specials
www.asource.com/cruisin/specials.html

Cruise.com
www.cruise.com

CruiseFun
www.cruisefun.com

City Guides

Headed to an unfamiliar city? These excellent city guide networks can help you get the most out of a city, even if you're a native. (See Chapter 1 for more information on city guides.)

CitySearch

www.citysearch.com

U.S. and Australian city guides: CitySearch uses local editorial teams to detail the restaurant, events, bar, club, community, and sports happenings in a bunch of American cities, a few Australian cities, Toronto, and soon, Scandinavia. The listings are comprehensive and the editorial consistently hits the mark.

CultureFinder

www.culturefinder.com

Find artistic events in the U.S.: Sometimes culture can prove hard to find, especially when you're visiting an unfamiliar city. Next time you feel that the opera is unattainable, visit CultureFinder. This nifty page locates highbrow culture in your neighborhood, or anyone else's for that matter.

Digital City

www.digitalcity.com

Guides to more than 30 U.S. cities: America Online produces these sometimes good, sometimes so-so city guides for most major U.S. metro areas. Good for listings, but a little uneven on the critical commentary.

Festivals.com

www.festivals.com

Locate festivals and events worldwide: Everyone loves a festival. Searching this massive database can greatly enhance any trip by finding some interesting local color. The site lists concerts, fairs, sports, hoedowns, and every other type of event possible to serve as a festival.

Sidewalk

www.sidewalk.com

Guides to a dozen U.S. cities: Sidewalk is the city guide series from Microsoft. New York, San Francisco, Seattle, and several other major U.S. cities are covered by locally based teams of writers, critics, and editors. Excellent restaurant, arts, and nightlife reviews.

TimeOut — Worldwide City Guides

www.timeout.co.uk

Global city guides: TimeOut guides focus on what to do and what to see in the world's great cities. As the online complement to a line of excellent, weekly magazines, TimeOut online can tell you what's going on from an insider standpoint.

What's Going On

www.whatsgoingon.com

Find events in the U.S.: This event database is notable for its nifty design features and whimsical editorial voice. The site looks like some sort of futuristic, hand-held device and the listings come equipped with an entire lexicon of icons denoting everything from the snob appeal of an event to the gluttony factor. Click the Intense-O-Meter to find out how an event rates with the editors; don't forget to find out where the Coolest Place on Earth is for each day.

Other Sites to Check Out

Cavemole's Guide to Boston
www.junie.com/cavemole.htm

culture*kiosque*
www.culturekiosque.com

SF Station
sfstation.com

Destination Guides

One of the great aspects of the Internet, especially for travelers, is the wealth of information about destinations. The following sites help you decide where to go, what to expect when you get there, and how to get around.

www.citysafari.com

City.Net

city.net

A destination search engine: Search more than 5,000 destinations using City.Net's vast compendium of knowledge. Using City.Net, you can research (and map) almost anyplace anyone has ever visited. After you select a destination, City.Net hooks you up with a comprehensive array of Web links that provide many different looks at the location, including links about history, geography, weather, travel and tourism, and economics.

CitySafari

www.citysafari.com

The life of the planet: CitySafari.com takes an innovative approach to destination guides, highlighting cities and regions that the news features because of holidays, events, or other timely notoriety. For example, CitySafari might highlight Dublin in honor of St. Patrick's Day or the City of Angels during Academy Awards week. CitySafari.com offers guides for many cities on each continent, even ones where no event is going down. Each guide provides the full rundown of accommodations, restaurant guides, nightlife, transportation, and everything else a traveler needs to know, by way of an appealing, easy-to-navigate design.

Fodor's

www.fodors.com

Comprehensive destination guides: Started by a Hungarian émigré, Eugene Fodor, in 1936, Fodor's claims that it's the largest publisher of "English-language travel information in the world" — and, heck, I believe 'em. The site was redesigned in 1998, making it easier to navigate through its considerable content. The home page highlights timely travel ideas and has terrific fixtures, such as a hotel and restaurant finder and a travel resource center.

Geographia

www.geographia.com/index.html

Explorations of exotic destinations:
Geographia doesn't burn away much time
explaining itself; it simply presents
information on exotic locations through
vivid photography, multimedia, and text.
The featured destinations change regularly, but you can always browse the site
by region.

The Insiders Guides

www.insiders.com

*Destination info for popular U.S. vacation
spots:* The Insiders Guides print guidebooks have been guiding travelers around
the United States for almost 20 years. The
online version is a welcome addition to
the online guidebook lexicon, containing
every bit of the great content found in the
print versions and more. Click the map of
the U.S. and you get a long list of topics
about the destination.

Leisure Planet

www.leisureplanet.com/TravelGuides

*A picture of your vacation is worth a
thousand words:* The South African
megasite Leisure Planet is one of the best
destination resources on the Web. You
can book hotels, vacations, and flights at
Leisure Planet, but its true strength lies in
its massive and well-organized database
of destination info. The site offers
detailed and well-written background
information as well as a vibrant slide
show for each destination it covers.

Lonely Planet Online

www.lonelyplanet.com.au

The bibles of independent travel: No
matter where you go, you're bound to see
motley backpackers pouring over dog-
eared copies of a Lonely Planet guidebook, and for good reason. Lonely Planet
publications are the premier sources of
independent traveler information, and
their Web site is no exception. In-depth

information on interesting and exotic
destinations, interactive maps and
photos, and a bulletin board for sharing
travel stories are all designed with the
independent traveler in mind. The site
also provides info on how to remain
healthy; and useful stuff to keep from
becoming lonely when in a far-off land.
Great links and an easy-to-use publication
order form make Lonely Planet Online
indispensable to the independent
traveler.

Rec.Travel Library

www.Travel-Library.com

*Destination info through personal travel-
ogues:* The Rec.Travel Library offers one
of the finest travel resources on the Web
in terms of researching trips and destinations. The Library consists primarily of
travelogues written by travelers like you
and me — well, I don't know about you.
Search the database by geographic
region; you get links to stories, guides,
and lots of other travel advice.

Rick Steves' Europe Through the Backdoor

www.ricksteves.com

European travel guides with flair: More
than just guidebooks, Rick Steves' guides
have a philosophy. After you check out
Rick's site, you may want to discard your
hotel reservations in favor of a footloose
and fancy-free backdoor style of travel.
Rick includes an online guide with tips,
detailed destination info, and a rundown
of how to survive in each country of
Western Europe (and a few others) on
minimal cash.

Rough Guides

travel.roughguides.com

Free, first-class guide books: Although this
British-based guidebook series has been
publishing selected guidebook titles
online in their entirety (every word from
the printed books) on the *Wired* magazine

Web site for several years, it now has its own address and a new look. The new site ups the ante even further for its competitors — every one of the 103 Rough Guides will eventually be available, free, online at the new site.

Web of Culture

www.webofculture.com

Cross-cultural communication: The various sections of Web of Culture help you find out all about the cultural customs in your destination area. Use the Educational section to find out about gestures used in foreign countries (among other fun stuff). The Reference section is perhaps the most useful, providing links to a variety of information for travelers headed abroad.

World Travel Guide

www.wtg-online.com

Sketch profiles of almost every country in the world: The World Travel Guide provides a quick overview of any country where your travels take you. Use the world map or the alphabetical listing to access a country's files. Every country listing includes details on accommodations, transportation, holidays, money, food, history, and much more.

Other Sites to Check Out

EatHere.com
www.eathere.com

Eurotrip
www.eurotrip.com

NetGuide Travel
www.netguide.com/Travel

PlanetRider
www.planetrider.com

Preview Travel Destination Guides
destinations.previewtravel.com

Roadside America
www.roadsideamerica.com

Route 66
route66.netvision.be

Travel Page
www.travelpage.com

Travelocity Destination Guides
www.travelocity.com/destg/

Discount Travel

Nothing's better than scoring a cheap flight or vacation deal. The following sites are a must for any travel bargain hunter. Of course, if you hate to save money on travel expenses, please refrain from reading these entries — they may save you more than you can stand.

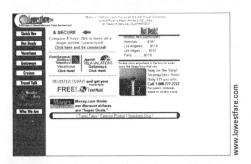

1travel.com

www.1travel.com

Discount travel agency: 1travel.com is one of the few online travel agencies that succeeds in its claim to provide discounted travel prices on travel products. Whether you want an all-inclusive vacation like Club Med or an around-the-world plane ticket, 1travel.com may have a deal for you. The site acts as a forum for travel suppliers (airfare consolidators and discount travel agents) to peddle their wares — sign up to receive free, customized weekly e-mail that alerts you to incredible, last-minute low fares.

Airtech.com

www.airtech.com

Cheap tickets for flexible flyers: Airtech operates on an interesting concept: Give them a four-day window of time and they guarantee to get you to Europe, the Caribbean, or to a U.S. city for an unbelievably low fare. It doesn't work, however, if you must be somewhere on a certain day. Find out all about this incredible service at the site.

Arthur Frommer's Outspoken Encyclopedia of Travel

www.frommers.com

One of the best discount travel sources on the Internet: Arthur Frommer's Outspoken Encyclopedia of Travel is the first place you look when you want to know what's happening in terms of discount travel opportunities, whether you seek a package tour, cruise, or airfare. Each day, the Frommer's staff compiles a newsletter of budget travel options that is *de rigueur* reading for anyone interested in saving some money on their next trip. You can read the newsletter at the Web site, or you can subscribe (for free) and receive it by e-mail. Each issue is archived, however, so before you make a purchase, it pays to search the Frommer's site.

Best Fares Magazine Online

www.bestfares.com

$

Bargain airfare advice and listings: You have to subscribe to get the really good stuff at this site (it's about $60 for a year's subscription), but Best Fares' free section has some good leads for individuals seeking discount airfares.

Cheap Tickets Inc.

www.cheaptickets.com

Purchase discounted airfares: Check in often with Cheap Tickets when you're searching for breaks on flights. The Specials section lists some mouthwatering fares — but are they available on the dates you want to travel? That is the question. . . .

Click-It Weekends

www.travelweb.com/TravelWeb/
   clickit.html

Last minute deals on hotel rooms: A service of TravelWeb, the biggest online computer reservation system for hotels, Click-It Weekends can help you find accommodations in major hotel chains for very little money. The catch: You must be willing to travel at the last minute. Bargains are posted each week for the coming weekend.

Hotel Reservation Network

www.180096hotel.com

Discounted rooms in great, American hotels: Hotel Reservation Network is one of my favorite travel services because it consistently delivers on its promise to save you loads of money on hotel rooms in major American cities (not to mention that the URL contains a toll-free number). After you find a cheap hotel room, book the room online or dial the toll-free number and speak to a representative. Even if the Marriott Marquis says they have no vacancy, check with HRN; the service buys blocks of rooms and often has rooms for sold-out dates.

The International Association of Air Travel Couriers

www.courier.org

Details on the art of courier flights: Perhaps you've heard tell of people who travel for ridiculously low airfares as a

D-16 Health and Insurance

courier. Basically, anyone can do it, so long as you are willing to donate your carry-on luggage allotment to a parcel. The IAATC site is the place to find out all about the intricacies of the process.

Lowestfare.com

www.lowestfare.com

Purchase discounted airfares: Lowestfare.com guarantees 20 percent off on most major airlines' published fares, both domestic and international routes, with widely varying results. Give 'em a try.

Priceline.com

www.priceline.com

 $

A revolutionary means of purchasing plane tickets: Priceline.com recently received a patent for its groundbreaking method of selling services and products. I offer a detailed explanation in Chapter 9, but here's the synopsis: You enter a reasonable price that you wish to pay for a given air route (you must have an up-to-date knowledge of airfares) and within an hour, Priceline.com tells you whether it can find an airline to supply the ticket. If they do find you a ticket, you've bought it — so be sure you want to go!

Travel Information Software Systems (TISS)

www.tiss.com

A database of consolidator airfares: Although the technology to sell so-called consolidator fares is still in the formative stages, you may have success in finding a discounted domestic or international airfare using the TISS system. (See Chapter 9 for more information on consolidators.)

Other Sites to Check Out

11th Hour Vacations
www.11thhourvacations.com

Airhitch
www.airhitch.org/

America West Surf N Go
www.americawest.com/eto/surfngo.asp

Bid4Travel
www.bid4travel.com

Cathay Pacific Travel Auction
www.cathay-usa.com/auction

Continental CO.O.L. Specials
www.flycontinental.com/cool

Epicurious Travel Detours
travel.epicurious.com/travel/d_play/
07_detours/detour.cfm

Fare Wars Mailing List
www.travelersnet.com/gr/listinfo.html

Learning Vacations' Travnews Newsletter
www.learningvacations.com/travnews.htm

Northwest Airlines Cybersavers
www.nwa.com/travel/cyber/cyber.html

Shoestring Travel
www.stratpub.com

TravelGram
news.travelgram.com/travelgram

TravelHUB
www.travelhub.com/club.html

TWA Hot Deals
www.twa.com/hot_deals/index.html

US Airways E-Savers
www.usairways.com/travel/fares/
esavers.htm

WebFlyer Deal Watch
www.webflyer.com/@deal/@deal.htm

Health and Insurance

Some planning and a few preventative measures can minimize the risk of getting sick during your travels. If you do run into health trouble abroad (heaven forbid), travel insurance goes a long way toward covering the financial cost. These sites should answer all your travel health- and insurance-related questions.

Center for Disease Control Travel Information

www.cdc.gov/travel

Health advisories for international travel: The Center for Disease Control is the world's authority on health safety for travelers. Before you head out into the world, check with the CDC to find out which inoculations and prophylactic measures you should take. The site offers detailed information about malaria and other common tropical diseases, as well as a section that rates the sanitation levels of cruise ships.

Travel Health Information Service

www.travelhealth.com

Travel healthy: Trust Dr. Stephen Blythe to administer heaping doses of solid medical advice for any journey. Dr. Blythe's page has information about all types of travel health concerns: food and water precautions, insect avoidance, sun protection and, of course, the dreaded traveler's diarrhea. You also get an excellent FAQ about travel insurance.

Travel Insurance Services

www.travelinsure.com

Travel insurance for individuals and groups: People often overlook travel insurance, mostly because they assume that their home insurance covers them should something go awry during their travels. Unfortunately, that's not always the case. Travel Insurance Services is one of many insurers that offer plans to cover medical, evacuation, and trip cancellation costs for travelers. The site details the costs involved in the various plans and provides a printable application form.

Other Sites to Check Out

Healthy Flying
    www.flyana.com

No Jet Lag
    www.nojetlag.com

Hotel Chains

All the big, international hotel chains now offer sophisticated sites on the Web. The following hotel chain sites offer similar services, allowing you to make reservations with a credit card, check out discounts and promotions, and scout out rooms with a click (or two) of the mouse. (Each site here requires registration.)

D-18 Online Travel Agencies

Best Western
www.bestwestern.com

Embassy Suites
www.embassysuites.com

Hampton Inn
www.hamptoninn.com

Hilton
www.hilton.com

Holiday Inn
www.holiday-inn.com

Hyatt Hotels
www.hyatt.com

Marriott
www.marriott.com

Ramada
www.ramada.com

Sandals Resort
www.sandals.com

Sheraton
www.sheraton.com

Other Sites to Check Out

Hilton Specials
www.hilton.com/specials/index.html

Holiday Inn Specials
www.holiday-inn.com/Promo.html

Hyatt Hot Deals
www.hyatt.com/hotdeals/index.html

Marriott Friday Specials
marriotthotels.com/friday/

Sheraton Hot Deals
www.sheraton.com/hot_deals/index.html

Yahoo! Hotel Directory
www.yahoo.com/Business_and_Economy/
Companies/Travel/Lodging/Hotels

Online Travel Agencies

The following full-service, online travel agencies have established themselves as the best places to research, reserve, and book airline tickets, hotel rooms, and rental cars. See Chapter 6 for a full description of how these sites operate. (Each site here allows online purchasing and requires registration.)

www.itn.com

Atevo
www.atevo.com

Expedia
expedia.msn.com

Flifo
www.flifo.com

Internet Travel Network
www.itn.com

Leisure Planet
www.leisureplanet.com

Preview Travel
www.previewtravel.com

Travelocity
www.travelocity.com

Publications and Travel News

Magazines, newspapers, travelogues, 'zines, brochures, newsletters, and all other writings are available online for travelers' edification. I consider the following sites required reading for dedicated travelers.

ABCNEWS.com Travel

www.abcnews.com/sections/Travel

Travel news and features: The latest news affecting travelers and a parade of regular features written by noted travel writers are handsomely displayed at this mega-news site. Check in regularly for the Deal of the Day, updated travel bargains from the pages of *Best Fares Magazine.* Other regular sections include the Crabby Traveler, an opinionated (and sometimes frustrated) column about various travel topics and the EuroFiles, that chronicles interesting happenings in Europe.

CNN Travel

www.cnn.com/TRAVEL

Travel news and guide: CNN uses its enormous reach and newsgathering strength to produce a dynamic travel page. Travel news, city guides, information on destinations, and many other travel tools make CNN Travel one of the most popular travel sites on the Web.

Search the enormous story archive for articles and multimedia that can enhance your trip.

Epicurious Travel

travel.epicurious.com

Refined travel writing: Brought to you by Conde Nast, the folks who publish *GQ* and *Vogue,* Epicurious Travel is an online journal aimed primarily at moneyed travelers. But even travelers who don't own a BMW can enjoy a peek at their deal of the week. The three main sections, Places, Planning, and Play, consistently cover a wide range of travel topics with quality writing.

National Geographic Traveler

www.nationalgeographic.com/media/ traveler

Travel features with great photos: Traveler adds to the tradition of the venerable *National Geographic,* illustrating expansive travel features with fantastic travel photography. Each story comes equipped with Web links and an invitation to contribute to the Traveler message boards with your own thoughts. The magazine is published online six times a year.

Salon Wanderlust

www.salonmagazine.com/wlust

Online travel magazine: Wanderlust is a terrific online magazine published each Monday at 6:00 p.m. Pacific Time. Each issue contains excellent feature writing about travel-related subjects, written by professional and sometimes well-known writers.

Underbelly

www.underbelly.com

Where not to go and what to do when you get there: This irreverent *e-zine* plumbs the depths of irony in various cities of the world. Its contributing writers range, in their own words, from "brooding and Byronic" to the "obsessive." Click the name of a world city to read the various musings.

U.S. State Department Travel Warnings and Consular Information Sheets

travel.state.gov/travel_warnings.html

Government reports on every country: If you're unsure about the safety of a destination, check the U.S. State Department's Travel Warnings site. The State Department maintains up-to-date listings for every country in the world, covering safety, health issues, and country information.

Web Surfer Travel Journal

edge.net/~dphillip/wstj.html

Lots of links and a love of travel: This one-man publication conveys the publisher's (Dan K. Phillips) love for travel and his embrace of the Internet through well-chosen Web links and nicely crafted, personal travel tales. Check in each month for a new issue or browse through the archived issues from months past.

Worldwide Brochures

www.wwb.com

Thousands of travel brochures: Even in the age of the Internet, sometimes it's nice to flip through a glossy travel brochure. Search the Worldwide Brochure database to find brochures, flyers, and pamphlets about destinations, resorts, and everything else that you can find in a brochure — the site offers more than 10,000!

Other Sites to Check Out

CIA World Factbook
www.odci.gov/cia/publications/factbook/index.html

Cyber-Adventures.com
www.cyber-adv.com/

Electric Book
www.electricbook.com

Everything's Travel
members.aol.com/trvlevery/media/index.htm

National Geographic
www.nationalgeographic.com

NetGuide Publications Directory
www.netguide.com/Publications

Newslink
www.newslink.org/news.html

Rec.Travel Library
www.Travel-Library.com/

Transitions Abroad
www.transabroad.com

Travelmag
www.travelmag.co.uk/travelmag

Traveloco
www.traveloco.com

Trippin' Out
www.trippinout.com

Newspaper Travel Sections

In print, newspaper travel sections generally appear only on Sunday. But online newspapers maintain travel sections each day that provide an excellent source of travel information.

Although every online paper has its own editorial style and design, the basic elements are similar for each: current travel news and features, a searchable archive of past articles and stories, travel tools (maps, current airfares info, weather forecasts), and various multimedia features. I include a detailed section about a specific online paper's features in Chapter 5. Here are the addresses of some of the best.

Los Angeles Times Travel Section

www.latimes.com/HOME/NEWS/TRAVEL

A travel section suited to L.A.: In the spirit of the city in which it makes its home, the LA Times Travel Section has a very glossy and colorful design. Engaging writing, with topics like "Hunt for the Perfect Hawaiian Shirt," keep the articles amusing.

New York Times Travel

www.nytimes.com/yr/mo/day/travel

Articles oriented towards destinations: Most of the New York Times Travel Section deals with destinations — the regular "What's Doing In" feature describes up and coming places to visit. Other sections include: The Practical Traveler, The Frugal Travelers, and Travel Q & A.

The Planet — The London Telegraph Travel Section

www.the-planet.co.uk

Hyper-designed travel section: Great design and multimedia offerings characterize this London newspaper's travel section. Read about a wide variety of destinations and travel advice.

USA Today Travel

www.usatoday.com/life/travel/ltfront.htm

An excellent travel reference: The so-called McPaper, USA Today, sports a travel section noteworthy for its many travel resources. You also find timely travel news and feature articles, as well as links to Preview Travel and Frommer's Guides.

Washington Post Travel

www.washingtonpost.com/wp-srv/travel/front.htm

A travel magazine within a newspaper: The *WP*'s travel section points you to either the latest travel news or an archived travel article. The magazine format allows for nice photography and easy access to a variety of resources.

Other Sites to Check Out

Chicago Tribune Travel
www.chicago.tribune.com/travel/index.htm

International Herald Tribune
www.iht.com

Miami Herald Travel
www.herald.com/travel

Rental Cars

Few areas of commerce are as well-suited to the Internet as rental cars. The following car rental companies' sites all allow you to view the fleet of available cars and make a reservation. I include a full description of the process in Chapter 8. (All sites under this heading allow online purchasing and require registration.)

D-22 Restaurant Guides

Alamo

www.goalamo.com

Avis

www.avis.com

Budget

www.budgetrentacar.com

Hertz

www.hertz.com

National

www.nationalcar.com

Restaurant Guides

Whether you're looking for the burger to end all burgers or a six-course French meal, plug in to the Internet and find a great restaurant in your destination city. Diners, family-style eateries, and fancy-schmancy establishments are online, waiting to be discovered.

www.cuisinenet.com

CuisineNet

www.cuisinenet.com

Find a restaurant in the U.S.: Traveling sure works up an appetite. Use this site to find tasty eats in many U.S. cities. Search the database by cuisine type, location,

price range, and amenities. Most of the listed restaurants are reviewed with text and numbers; some even have menus and photos.

The Zagat Survey

cgi.pathfinder.com/
@@3RgX2QUAZNX8Wemv/cgi-bin/
zagat/homepage

Famous U.S. dining guide: Zagat's little brown books have become ubiquitous items for restaurant connoisseurs. Now you can access the pithy reviews online, organized by city, for free.

Other Sites to Check Out

Dine.com
www.dine.com

Dinner and a Movie.com
www.dinnerandamovie.com

EatHere.com
www.eathere.com

Fodor's Restaurant Index
www.fodors.com/ri.cgi

The Kosher Restaurant Database
www.shamash.org/kosher/krestquery.html

KosherLink
www.kosherlink.com/

Menus Online
www.menusonline.com/

Sushi World Guide
www.sushi.infogate.de

World Guide to Vegetarianism
www.veg.org/veg/Guide

Special-Interest Travel

In cyberspace, you can find sites geared to every type of traveler. The following represent a sampling of sites that exist for disabled travelers, women-only tours, study and work abroad, family travel, senior travel, and gay and lesbian travel.

Access-Able Travel Source

www.access-able.com

Comprehensive info for disabled travelers: Travelers with disabilities need look no further than this detailed and devoted site. Find out about accessible destinations and tour operators that specialize in products for disabled travelers.

ElderTreks

www.eldertreks.com

Interesting trips for mature adults: ElderTreks is a Toronto-based travel agency that specializes in adventurous trips to exotic destinations for people over 50 years old. The trips, which you can easily explore via the nicely designed and comprehensive Web site, consistently earn high marks from travelers.

Family.com Travel Category

family.disney.com/Categories/Travel

Hit the road with the family: Need a few ideas for the next family vacation? Family.com (a Disney site) can help. Read the feature articles or search the archives to find trips the whole family can enjoy. You can also find links to sites for Disney's theme parks.

Gayscene

www.gayscene.com

Destinations info for gay, lesbian, and bisexual travelers: Explore more than 3,000 destination listings by clicking the world map or browsing by region. Listings include bars, clubs, hotels, and personal ads.

PlanetOut Travel

www.planetout.com/pno/travel

Travel info for gays: Read about gay-friendly destinations and the well-written feature articles in the travel section of PlanetOut, a great lifestyle site. Travel story categories include Fun in the Sun, Outdoor Adventures, and Weekend Getaways.

Rainbow Adventures for Women

www.rainbowadventures.com

Adventures for women over 30: Each year, Rainbow Adventures, a Montana-based tour operator, takes groups of women on some great trips. Check the Web site to see the scheduled trips and prices.

Studyabroad.com

www.studyabroad.com

Info for student travelers: Spending time studying in a foreign country can be a valuable experience. So many programs are available today, though, that you need a comprehensive Web site to sort through them. Studyabroad.com gets straight A's for its detailed listings of study programs in more than 100 countries. You can search for programs by country and subject.

Wild Women Adventures

www.wildwomenadv.com

Adventures for women: Before you visit Wild Women Adventures, make sure that you're ready to shed your inhibitions and delve into some adventurous travel. Billed as the ultimate guide to fab fun, Wild Women is your passport to destinations all over the world through travel agents who specialize in women's travel. They also offer "advice for recovering good girls."

Other Sites to Check Out

1travel.com's Honeymoon Guide
www.1travel.com/honey.htm

American Airlines Senior Fares
www.americanair.com/aa_home/servinfo/
senior.htm

American Institute for Foreign Study
www.aifs.org

Continental Airlines Senior Fares
www.flycontinental.com/products/senior/

**Council on International Educational
Exchange**
www.ciee.org/

Elder Hostel
www.elderhostel.org/

EscapeArtist.com
www.escapeartist.com

Family Travel Forum
www.familytravelforum.com

Family.com Travel
family.disney.com/Categories/Travel/

Honeymoons.com
www.honeymoons.com

The Mining Company's Travel with Kids
travelwithkids.miningco.com

Modern Bride's Honeymoon Planning
www.modernbride.com/
honeymoonplanning/index.html

Sta Travel
www.sta-travel.com/index.html

Transitions Abroad
www.transabroad.com/

TWA Senior Fares
www.twa.com/html/vacation/toursp.html

United Airlines Silver Wings Plus
www.silverwingsplus.com/

US Airways Senior Fares
www.usairways.com/travel/fares/
sen_trav.htm

Trains and Buses

These sites can help you get around the surface of Planet Earth via good old-fashioned train or bus. Don't forget to cruise these sites before you get on board.

Amtrak

www.amtrak.com

America's passenger trains: All aboard! Now you can purchase train tickets online using Amtrak's easy-to-use reservation system. Find out about special promotions, schedules, fares, and the status of trains in transit.

European Rail Travel

www.eurorail.com/railindx.htm

Plan European train trips: Anyone who plans to travel on a European railroad can benefit from this Euro-rail primer. The site furnishes information about everything from basic facts on European trains to detailed, country-by-country timetables. Search the database for schedules and ticket information.

Greyhound Bus Lines

www.greyhound.com

Leave the driving to them: Find out about the routes and ticket prices for America's largest bus line. Currently, you can't purchase tickets online, but at least you can see what's available.

UK Railways on the Net

www.rail.co.uk/ukrail/home.htm

Rail travel in the U.K.: Most European countries now have Web sites for their railroads, but the U.K. site is notable for its handsome design and ease of use. And you can find out about the London to Paris route through the Chunnel.

Other Sites to Check Out

Cyberspace World Railroad
www.mcs.com/~dsdawdy/Parlor/parlor.html

Eurail.com
www.eurail.com

European National Railways and Timetables
mercurio.iet.unipi.it/misc/timetabl.html

Rail Europe
www.raileurope.com

Rail Serve
www.railserve.com

Rail Travel Center
www.railtvl.com/

Trans-Siberian Railroad Page
www.xs4all.nl/~hgj/

The World by Rail
www.trippexplorer.com

Travel Agents and Tour Operators

Nowadays, virtually every travel professional does at least some share of business over the Internet, even if only to e-mail customers. These sites enable you to find and contact travel agents (not online travel agencies where you can book tickets on the Web) and tour operators that suit your individual needs.

American Society of Travel Agents (ASTA)

www.astanet.com

A huge database of reputable travel agents: The American Society of Travel Agents is the best-known and largest travel industry trade association (the largest trade association for any industry, for that matter) in the world. Click Travelers to access the directory of travel services that ASTA provides. ASTA holds its member agents to a high standard of integrity; use the Travel Directory to search the massive database for agencies and other ASTA-approved travel suppliers.

Club Med

www.clubmed.com

World renowned all-inclusive resort: Club Med is probably the best known resort chain in the world. Visit its site to explore all the resorts, or, in Club Med-speak, *villages.* If you know where you want to spend your vacation, choose the country from the pull-down menu. You also can use the site's search features to find your ideal village.

InfoHub Specialty Travel Guide

www.infohub.com

Find the tour for you: You know what you want out of a vacation, but you don't know how to put it together. InfoHub lets you input a set of vacation or tour criteria (destination, activity, travel period, and price) and then searches its database to find tour operators that can make your trip happen. Tours and info are regularly updated.

Resorts Online

www.resortsonline.com

Find a resort by activity: Click the icon that denotes your interest, and Resorts Online finds you a list of resorts where you can golf, scuba dive, ski, gamble, or just sit on the beach. You need to choose the region of the world where you want to vacation.

TravelFile

www.travelfile.com

Find tour operators and travel services: Input a destination into the search box and TravelFile produces a list of travel-related services, including tour operators, accommodations, attractions, information offices, and transportation. The featured tour operators have their own informational pages on TravelFile, describing their services and providing contact information.

Travelon

www.travelon.com

Find a cruise, resort, or adventure: Travelon is like a big, interactive travel catalog. Tour operators, cruise lines, and resorts enlist the services of Travelon to connect with travelers. Choose the type of vacation you seek and then select the features that are most important to you, such as activity, date of departure, price, destination, and so on. After prioritizing, Travelon comes up with a list of travel options that includes hypertext links to the companies that provide the travel.

Other Sites to Check Out

Carlson Wagonlit Travel
www.travel.carlson.com

Sightseeing.com
www.sightseeing.com

Traveler.net
traveler.net

TravelFile
www.travelfile.com

TravelHUB
www.travelhub.com

Travel Tools

In addition to allowing you to research your trip and purchase tickets, the Internet also includes some super-practical tools for travelers. Want to know the weather in Ireland before you arrive (hey, it may not be raining — you never know)? How about checking whether Uncle Roger's plane is still coming in at the scheduled time? You can do these things, as well as generate maps, find Internet cafés worldwide, travel on a budget, build a Web page, find the distance between two points, find resources for laptop travel, convert currencies, and translate languages.

www.hotmail.com

ArtofTravel.com

www.artoftravel.com

See the world for $25 or less per day: From where I'm sitting, John Gregory has the right idea. He published his book, *How to See the World,* all 100,000 words, in its entirety, online. Check out his useful advice for budget travel, and, if you're a publisher, think about putting his book in print!

The Cybercafe Search Engine

cybercaptive.com

Find an Internet café: You can now find Internet cafés in almost every country in the world. Travelers can send and receive e-mail at these cafés; some have Web access as well. The Cybercafe Search Engine lists more than 1,900 cafés in 109 countries — search the database before you leave if you want to know where to connect.

Homestead

www.homestead.com

Build a Web page: Homestead is a free Web hosting service that makes it extremely easy for anyone to build and maintain a Web page. You need not have any programming experience; Homestead walks you through the process step by step. (I recently heard about a group of friends who went on a trip in Europe, built a Web page at a cyber-café in Paris, and then posted photos to it periodically during their trip to let their friends and family follow their journey.)

Hotmail

www.hotmail.com

Free Web-based e-mail: Access an e-mail account from anywhere on the planet with Web access through a freemail account, courtesy of Hotmail (a Microsoft site).

How Far Is It?

www.indo.com/distance

Distances between cities: You can do just two things at this neat little site: Enter two cities or two map coordinates and it tells you the distance (in miles, kilometers, and, for you sailors, nautical miles) between the two points. You can then have the site produce a map, if you so desire.

Intellicast

www.intellicast.com

Worldwide weather forecasts: The weather isn't just for small talk anymore. Now it's a full-blown fascination thanks to Intellicast's unbelievable weather megasite. Users get many different looks at weather as it happens all around the world through technicolor satellite imaging, extended forecasts, and detailed meteorological reports. Sports enthusiasts can make use of the ski, golf, boating, and NASCAR reports.

iPass

www.ipass.com

Global Internet roaming: iPass has developed a network of Internet service providers, allowing mobile computer users to connect from anywhere without having to incur expensive long distance phone charges or maintain multiple ISP accounts. Find out about their service and prices at this site.

itList

www.itlist.com

Online bookmark manager: Those of you who spend much time on the Web know the value of a bookmarks/favorites file. But what to do when you're in Bali and your bookmarks are in Dallas? itList is an

D-28 Travel Tools

online bookmark manager. Transfer your bookmarks, for free, to the site's database and ... voilà! You can now access your bookmarks anywhere in the world at the itList Web page.

The List

thelist.internet.com

Find an Internet service provider (ISP) almost anywhere: The List is the single biggest listing of ISPs around the world that I've come across. Search the database by area code or country code. Especially useful for laptop travelers.

MailStart

www.mailstart.com

Check your e-mail from anywhere using the Web: Those clever Internet people have done it again. Now you can check your e-mail account from any browser by visiting the MailStart site. Simply enter your e-mail address and password and the site magically accesses your POP mailbox, enabling you to read, send, or delete mail messages — free of charge. The service does not yet work with AOL accounts or with networks protected by a firewall. (See Chapter 13 for more information.)

MapQuest

www.mapquest.com

Maps made to order: You no longer have an excuse for getting lost. A visit to MapQuest yields door-to-door instructions and full-color maps for any U.S. destination. MapQuest also locates and maps any location worldwide. Just print out the map and you're ready to go. (See Chapter 11 for more details.)

The Mining Company Travel Section

home.miningco.com/travel

Directory of Internet travel information: The Mining Company does a nice job of organizing all their Internet guides, and each major topic has its own dedicated expert. For travel, you get separate guides for the big topics, such as active travel, air travel, budget travel, and others. The site also includes loads of links for destinations and types of vacations.

NetGuide Travel Channel

www.netguide.com/Travel

One heck of a site!: Okay, I may be a little biased, because I'm the former producer of the NetGuide Travel Channel. All personal feelings aside, the site offers a great guide to the enormous amount of travel info on the Internet. Each day, the Travel Channel reviews an outstanding travel Web site and adds the review to the enormous, searchable database. It also has informative feature articles about destinations, types of travel, and discounts.

Travel.Org

www.travel.org

Web travel directory: Use Travel.Org when you want to find travel information on the Web. The top-level directory headings deal mostly with destinations (Europe, Asia, and so on), but you can also find headings for Airlines, Information, and Lodging. Enjoy tons of good link choices and a free e-mail newsletter.

Travlang

www.travlang.com

Online language translator: Ever try to express yourself without speaking a word of the native tongue? Before your next trip abroad, spend a few moments with the basics at Travlang. Travlang has an enormous amount of language resources, including two-way dictionaries, translators that speak, and language chat rooms.

TheTrip.com's Real Time Flight Tracking

flight.thetrip.com/flightstatus/ index.html

Track flights in the United States: Anyone who has spent hours at an airport waiting for a plane to arrive can appreciate the value of a flight tracker. TheTrip.com offers a really cool flight tracking application that uses real-time flight info from the FAA, free of charge. To check on a flight, simply enter the flight number and the airline. You can choose a graphical version that shows a visual representation (which is pretty cool) or a faster-loading text version.

The Universal Currency Converter

www.xe.net/currency

Current exchange rates and currency conversion: Ever try to convert Turkish Lira to Japanese Yen? It ain't easy. The Universal Currency Converter has the latest exchange rates and allows for easy conversion from one currency to another. (See Chapter 10 to read about other features.)

Yahoo! Travel

travel.yahoo.com

A directory of all things travel on Yahoo!: Yahoo! Travel serves as a great launching pad for accomplishing myriad travel goals. Book a flight, research a destination, find out travel news, and access all the Yahoo! travel categories from one happy page.

Other Sites to Check Out

AccuWeather
www.AccuWeather.com

American Passport
www.americanpassport.com

CMPnet Mail
www.cmpnetmail.com

The Definitive Table of Real Time Traffic Information (US)
www.itsonline.com/rttable.html

G3 Visas
g3visas.com/index.htm

Instant Passport
www.instantpassport.com

Kallback.com
www.kallback.com

Maps On Us
www.mapsonus.com

Mastercard ATM Locator
www.mastercard.com/atm

Net Café Guide
www.netcafeguide.com

Rand McNally Road Construction Listings
www.randmcnally.com/construction/ index.htm

RWA Direct Traffic
rwa.metronetworks.com/RWADirect.HTML

SmarTraveler Traveler Information Services
www.smartraveler.com

Travel Document Systems
www.traveldocs.com

US Passport Services
travel.state.gov/passport_services.html

Visa ATM Locator
www.visa.com/cgi-bin/vee/pd/atm/ main.html

Part III

Plugging In to Plan and Prepare Yourself

The 5th Wave   By Rich Tennant

"I love these online travel tips, like how _not_ to look like a tourist. Imagine– I was gonna get off the plane in India with a goofy camera around my neck."

In this part . . .

After you've found a place to go and made the arrangements, you need to prepare for the trip. The Internet is full of expert travel advice and nifty travel tools. This part shows you where to find the tools and resources to minimize risks (and know what to pack). I also explain how to connect with a vast pool of experts — your fellow travelers. And for those of you that simply can't bear to leave the Internet behind, I include a chapter about staying connected from anywhere in the world.

Chapter 10

Healthy, Wealthy, and Wise

- -

In This Chapter

▶ Getting your traveling papers in order

▶ Knowing travel conditions before you leave

▶ Converting currency online

▶ Managing travel money

▶ Locating ATMs worldwide

▶ Checking out online health resources

- -

*T*his chapter shows you how to use the Internet to gear up for a trip — next time you need a passport, visa, location of an automated teller machine, or the conversion rate for Yen to Marks, turn to the Internet. You can conveniently take care of the predeparture drudgery online so you can get to the good stuff: crossing borders and buying souvenirs.

Papers, Please: Getting Your Travel Documents in Order

If you've ever been to your country's passport agency, you probably don't want to return anytime soon. Long lines, foul-tempered bureaucratic clerks, and endless forms are all good reasons to submit your passport application online. And if you need your passport issued or renewed in a hurry, most online passport services expedite passport requests, sometimes supplying a passport in as little as 24 hours. Many countries now allow their citizens to apply for a passport on the Internet.

As for visa and country entry requirements, the Internet is a natural. Most countries have an official government Web site that you can visit to read about entry procedures and visa regulations. In addition to the official government sites, there are several sites that act as embassy encyclopedias, listing the entry info, consulate locations, and visa news for nearly every country in the world, all in one convenient location.

U.S. State Department's Passport Services Web page

If you're an American citizen, your tax dollars have created a very useful and informative site — you didn't know you had a Web site, did you? The U.S. State Department's Passport Services Web page (`travel.state.gov/passport_services.html`), Figure 10-1, provides a great starting point for Americans who need to get their travel papers in order.

Visit the State Department's Passport Services page when you have any questions regarding traveling papers. The site allows you to:

- ✔ **Find a passport office.** Or "passport acceptance facility" in the language of bureaucracy, where you can pick up and submit applications. The site offers a state-by-state listing.

- ✔ **Get fees for passports.** Find out how much you need to pay for a new passport and passport renewals.

- ✔ **Download a passport application.** You need a piece of software called Adobe Acrobat Reader (free to download from the site) before you can print out the application. After you have the form, you can avoid the passport office entirely and submit your application by mail.

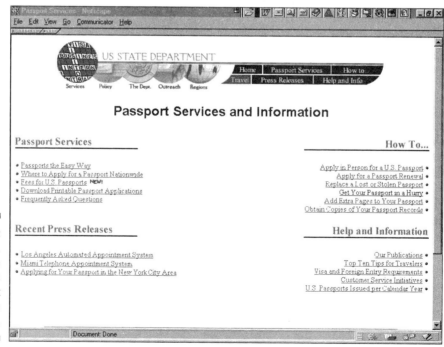

Figure 10-1:
The U.S. State Department's Passport Services page.

✔ **Directions on how to apply for and get a passport in a hurry.** The
How To section answers all your questions.

Before you visit a private passport agency, online or in person, get the
straight dope direct from the government. That way you can avoid getting
inaccurate information.

Other official government passport sites

The U.S. is not the only country that has passport information online. The
following countries offer excellent passport resources:

✔ **Canadian Passport Office** (www.dfait-maeci.gc.ca/passport/
passport.htm): Though you can't submit an application online, this
site should tell you all you need to know to obtain a Canadian passport
in Canada or in the U.S.

✔ **UK Passport Agency** (www.open.gov.uk/ukpass/ukpass.htm): The
British government offers most of the same passport services as the
U.S. State Department's Passport Services Web page, which you can
read about in the preceding section.

✔ **Britain in the USA** (britain-info.org/BIS/CONSULAR/
PASSVISA.SHTM): This site is for British citizens living in the U.S. who
wish to obtain a British passport in the U.S. or for those of any nationality wishing to obtain visas for the U.K.

✔ **Passports Australia** (www.dfat.gov.au/passports/pp_home.html):
Download a passport application form or just find out the details
(including fees) about obtaining an Australian passport.

If you want info on a specific country's passport regulations, find out if the
country has an official government passport page. It may take a little
searching, but start your search in the Yahoo! Government section in the
countries subcategory (www.yahoo.com/Government/Countries).

Private agencies for American passports

In addition to using an official government passport agency to obtain a
passport, Americans can get their passports issued by private passport
agencies. Many of these agencies now have Web sites; Yahoo! offers a
category listing, called Passport Services (www.yahoo.com/Business_
and_Economy/Companies/Travel/Passport_Services), which lists
most of these private agencies' Web sites.

Most online passport agencies offer similar services that focus on getting
your passport as quickly as possible. Of course, private agencies expect to
be compensated for their speed.

Most agencies have similar procedures for expediting passports. Each charges U.S. $100 to deliver a new passport (for someone that has never held a U.S. passport) in 24 hours. You still must sign the official government form in front of an authorized acceptance agent — usually your local post office can provide an authorized witness — and pay the $95 government processing and expediting fee. You then send all the required materials to the expediter (via FedEx or another overnight delivery service) and it sends back your valid passport.

If you need a passport renewal, these agencies will expedite your renewal (within 24 hours, same process as above) for the same U.S. $100 fee, but the government fee is $75 for renewals and it is not necessary to have an authorized acceptance agent witness the signing.

These agencies also gladly process standard passport applications (non-expedited) for a U.S. $50 fee. You get the passport in three to five business days — much faster than if you do the application yourself through a U.S. Passport Agency, but there's no $50 fee if you do it on your own.

The two sites I mention in this section are generally acknowledged to be among the most reliable on the Net, and I've found them easier to use and navigate than their competitors:

- **Instant Passport and Visa (www.instantpassport.com):** Can deliver a passport in 24 hours. All the steps are clearly outlined and you can download and print out the necessary government forms. The service also expedites visas for most countries, with a specialty in Brazilian, Chinese, Indian, and Russian visas. The expediting fees for visas vary depending on whether you are a tourist or a business traveler.

- **American Passport Express (www.americanpassport.com):** Provides 24-hour passport processing and also charges U.S. $100 for the service. Follow the steps to print out the form and submit the required materials. This service doesn't process visa applications.

Finding visa requirements and embassies online

In order to enter many countries of the world, you need to have a *visa,* or formal permission, which allows governments to monitor the comings and goings of its visitors.

Usually, you must obtain the necessary visas (directly or indirectly) from an embassy or consulate of the nation you plan to visit. You can either contact the consulate yourself or use a visa service to acquire a visa.

Before you head to the embassy, consulate, or visa service, take a moment to look at the consulate site of the country you plan to visit, just to know the facts. In general, the official embassy sites are the best places to look for visa information. The best way to locate these official pages is to use either of the following two sites:

- ✔ **Governments on the WWW** (www.gksoft.com/govt/en/representations.html): This no-frills site has an alphabetical listing of links for every country in the world that maintains consulates. Follow the link to the consulate nearest you.

- ✔ **The EmbassyWeb** (www.embpage.org): The EmbassyWeb just completed a renovation of its site, making access to the vast amount of information about diplomatic offices worldwide very easy to navigate. Click Diplomatic Offices and then choose your home country to find the nearest consulate or embassy.

You can also find individual consulate and embassy sites by entering a phrase such as **Brazil embassy** or **Italian consulate** in a search engine. For example, plugging the phrase **Brazil embassy** into Yahoo! (www.yahoo.com) should turn up an official government site for Brazil — it does (www.itu.org.br/itembassy).

Obtaining visas online (Americans only)

You can always secure a visa by contacting a country's official diplomatic office. But if you live far from a consulate or don't want to deal with the bureaucratic red tape, then you can make use of intermediary services that can obtain a visa for you.

Entry requirements vary depending on your country of residence; most of the visa procuring services on the Internet are geared towards Americans — a fact that is sure to change over time.

The following sites specialize in providing Americans with visas to a wide range of countries. However, if you live in a major gateway city (for example, New York, Los Angeles, San Francisco, Washington D.C., and so on), where applying for a visa in person is relatively hassle-free, I recommend doing the work yourself and avoiding the fees associated with a visa service.

Travel Document Systems

Travel Document Systems (www.traveldocs.com), Figure 10-2, has been helping travelers obtain visas since 1985; it would be pretty safe to say they know their way around the diplomatic community in Washington D.C.

To find out about a country's entry requirements, either use the map of the world or click the first letter of the country's name on the navigation bar. Each country has its own page with links to information about the people, geography, history, travel conditions and, of course, entry requirements,

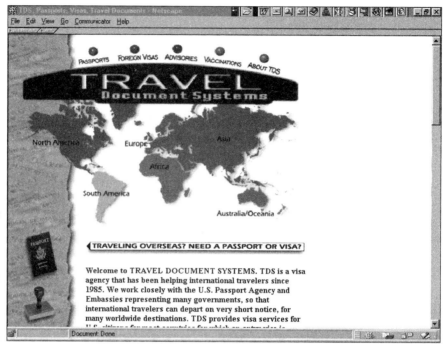

Figure 10-2:
The
Travel
Document
Systems
home
page.

and visa applications. Also included are links to online guidebook pages for the country.

Click Entry Requirements to view the cost and restrictions of the visa. TDS generally charges between U.S. $30 and $50 to process visa applications; you must also pay the country's consular fee, which varies widely. If you wish to apply for a visa, round up all the requirements specified on the page and mail them to Travel Document Systems. They then hand-carry your request to the country's embassy, and the visa application should be processed in less than a week. TDS then returns the authorized visa to you by old-fashioned postal mail.

G3 Visas and Passports

In its own words, G3 Visas and Passports (g3visas.com/index.htm), Figure 10-3, specializes in "obtaining visas and passports under very tight time constraints and with less than perfect documentation."

Like Travel Document Systems, which I discuss in the preceding section, G3 Visas and Passports is located in the Washington, D.C. area; the service hand-processes all applications and shepherds them quickly through the necessary offices.

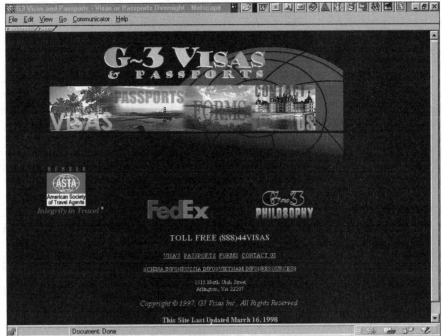

Figure 10-3:
The G3
Visas and
Passports
home page.

To find the entry requirements for a given country, click Visas on the G3
Visas and Passports home page and use the pull-down menus to select your
country and the length of stay. Check on the Forms page to see if your destination country has a downloadable form; if not, you need to either e-mail G3
and request a form or call them toll free at the number provided at the site.

Call and talk to a consultant in any case, just to make sure that everything is
squared away. The last thing you want is to arrive in some foreign country
and have to deal with red tape.

Know Before You Go: Travel Advisories and Conditions

More and more people are discovering the joys of visiting places off the
beaten track. Unfortunately, some of the most fascinating destinations you
can travel to have unstable political and environmental conditions that can
change in an instant.

In the past, travelers had to rely on sketchy hearsay and outdated government reports for predeparture safety info. Nowadays, you can get reliable hearsay and up-to-date government reports that tell you the current travel conditions anywhere in the world — by way of your digital friend, the Internet.

Thanks, Uncle Sam!

The U.S. government supplies online information that travelers of all nations should take advantage of before embarking to a foreign country.

The U.S. State Department

Any time the U.S. State Department feels that political instability or other conditions in a country make travel there unsafe for Americans, it issues a Travel Warning or Public Announcement. You can get the full text of these announcements at the U.S. State Department Travel Warnings and Consular Information Sheets page (`travel.state.gov/travel_warnings.html`), Figure 10-4. In fact, within hours of an international event affecting U.S. travelers or expatriates, the site is updated with the latest safety information.

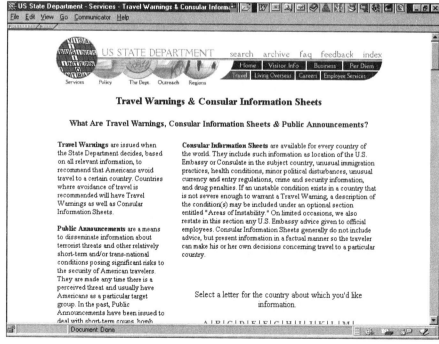

Figure 10-4:
The U.S. State Department Travel Warnings and Consular Information Sheets page.

Navigate through the countries by using the alphabetized listings. Click the first letter of the country you want to read about and you go to the applicable part of the list of announcements.

In addition, the State Department also produces Consular Information Sheets for every country of the world, detailing "the location of the U.S. Embassy or Consulate in the subject country, unusual immigration practices, health conditions, minor political disturbances, unusual currency and entry regulations, crime and security information, and drug penalties." Good stuff to know.

To check on a specific country's report, select the first letter of the country from the alphabetical links. Each country has a dated Consular Information Sheet that may or may not have been updated in recent months. These reports are updated as conditions change, so if a country's sheet has not been updated, it means that conditions have not changed significantly since the posting. Further, if you see a Travel Warning posted with the Consular Sheet, then you should know that there is something going on in that location that you wouldn't find at Disney World.

The CIA World Factbook

You don't have to be a spy to make use of the CIA World Factbook (`www.odci.gov/cia/publications/factbook/index.html`), Figure 10-5.

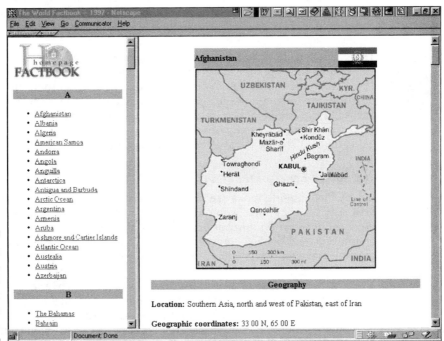

Figure 10-5:
The CIA
World
Factbook
countries
home page.

The Central Intelligence Agency of the United States (CIA) maintains detailed files on every country of the world, to, er, better *understand* them. The empirical data about every country of the world (populations, gross national product, and so on) is collected in the World Factbook; you can now access this compendium of world info at the CIA Web site. The information is useful because it enables you to know the ethnic makeup of a country, the climate, and the level of development, vis-à-vis other countries of the world. All information that can come in handy when you are packing for the trip.

The Factbook is organized very simply. Scroll through the list of countries on the left of the page; click your destination to read all sorts of interesting facts and statistics about the place. Also included for each country are detailed maps and the country's flag.

My favorite listing is the county's comparative size to the U.S. (though, if you're not familiar with U.S. geography, it's of little use). For example, the site states that Isle of Man is slightly more than three times the size of Washington D.C.

News from the field

Reading travel news provides another good way to find out about current conditions at destinations around the world. The following sites offer travel discussion on the Web and are great places to read news about travel conditions.

Travel sections in online newspapers, as described in Chapter 5, provide excellent sources of up-to-date information. Most online newspaper sites are searchable; use the name of your destination as a keyword in the search. In addition, the Usenet newsgroups (which I talk about in Chapter 13) give you access to the advice of travelers who have been there and done that; if there's a problem crossing borders in Thailand or a high incidence of theft going on in Costa Rica, travelers are talking about it in newsgroups.

The not-so-Lonely Planet Online

Lonely Planet guidebooks are known throughout the world as some of the best. The Lonely Planet Web page (www.lonelyplanet.com.au) has two great sections for finding out pointed bits of news about destinations' conditions. And because most of the people who use Lonely Planet are independent travelers, you can be sure that people are speaking from experience:

  ✔ **The Scoop - Travel News This Week** (www.lonelyplanet.com.au/news/newsweek.htm): This section, shown in Figure 10-6, contains excerpts of the world news that pertains to travelers; the site focuses on some of the most popular destinations. A dengue fever outbreak in New Delhi? Check here to see what's going on.

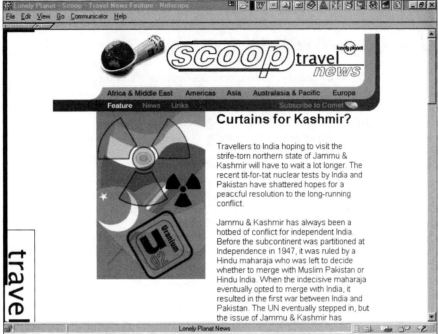

Figure 10-6:
The Scoop -
Travel
News
This Week
home page.

✔ **The Thorn Tree** (www.lonelyplanet.com.au/thorn/thorn.htm):
Lonely Planet's bulletin board for travelers. The site arranges the posts
by geographic region and special interests. Travelers regularly post to
this bulletin board from the road or upon returning from a trip. Pose a
question and some knowledgeable traveler somewhere may answer it.
A recent post by a young woman asked about the safety concerns of a
woman traveling alone in Thailand. Several women quickly responded
with posts that offered safety advice and even recommendations for
guest houses. But all agreed that Thailand is a safe place for women to
travel unaccompanied, as long as precautions are taken.

CNN Travel

The reputation of CNN's vast news gathering capability draws travelers to
the widely-visited CNN Travel Page (www.cnn.com/TRAVEL). Here you find a
good place to check for articles about your destination. Use the search
feature and keywords to search the entire CNN site for stories about a
specific country or region.

For example, before I went to Cambodia last year, I conducted a search using
Cambodia as a keyword and found more than 200 articles that contained the
word Cambodia. The articles I read gave me a feel for the tensions in that
country and told me some places to definitely avoid.

Francs to Yen and Back Again: Online Currency Converters

Mathematically-challenged travelers hate to convert money. If you belong to this oft-frustrated group, have no worries. Many sites on the Web convert currency with the push of button, eliminating the gnashing of teeth and pulling of hair that sometimes accompanies these conversions. Even more important, these sites always use the most current exchange rates. And they don't cost a dime, a rupee, or a baht, for that matter.

Online currency converters are a snap to use. You specify the currency you wish to covert and the currency you wish to covert it to (for example, U.S. dollars to lira). You then click a button, and voilà — your U.S. dollars have found their equivalent sum in lira.

As an example, I'd like to walk you through the conversion at the very popular Universal Currency Converter (www.xe.net/currency), Figure 10-7. Most other converters follow an identical, or very similar process.

After you arrive at the Universal Currency Converter, follow these steps to see how your money matches up against any other currency:

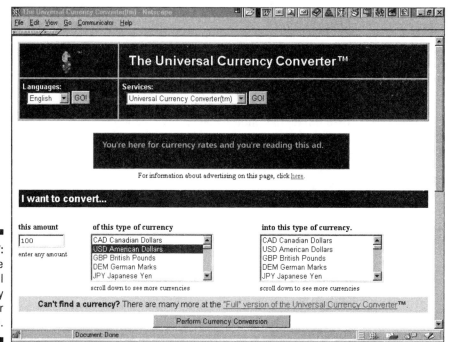

Figure 10-7: The Universal Currency Converter home page.

A great tool for business travelers

Xenon, the company that brings you the Universal Currency Converter, also offers its Travel Expenses Calculator (www.xe.net/currency/expenses) online. Xenon designed the Travel Expenses Calculator with the business traveler in mind.

To calculate the amount you paid for that dinner with clients in Italy, enter the cost of the dinner and the currency used (lira), the date of purchase (the past exchange rates are archived), your home currency, the percentage your credit card charges for foreign purchases, and hit Calculate. Now you know just how much to submit on your next expense report.

1. **Enter the amount you'd like to change into the box labeled "this amount" at the far left.**

2. **Select the type of currency you're starting with by scrolling through the currencies in the next box.**

3. **Select the currency you wish to convert to and click Perform Currency Conversion.**

If you don't see the currency you wish to convert to, click the link for the Full Version of the Currency Converter (www.xe.net/currency/full). This version operates exactly the same, just with more currencies to choose from.

The site then displays the conversion using the latest exchange rates.

The Universal Currency Converter can operate in several languages. Use the pull-down menu at the top of the page to switch to the language you wish to use.

If you want to compare various currencies to one base currency, use The Interactive Currency Table (www.xe.net/currency/table.htm). Select the base currency and the site generates a table of exchange rates for dozens of world currencies. Just think of the fun stuff you can buy with 270,000 Turkish Lira!

Fortune Tellers: Locating ATMs Worldwide

The global economy is revolutionizing the world at an astounding rate. Soon, the acronym ATM (automated teller machine, for those of you living in a cave), may be the most widely recognized word on the planet.

Indeed, you can now use your bank card to access your home checking or savings account in some unlikely places. Last year, I withdrew about 600,000 Vietnamese dong (about U.S. $50) from a bank machine in downtown Saigon.

Using bank machines to restock your wallet while traveling provides an excellent alternative to carrying loads of currency and travelers checks. ATMs are also a good way to avoid paying fees for money exchange, and they usually give a very good exchange rate. The Internet can help you locate all the ATMs you might need during your trip before you leave.

Finding ATMs using the Internet

Like the Internet, ATMs are connected to a network of computers. In order to make use of ATMs around the world, you must make sure that your bank participates in one of the two major ATM networks run by the two big credit card companies, Visa and Mastercard. Your bank card should have symbols on the back denoting the ATM networks in which it will work. But to be sure, ask your bank before you leave at which types of machines you can use your card internationally.

Visa and the Plus Network

The Visa ATM network is called Plus. If your bank card has the Plus symbol on the back, you can withdraw money from any bank machine that displays the symbol. You can also use your Visa card to get a cash advance at these machines if you have a personal identification number (PIN). You can obtain a PIN by contacting Visa or Mastercard before you leave; it's *extremely* helpful to have in a pinch.

To locate a Plus machine, visit the Visa Web site (www.visa.com). Click the ATM Locator link (www.visa.com/cgi-bin/vee/pd/atm/main.html), Figure 10-8.

Using either the map of the world or the pull-down menu, select the region in which you wish to find an ATM. After you select the country, you must select at least a city (you can narrow your search by entering a street or postal code) and then click Submit. The results display the address of the machine, the operating hours, and the bank affiliation.

You can also use the ATM Locator to search for ATMs in airports by clicking Airport ATMs and perusing the list of world airports.

Mastercard and the Cirrus Network

The Mastercard ATM network is called Cirrus, and it offers many of the same services as the Visa network. Check to see if your bank card has the Cirrus symbol — if so, you can withdraw money from any Cirrus machine anywhere in the world.

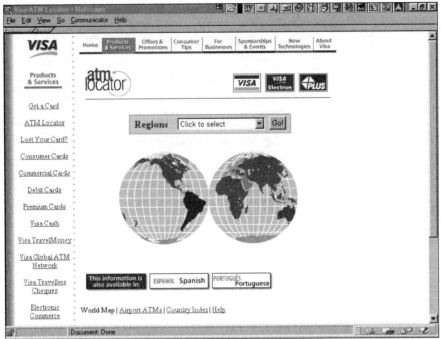

Figure 10-8:
The Visa
ATM
locator.

To find an ATM that allows you to use your Cirrus card, visit the ATM locator page (www.mastercard.com/atm), Figure 10-9.

Select the region of the world you wish to search (or click Airports to find an airport ATM), and then select the city. You can even limit your search by naming a street. Some listings contain a Map It! button — click the button to view a map showing the location of the ATM.

In order to use any credit card in an ATM, you must have a PIN number. Check with your bank before you leave to make sure your PIN number is current and active.

Finding traveler's check offices

I invariably run out of traveler's checks in the middle of a trip. Then I just have to hope that I can find an American Express office nearby where I can buy more checks with a credit card.

If I were smart, I'd use the Web to check where the offices are located before I departed. Then I wouldn't have to spend hours speaking broken Thai to find the nearest office. I guess for me, it's part of the fun. If you prefer to spend your time abroad shopping, sightseeing, or sitting by the beach,

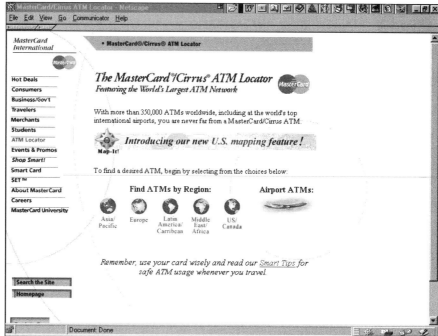

Figure 10-9:
The
Mastercard/
Cirrus ATM
locator.

research the location of traveler's check offices in your destination area before you leave. Don't forget to print out a list of the locations once you find them!

American Express

To use the American Express Office Locator (www6.americanexpress.com/ travel/index.html), Figure 10-10, click Travel Resources and then Travel Offices.

Select the region you wish to search and then choose the country. The listing for the individual offices gives the address, phone number, and hours of operation. If you need help finding the office, you'll have to give them a call — the site offers no mapping features. All American Express offices have English-speaking employees. They're fun to chat with.

Thomas Cook

Thomas Cook is like the American Express of the U.K. It provides a variety of travel services, including the issuance of travelers checks.

You can find Thomas Cook offices in many countries of the world by using the online office locator (www.thomascook.com/cgi-bin/wfu-com), Figure 10-11.

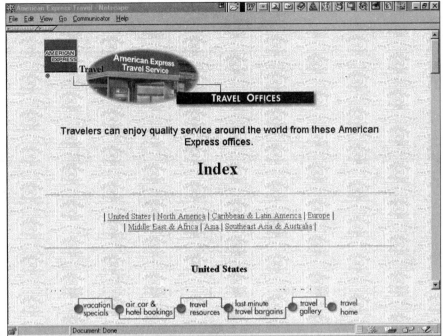

Figure 10-10:
The
American
Express
Office
Locator.

Figure 10-11:
The Thomas
Cook Where
to Find Us
page.

Use the Where to Find Us page (there's a link at the bottom of the page) to locate Cook offices worldwide. Select a country from the list by highlighting it with your mouse, and then check the box next to the type of service you are trying to find in that country. Further refine your search by typing in the name of a city within your destination country. When your search is all set, click the Find Us button. The site then searches its database for matches and returns a list of offices that meet your criteria.

At Least You Have Your Health — Right?

Trust me on this: there's nothing scarier than falling ill in some remote corner of the world. Ever seen a hospital in a developing nation? A wonderful vacation can quickly turn into a nightmare with the first onset of an illness. Even a nasty case of jet lag can waste precious days.

How can the Internet help me stay healthy, you ask? Well, you can find tons of knowledge and information about destinations' health hazards, preventive measures, and general travel health advice online. An ounce of prevention. . . .

Searching for travel health info

Yahoo! has a subcategory devoted to the topic of travel health (www.yahoo.com/Health/Travel). Delve into those links to find sites such as Travel Health Online (www.tripprep.com/index.html), which acts as an encyclopedia of travel health topics. In the Yahoo! links you also find a page about how to avoid altitude sickness (www.princeton.edu/~oa/altitude.html) and many other gems. This listing is probably the best of its kind on the Web.

You can also use the search engines by plugging in keywords such as **travel + health** and the name of your destination. But this method is less likely to provide as focused a list as Yahoo!

The Center for Disease Control Travel Information page

The Center for Disease Control (CDC) is a U.S. government agency and is the most respected authority on diseases in the world. The CDC's Travel Information page (www.cdc.gov/travel/travel.html), Figure 10-12, offers a definitive resource about regional health concerns around the world.

If you want to know which, if any, vaccinations or other prophylactic measures to take before departing on a trip, you should look no further than

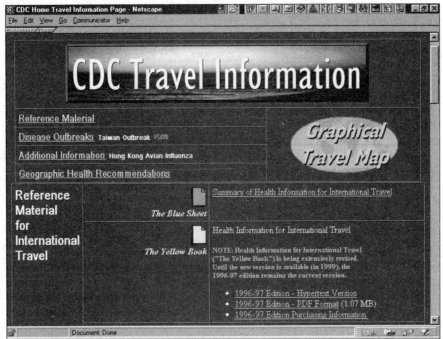

Figure 10-12:
The CDC
Travel
Information
page.

the CDC Web site. Using the map of the world, select your destination by choosing a region. The CDC prepares and updates travel fact sheets for each region of the world that contain the latest disease and vaccination recommendations. Specific countries are detailed within each section, and links throughout the site help you navigate to more information about diseases and precautionary measures.

The CDC is particularly helpful with its breakdown of the risks and treatment of malaria (a very common problem in tropical and subtropical regions). The CDC concisely lays out the pros and cons of the various ways to treat and prevent this disease.

The site also offers a section on the most common travel illness, travelers diarrhea (gasp!). This affliction affects almost every traveler at some point in their life, and you will benefit immensely by knowing the reasons for its occurrence and how you can avoid its unpleasant grasp.

One more interesting section on the CDC site regards cruise travel. Though it may not have occurred to you (I never thought of it), cruise ships could conceivably roam the world collecting nasty bugs and pass these on to unsuspecting cruisers. The CDC inspects every cruise ship that holds 13 or more passengers. Before your next cruise, you may want to read the CDC inspection logs for your boat and make sure it got a satisfactory rating.

Avoiding "airborne" illness and jet lag

I've always disliked flying. After I read some of the info on the Web about the health hazards of air travel, I've now become nearly phobic. But, I'm a bit of a hypochondriac to begin with, and the good news is that you can do some simple things to minimize your risks and reduce the effects of jet lag.

Healthy Flying

Diana Fairechild spent "21 years and 10 million miles as an international flight attendant," and she now offers her hard-won advice to you free of charge on her Web site, Healthy Flying (www.flyana.com), Figure 10-13.

The site contains practical advice about the nastier aspects of air travel: recycled air, airline food, and blocked ears to name a few. You also find advice about avoiding jet lag and the fear of flying. Use the links on the home page to navigate through the information.

No Jet Lag

Business travelers and other members of the jet set know how debilitating the effects of jet lag can be. Next time your travels require you to cross many time zones, check out the No Jet Lag site (www.nojetlag.com) for advice on how to keep your body clock in tune with the environment. The site is easy to navigate; the topics associated with jet lag are outlined on the home page. Just click to explore.

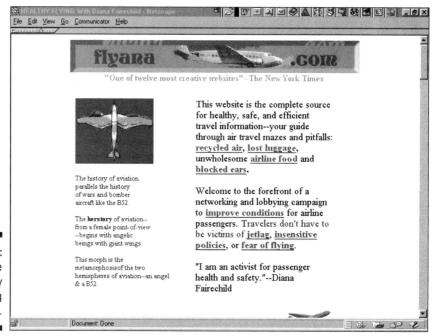

Figure 10-13: The Healthy Flying home page.

Chapter 11

Checking the Weather and Finding Your Way

*E*ver been rained on at the beach? Or arrived at a ski resort to find the trails covered in slush? The Internet can help you avoid these unpleasant scenarios. By using the Internet, you can always know the current weather conditions at any destination on the planet, plus you can find out what the weather has in store for the duration of your stay. This chapter helps you know exactly the right clothes to pack and what to expect from Mother Nature during your travels.

Chapter 11 also examines a few of the most popular mapping and routing sites on the Web. Even if you're someone who gets lost in your own neighborhood, once you get the hang of these cool mapping applications, you'll have to put some serious effort into getting lost.

The Rain in Spain — Or Anywhere Else

On the one hand, life would be pretty boring without storms and wind; but on the other hand, it's no fun (and sometimes dangerous) to travel in bad weather. Whether you're a leisure traveler, frequent business traveler, or an amateur meteorologist, you can make your travels much smoother by planning for the weather using the Internet.

The best weather Web sites provide a wide range of advanced weather technology, including the following features:

- ✔ Current weather and conditions for numerous locales
- ✔ Extended forecasts
- ✔ Satellite imagery
- ✔ A variety of weather radar maps
- ✔ Customization ability
- ✔ Special weather features, historical data, and news reports

Mapping and weather sites are necessarily heavy on graphics. If you have a slow connection, prepare for longer downloads on some sites.

The weather technology available on the Internet allows skiers to get the current snow conditions and cruisers to check the status of tropical storms. If you're driving somewhere, you can log on to the Internet to find out if the roadways are flooded. Or maybe you just want know what to wear outside your door. Read on!

Great weather Web sites

You don't have to look too far on the Web to find tons of weather info. Check out the Yahoo! weather category listing (www.yahoo.com/news_and_media/weather) and you find a mind-boggling number of listings. Thank goodness that you don't have to plow through all of these sites to find the good ones — I've already done all that for you.

I stick with the big weather sites, because these generally have the reach and technology to provide accurate conditions and forecasts. The rest of this section presents a couple of my favorite weather sites

AccuWeather

AccuWeather (www.accuweather.com), Figure 11-1, has been a leader in the field of weather forecasting for many years; many professional news services use AccuWeather data to prepare their own weather reports.

To get a quick check of the weather in a specific city, enter the city's zip code or name into the box under the heading Enter Your Local City on the home page. For U.S. weather forecasts, AccuWeather presents you with a look at the current conditions by way of three satellite radar maps (national Doppler radar, local Doppler, and a satellite map of the cloud cover). AccuWeather also shows you a five-day forecast for the city with high and low temperatures for each day.

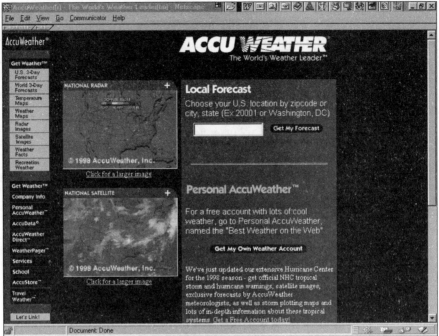

Figure 11-1:
The
AccuWeather
home page.

For worldwide five day forecasts, click World in the left-hand navigation bar. You can then select a country and a city from the menus that represent the different continents of the world. You can also click one of the world regions under World Satellite Features for satellite views of the cloud cover.

AccuWeather also allows you to create a personalized weather page that you can set to automatically look up the weather in the area you want to know about. The service has a subscription fee; you can have a free 30 day trial, but after the trial, you must pay a monthly fee, according to a sliding scale. For personal use, it costs $4.95 per month. For educational or corporate use, the fees are a bit higher. Follow these steps to set up a personalized weather page for the trial period:

1. **Click Sign Up for Premium Service on the AccuWeather home page.**

2. **Enter your personal information, a username and password, and the location (using a zip code or city name) for which you want the forecast.**

3. **Choose the title you wish to have displayed for your personalized page and then click Submit.**

   I use Noah's Weather as the name of my personal weather page, but you'll probably want to choose something that's a little closer to home.

4. **On the next page you must choose a user name, a password, and enter your credit card information.**

A valid credit card is required, even for the free 30-day trial period. If you choose to give the free trial a go, be advised that you may not get a warning when the free period ends — your credit card will automatically be billed.

5. **Hit the Go! button.**

The site then displays your page with forecasts and maps for the region you selected.

You can quickly access the weather info you use most often by either bookmarking your customized weather page or setting it as your home screen (the page that comes up when you turn on your browser).

Sun worshippers will appreciate the Recreation Weather section at AccuWeather. Clicking the Recreation Weather button (on the left navigation bar) brings you to a page where you can choose to view either the Beach and Boating Forecast or the Ray Ban UV Index. Beach and Boating, as you might guess, gives the coastal weather conditions for 44 regions of the U.S., complete with tanning index and wave heights. The Ray Ban UV Index uses a map of the U.S. to show where the ultraviolet light levels are the highest and most dangerous each day. Don't forget your sunblock.

Intellicast

The clean design at Intellicast (www.intellicast.com), Figure 11-2, makes finding the weather in your neighborhood or across the globe an easy task.

You can use either the links on the left side of the page or on the top to navigate through the various sections of the site, which include the following:

- ✔ **USA Weather:** Maps and forecasts for the U.S.
- ✔ **World Weather:** Worldwide maps and forecasts.
- ✔ **Travel:** Forecasts geared towards travelers.
- ✔ **Ski Reports:** Check the snow conditions at resorts around the world.
- ✔ **Health:** Reports on the impact of weather on your health.
- ✔ **Almanac:** Facts and statistics from the world of meteorology.

For weather information about cities in the U.S., click USA Weather to access a map of the U.S. Click the appropriate city, or if the city you want to check didn't make the map, use the list of links below the map to locate your city or region. A city's weather listing on Intellicast gives the four-day forecast as

Figure 11-2:
The
Intellicast
home page.

well as the expected high and low temperatures. To see the various satellite maps and radar views (like you see on the evening newscasts), click the links on the left side of the page. You can choose from the following views:

- ✔ **Radar:** Use Radar to see precipitation and storm action.

- ✔ **Radar Loop:** A composite of several radar images, taken at timed intervals, looped together. Use this map to watch the progress of a storm. It's a cool feature but beware— it takes time to load each image, and the loop doesn't run until all the images are loaded.

- ✔ **Radar Summary:** A type of radar that provides detailed storm info.

- ✔ **NEXRAD:** An advanced radar system that shows weather events with more accuracy than other radar systems.

- ✔ **Satellite and Satellite Loop:** The satellite image is taken by a satellite orbiting the Earth and allows you to see actual photos of clouds and storm systems. The Satellite Loop is similar to the Radar Loop, just with satellite images instead of radar scans.

My favorite map is the radar loop; it takes a little while to load, but after you get it, you can watch the movement of storms across the region. It beats watching the nerdy weatherman on your local news by a long shot.

Unfortunately, these maps are only available for the U.S. For the rest of the world, Intellicast has four-day forecasts and satellite images for your weather viewing pleasure.

For a look at current weather conditions and forecasts for other places in the world, click World (duh!) and select the region or city you wish to know about. If your inner Celsius to Fahrenheit converter is not all it should be, use the one provided by the site (on the left navigation bar) to translate the scale into a recognizable number.

The Travel section at Intellicast quickly shows you the weather in dozens of cities in the U.S.; click the city name to see a more detailed report. If you and the family are heading out to the U.S. National Parks, make sure you stop in at the section specifically for parks' forecasts. In addition, the site offers a section devoted to golfers, skiers, and sailors to address the specific weather-related needs of those who putt, schuss, and tack.

Finally, Intellicast features Dr. Dewpoint, an expert meteorologist, who discusses the most compelling weather stories of the day in detail. (I just read about the coming of La Niña, El Niño's sister. I think it's going to be a cold winter.)

Seeing the weather for yourself with Webcams

A *Webcam* is a device that takes pictures of its subject every minute or so; then it transmits those images instantaneously to the Internet, where the pictures can be viewed on Web pages. Thousands of Webcams are set up around the world, hooked up to the Internet, transmitting images of everything from Pike's Peak to a fish bowl in someone's living room.

Several sites have organized networks of Webcams and links to Webcams, enabling you to take a peek at the current conditions with your own peepers. It can be fun to check out a current photo of, say, a ski resort that you'll be visiting in a few days.

Webcams rarely tell you anything concrete about the weather beyond what you can see on your screen. Don't rely on a Webcam picture to plan your wardrobe for the day — even if the sun's shining in the Webcam picture, it may still be 34 degrees!

Resort Sports Network

Resorts Sports Network (www.rsn.com), Figure 11-3, maintains a network of Webcams at ski resorts across North America.

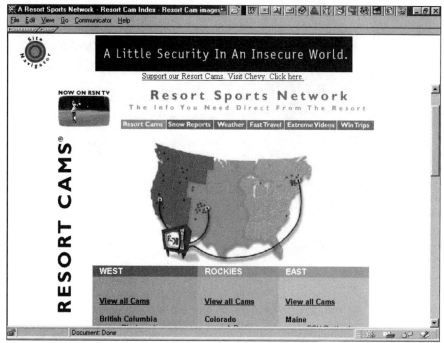

Figure 11-3:
The Resort
Sports
Network
Resort Cam
Index page.

Click Resort Cams to access the menu of cams, and then select the resort you want to look at. The image on the page has the date and time it was taken, making it easy to check that the image is current. You can also go into the archives to look at shots taken on other dates.

And the best part: You can send a photo from the Webcam as an electronic postcard to a friend's e-mail address. Simply click the postmark above the image and fill in the address and your message. "Wish you were beautiful, the weather is here!"

Leonard's Cam World

Somebody named Leonard put together a monumental listing of Webcams around the globe at Leonard's Cam World (www.leonardsworlds.com/camera.html), Figure 11-4.

If you want to take a look at some obscure corner of the world, chances are you can find a link to a cam on this site, which currently lists over 1,500 cams. Leonard organizes the links by state and country; click the state or country and choose from the array of different cams. Good old Leonard also highlights cams that he considers "special"— at last check, the site was spotlighting cams on the home page that showed the big surf caused by an Atlantic hurricane.

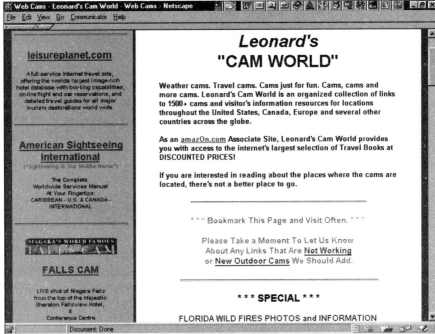

Figure 11-4:
Leonard
sure loves
Webcams.

The moral of this site is that you never know when you have a camera trained on you — your best bet is to just smile a lot.

More Webcams

You can use the following pages to find lots of cool cams:

- ✔ **Yahoo! Listing of beach cams** (www.yahoo.com/recreation/outdoors/beaches/beach_cams/): Sun, sand, surf, and the Internet. You'd be surprised at how well they go together.

- ✔ **Around the World in 80 Clicks** (www.steveweb.com/80clicks): Travel around the world via 80 different Webcams. Fun for the whole family!

- ✔ **Random Camera** (www.xmission.com/~bill/randcamera.html): Click the random camera logo and you are plugged into a random Webcam somewhere in the world.

(Don't) Get Lost!

Some people can't help it. Their brains are wired in such a way that right and left, north and south are hopelessly irreconcilable. These hapless souls, the directionally challenged, are perfect candidates to use online mapping sites.

Even if you consider yourself to have a good sense of direction, online mapping sites can help you plan a road trip, aiding you in getting from point A to point B without a blow to your ego. Or, if you simply have a love of maps, you'll enjoy playing with these fun and easy-to-use sites. These sites offer additional features that travelers will appreciate: Mapping sites are equally adept at generating maps as well as driving instructions.

Mapping and routing Web sites

I remember the first time I tried using an interactive, online mapping site. I was amazed that I could type in two addresses and, after a few moments, a clear, well-drawn map between the two points would appear on the screen. Since that day several years ago, mapping sites have added many bells and whistles that make them even easier to use.

The following three sites have proven themselves to be the best bets when you are in need of a map:

- **DeLorme's CyberRouter** (www.delorme.com/CyberMaps/route.asp)
- **MapQuest** (www.mapquest.com)
- **Maps On Us** (www.mapsonus.com)

Each of the preceding sites can draw you a map of any place in the U. S. and provide driving directions if you enter a starting and destination point. The map quality is fairly equal on each. MapQuest and Maps On Us differentiate themselves by allowing you to enter exact starting and destination points for driving instructions (door to door), while DeLorme's CyberRouter only creates city-to-city directions.

Using these mapping sites is easy, and the process is very similar on each. MapQuest is probably the most popular and has the most features, so I break down the MapQuest site's nuts and bolts for you in the next section to guide you in using other mapping sites. The last thing you want to do is get lost while using a mapping site.

MapQuest

Beneath the bright, happy exterior at MapQuest (www.mapquest.com), Figure 11-5, lurks some serious mapping technology. Produced by GeoSystems, a leading cartography and geographic products company, MapQuest is a great service for travelers.

Finding a map with the MapQuest Interactive Atlas

If you want to see a map of a particular city, click Interactive Atlas on the MapQuest home page, which unleashes the form shown in Figure 11-6.

Input an address, city, state, or zip code into the spaces provided. You don't need to fill in every field, but the more you fill in the more likely you are to get the correct map. For example, I entered only *Atlanta* (no state, no zip code), hoping to turn up a map of the Georgian metropolis. But without more information, the Atlas returned thumbnail maps of every Atlanta in the U.S. — who knew there was an Atlanta in California? However, when I entered *Atlanta, GA,* I got the right map immediately.

After you have the right map, you can zoom in and out for a better look at specific locations using the controls on the left of the map. Street level reveals details down to individual streets, while State gives you a map of the entire state. Simple enough, right? Click the compass directions on the corners of the map to adjust the map's viewable area in a desired direction.

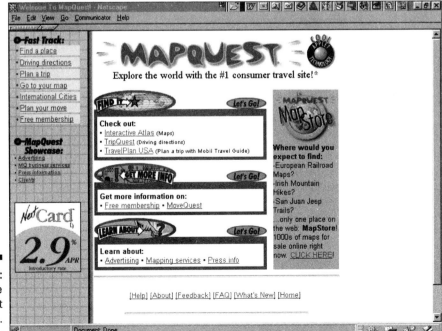

Figure 11-5:
The
MapQuest
home page.

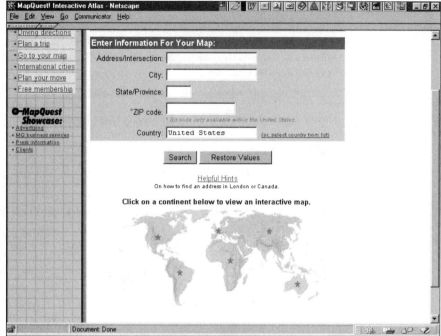

Figure 11-6:
The
Interactive
Atlas query
page at
MapQuest.

You can click the map itself to perform a few functions. By using the small check boxes at the bottom of the map, select whether you want to re-center the map on the spot you click or zoom in on the spot. You can also use the check boxes to help you identify the various icons on the map.

Adding places of interest to a map

Say you're going on a business trip and have reserved a hotel room that is far from the airport. Instead of struggling to find the hotel with your rental car, use MapQuest's features that allow you to customize a map, placing icons that denote points of interest, wherever you'd like on the map. You can then print out copies that you can read while driving (just keep one eye on the road).

In order to customize a map with points of interest, you must first establish a MapQuest membership, free of charge. From the home page, click Free Membership under Fast Track. Enter your name and e-mail address and you're ready to make a customized map by following these steps:

1. **Using the Interactive Atlas, find a map of the area you wish to customize.**

   For example, you might choose your home town.

2. **Select, from the list on the left of the map, the POIs you wish to have noted on the map.**

   For example, if you want a specific type of POI, such as just train stations and not all transportation, click the Transportation link and select only train stations.

3. **Click Update Map to show the POIs you selected.**

If you want to add your own POI, check Personal and follow these steps:

1. **Click Add/Edit My POIs.**

   After the map finishes loading, click the radio button at the bottom of the map labeled Add/Edit POI.

2. **Click the exact spot on the map that you wish to establish as a POI.**

   When you place a new POI on a map, zoom in to the street level, so that you carefully select the exact location.

   After clicking the location on the map, you see a new map that has a question mark on the spot you selected.

3. **Using the form below the map, enter the info about this location.**

4. **Click Save Information.**

   Your map is now customized with your POI. Figure 11-7 shows a map that I pretended to customize with the location of my house (just in case I get lost). *Note:* This is not really the location of my home, so don't go looking for me there!

5. **Click Exit Add/Edit Mode.**

After your map is set to go, you can, using the buttons below the map, e-mail it to a friend, print it out, or save it. You can print out several maps at different levels of detail (zoom in or out) and use them to direct people to the party at your house.

Using TripQuest for driving directions

All the top mapping sites provide driving directions. You enter your starting point and destination, then the software churns for a moment and produces a set of turn-by-turn directions from point A to point B.

Here's how to use the MapQuest mapping system, TripQuest:

1. **Click TripQuest on the MapQuest home page.**

   You see the TripQuest query page, shown in Figure 11-8.

Figure 11-7:
My
(pretend)
house on a
customized
map.

2. **Use the form to enter a starting point (it can be as general as a city or state) and a destination (same deal).**

   You can also use the pull-down menu to select a point of interest for either the starting point or destination. For example, if you select airports in New York, the system will ask you if you want directions to/from JFK Airport or LaGuardia.

3. **Select the type of directions and maps you want.**

   TripQuest can make a map of city-to-city directions for almost any cities in North America. For door-to-door, each door (so to speak) must be in the same region, as classified by TripQuest — click the link entitled What's the difference? to see a map of regions.

   You also must choose the type of route map you wish. The default setting is an overview map of the route with text of directions. If you want door-to-door directions, try selecting turn-by-turn directions (aren't you glad I'm giving you step-by-step instructions?). This setting gives you a small map for each segment of the trip. It's impossible to get lost! If you feel you don't need any stinking maps, you can select text only.

4. **After you enter your starting and destination points, either click Calculate Directions (which immediately plots the route) or select Door-to-Door Options to specify how you want your door-to-door directions presented.**

The options allow you to choose how you want the directions calculated: by the fastest or most scenic route, to avoid certain type of roadways, and so on. After you have chosen the way you want your directions presented, click Calculate Directions to generate the map and directions.

Reading the directions is a cinch. You get an overview map of the route and a breakdown of each turn, with a small, thumbnail map next to the direction's text for navigation. You can print out this page and take it with you on the road.

The directions produced by mapping software are usually accurate; that is, they *do* tell you one route for getting from point A to point B. However, even though the computer may think its found the fastest route, the directions may not be the fastest or the wisest route available; no computer can know that one route has construction or consistently has traffic at a certain time of day. Let someone with an organic brain, not a computer, examine a map for more logical routes.

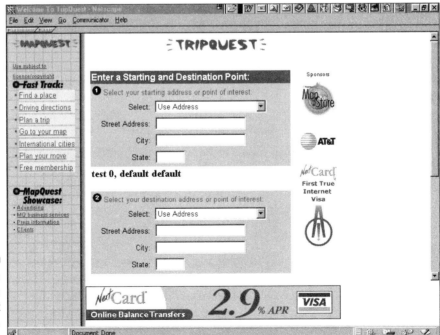

Figure 11-8:
The TripQuest query page.

Maps of international cities

MapQuest is not just for North Americans. Its database contains detailed maps of many cities of the world.

To access a city map for a location outside North America, click International Cities on the home page and use the clickable world map to find maps of cities on every continent.

Satellite maps for spies and astronauts

Though few travelers will ever need a map made from satellite images to aid in their terrestrial navigation, it's nice to know that they are available.

The Microsoft site TerraServer (www. terraserver.com) delivers a look at the world from a different perspective — space. The next time you want to see what your house, vacation spot, or office looks like from space, simply log on to the TerraServer and input the appropriate address.

The map of the world on the home page has green shaded areas that denote areas for which there is an available satellite image in the database. You can click the map or use the Find a Spot on Earth function to enter an address or city. The maps are incredibly sharp and you can zoom in and out to reveal greater or less detail. Click Famous Places to see some well-known locales from a different perspective: Space.

Who knows, maybe Bill Gates's next move is to buy photos of every human on the planet and put them in a database. I wouldn't be surprised.

Chapter 12
Staying Connected Worldwide

● ●

In This Chapter

▶ How to find cyber-cafés online

▶ Getting free Web-based e-mail

▶ Tips for laptop travelers

▶ Global Internet Service Providers

● ●

*T*he world is rapidly becoming a big ball of interconnected wires. Soon, for better or for worse, you won't find a place in the world that doesn't have access to the Internet, especially if you travel with a laptop computer.

This chapter shows you how to take advantage of the Internet while you're on the road — whether you're in Calcutta or California.

Cream, Sugar, and E-Mail — Internet Cafés

E-mail is the aerogram of the digital age. Having access to e-mail while traveling can be a great comfort and a useful tool when you're far from home. Most major cities (and many smaller burgs) now have cafés, called *cyber-cafés,* that provide access to the Internet for a nominal fee. You can send and receive e-mail as well as surf the Web from these cafés.

Cyber-cafés are sprouting up in the most unlikely places — last year, I sent e-mail to everyone back home from a café (that had no coffee, just tea) in downtown Katmandu, Nepal. Also, I checked flight information and researched destinations from the airport computer center in Singapore.

If you plan on making use of e-mail or the Internet while you travel, try to locate cafés and other Internet access points before you leave. And the best way to do this is, of course, by using the Internet.

Yahoo! has a category devoted to cyber-cafés (www.yahoo.com/Society _and_Culture/Cultures_and_Groups/Cyberculture/Internet_Cafes/ Complete_Listing) that lists café directories and individual café pages. Use your browser's Find feature (probably under the Edit menu) to search for keywords in the enormous list. For example, if you want to locate cyber-cafés in France, you may find a directory or site in the list that can help. Use Find to search for the keyword **France**.

Yahoo! also has a listing of online indexes (www.yahoo.com/Society_and _Culture/Cultures_and_Groups/Cyberculture/Internet_Cafes/ Indices) that are very helpful in locating cyber-cafés. Following are a few of the best:

- **The Cybercafe Search Engine** (cybercaptive.com): This directory is updated almost daily, and at last check, it listed 1,822 cafés in 107 different countries, as well as more than 1,600 other Internet access points (such as hotel business centers). You can search the database by city, state, or country and find listings that consist of a physical address, a phone number, and a link to a the café's Web site.

- **The Internet Café Guide** (www.netcafeguide.com/frames.html): This directory lists more than 1,700 cafés worldwide and more than 900 public access points. To search the database, you can enter keywords, or terms, into the search box and choose the search setting (all terms, any terms, or as a phrase). Most listings give you descriptions of the services offered, and all listings have addresses and other contact information.

  The site also includes a useful section regarding cyber-café tips and tricks. Look here for advice that deals with issues involving updating and maintaining a Web site from a cyber-café.

- **Traveltales.com Cybercafe Listing** (traveltales.com/~steve/ cafes): I like this directory because it lists 500 or so cafés by country. Click a country to see an address (both real world and cyber), hours of operation, and information about the hardware and software of the listed cafés.

- **Alt.cybercafes:** This is a Usenet newsgroup (see Chapter 13 for a description of how newsgroups operate) dedicated to cyber-cafés. Posting a question on this group is a good way to find cafés in out-of-the-way places. Also, the other travel newsgroups can help you locate Internet access points.

Just because you see a café listed in a directory doesn't mean that it still exists. Cafés come and go with amazing speed. If you are depending on having Internet access at a certain location, use the contact information from the directory listing (usually an e-mail address) to find out whether the café plans on being there when you arrive to collect your e-mail.

Free E-Mail!

You probably have an e-mail account at work or through your ISP at home. These accounts work just fine when you're at the office or dialing up from home. But checking your mail while you're traveling is much easier if you set up a Web-based e-mail account.

You don't often get something for nothing, but many Web sites offer you just that. Instead of using a piece of mail software, all you need is a Web browser to send and receive e-mail. You can find more and more services through the Web that offer free e-mail accounts to anyone who asks — the only price you pay is having to look at advertisements. And when you're on the road, you can check your *free-mail* (rhymes with *e-mail,* you know) from any computer that has Web access.

Web-based e-mail resembles other e-mail accounts. In terms of privacy, it's fairly safe (no e-mail system is 100 percent guarded against hackers), but you should think twice about sending highly sensitive information (credit card numbers, and so on) through a Web-based e-mail system. Business travelers may want to think about making other e-mail arrangements if they want to make sensitive business transactions.

Web-based e-mail works basically the same as other accounts. You can forward mail, reply to groups, use a signature, and send attachments just as you do with a regular e-mail account.

Using Web-based e-mail

Giving out e-mail accounts free for the asking is a good business model. This practice essentially guarantees that users return to the same Web site again and again to check for their mail. And when they return, they have no choice but to check out the advertising. That explains why so many major sites are offering mail services!

The Microsoft Hotmail (www.hotmail.com) site, Figure 12-1, is one of the best known and most widely used World Wide Web free-mail sites. Most free, Web-based e-mail performs in a similar fashion to Hotmail. I speak about Hotmail because I have had good experience using it — millions of users can't be wrong, can they?

Signing up for an account at Hotmail is a simple process. Just follow these steps:

1. **From the home page (www.hotmail.com), click Sign Up Here! to subscribe.**

2. **Read the user agreement and, if you are feeling agreeable, click I Accept.**

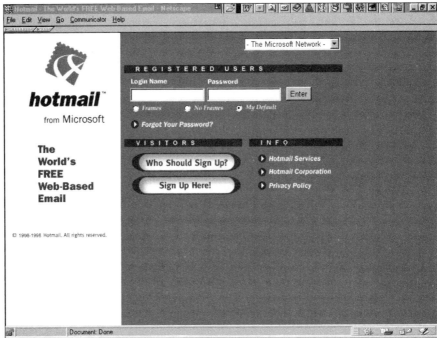

Figure 12-1:
The Hotmail
sign-in
page.

I hope that you read the fine print about accepting Bill Gates as your personal postmaster.

3. Fill out the subscription form.

You must choose a user name and password, and provide a bit of personal information. The user name you choose doesn't have to be your own name, but it's the name that people will see when they read your mail — choose carefully.

4. Confirm your user name and password, and choose a hint for remembering your password.

You now have an e-mail account like the one shown in Figure 12-2. Your new address is your `username@hotmail.com`

The e-mail features in Hotmail are very similar to those in a standard e-mail program. You have the Inbox, where you check for new messages, a Compose area, where you write new mail, an Address Book, where you keep your friends' e-mail addresses, and so on.

To check your mail, go to the Hotmail site and enter your user name and password. Click Enter and you are automatically dropped into your inbox. The number of new and old messages is displayed at the top of the page.

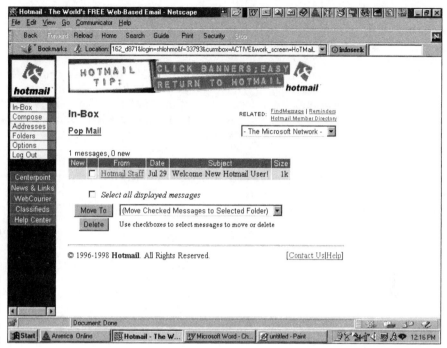

Figure 12-2:
A Hotmail
inbox page
with one
e-mail
message.

If you need to brush up on your e-mail skills before hitting the road, check out *E-Mail For Dummies,* 2nd Edition, by John R. Levine, Carol Baroudi, Margaret Levine Young, and Arnold Reinhold, published by IDG Books Worldwide, Inc.

If everyone you correspond with has your regular office or home e-mail address, how can you use a free-mail account to check mail? Most mail programs allow you to forward mail to another address. Check with your ISP or the help section of your mail program to find out how to forward your mail to another e-mail address.

In addition to Hotmail, the following Web sites also offer free-mail:

- ✔ CMPnet Mail (www.cmpnetmail.com/member/login.page)
- ✔ Excite Mail (www.mailexcite.com)
- ✔ Supernews (wyrm.supernews.com)
- ✔ Yahoo! Mail (mail.yahoo.com)

Checking your existing e-mail from the Web

In addition to forwarding your e-mail to a Web-based account (see the preceding section), you have another option for checking your office or home accounts from a remote location. MailStart.Com (www.mailstart.com), Figure 12-3, offers a nifty service that can check almost any POP (*post office protocol* — the standard type of e-mail account) mailbox from any computer with Web access.

MailStart.Com can't access America Online accounts nor e-mail servers protected by a *firewall* (a software program that keeps people from accessing your computer), which includes many corporate systems. But for the majority of mail accounts, MailStart.Com works amazingly well and is a terrific way to keep in touch from abroad.

To check your e-mail, enter your e-mail account's address (yourname@domain.com) and your password into the provided boxes on the MailStart home page. MailStart.Com then accesses your mail server and allows you to read, compose, and send mail from any computer. Your messages will still be accessible when you return to your home computer.

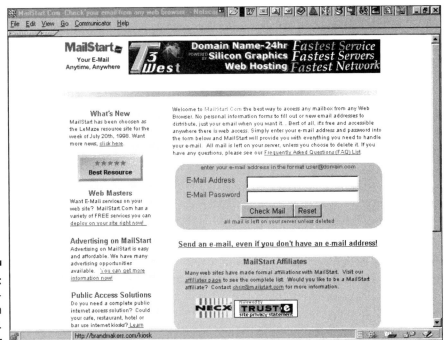

Figure 12-3:
The Mail-Start.com home page.

Instant messaging

Those of you who use America Online may already use instant messages (IM). Instant messaging allows you to communicate in real time: That is, you type a message at your computer and your friend, sitting at his or her computer, receives the message as soon as you click Return.

To use instant messages, the person you want to communicate with must have the same instant message software. If you or your friends aren't AOL members, you can download the IM software from the AOL Web site (www.aol.com/aim). Excite also produces a similar application, available free for download, at (talk.excite.com/communities/excite/pal).

When you go on a trip, you can have a discussion without racking up a mammoth phone bill (assuming that you have a low-cost Internet connection). And your typing skills are bound to improve.

Other sites on the Web, including Yahoo! Mail (mail.yahoo.com), offer the same mail-checking service as MailStart.Com, and new sites appear continually as this service becomes more popular with users.

Laptop Globetrottin'

I dare you to try to separate a business traveler from his or her laptop computer. You're likely to get bitten — or worse — and with good reason. Laptops have become the essential lifeline and business tool for persons away from their offices. Even leisure travelers are finding that a notebook computer can be a very useful item to have amongst their luggage — it comes in handy when you want to write some e-mail, make a journal entry, or play a game of solitaire.

But as helpful as it is, mobile computing carries its own set of concerns:

- How and where can you connect to the Internet?
- Will you have the correct electrical plugs and power adapters you need to run the computer?
- Is it safe to take your computer where you're going?
- What kind of technical support can you find if you run into problems?
- Can using your computer on the road contribute to loss of sanity?

Before you head out on the road with your laptop, be sure that you are well versed in your destination's connection requirements. Also, make sure that you always secure your machine; thieves prey upon travelers carrying laptops. The last thing you need is to loose valuable data and contact information. No one can hear you scream from abroad.

The biggest challenge laptop-equipped travelers face is finding a reliable Internet connection. Phone lines and connection protocols vary widely from country to country. Luckily, you don't have to find out things the hard way. Many fine Web sites have all the information you need to successfully connect from anywhere on the planet. Well, anywhere you can find a phone line.

The first step toward successful connections is making sure that you have the *right stuff* — equipment, that is. You need to do some research about power supply cords and adapters, phone jacks, and modems. Proceed directly to Walkabout Travel Gear (`www.walkabouttravelgear.com`) to find out what you need to know.

Walkabout Travel Gear has a page entitled *Solving the Riddle of Worldwide Computer and Modem Use* (`www.walkabouttravelgear.com/modem.htm`). You can order the equipment you need from the extensive selection of plugs, telephone adapters, transformers, and modem gear, as well as answer most of your mobile computing questions by reading the terrific FAQs.

Walkabout even sells *acoustic couplers,* those old style modems that connect directly to the mouth and ear pieces of a phone receiver. True road warriors swear by acoustic couplers as a surefire means of connection, regardless of a country's technological level.

The Walkabout site also offers the following information that can aid the cyber-minded traveler:

- ✔ **The Walkabout Worldwide Phone Index** (`www.walkabouttravelgear.com/phone.htm`): Tells you what type of adapters you need for each country.

- ✔ **The Walkabout Worldwide Electricity Index** (`www.walkabouttravelgear.com/phone.htm`): Shows you which electrical adapters you need for each country.

- ✔ **Tips for Digital Nomads** (`www.walkabouttravelgear.com/digital.htm`): Offers a great collection of tips and advice from real-life laptop travelers.

In addition to Walkabout, the following sites offer helpful information about connectivity issues:

- ✔ **Roadnews** (`www.roadnews.com`): Look for the link to resources for the computer-equipped traveler.

- ✔ **LaptopTravel.com** (`www.laptoptravel.com`): Although the site features mostly electrical adapters for sale, it also offers some good advice on getting connected.

> ✔ **Mobile Computing Magazine's 101 tips for business travelers**
> (www.mobilecomputing.com/articles/1997/09/9709cs.htm): You
> find some good ideas at this site, such as the tip to unplug your PC card
> when not in use because it consumes battery power.

The World Shall Provide an ISP

Another major issue facing laptop travelers, especially those that frequently
travel abroad or conduct a lot of business from the road, is finding a cost-
effective means for connecting to the Internet. If you are in a foreign country, the cost of dialing in to your domestic Internet Service Provider (ISP)
could be astronomical. The solution is to find a local ISP or become a
member of an ISP network.

I spy an ISP

Finding Internet Service Providers anywhere in the world is best accom-
plished on the Web. The List (thelist.internet.com) is probably the
most comprehensive ISP listing, with over 4,850 listings worldwide.

The List is simple to use. You can search the database by U.S. or Canadian
area code (phone), by country code (select from a list), or by selecting U.S.
or Canada and then using a map. Most ISP listings give you a brief description of the services offered, the price of the service, and contact information.

Don't try to set up a connection with an ISP from the road — you need to set
up an account with an ISP before you leave for your trip, so that you can
equip your computer with any necessary software or dial-up settings (your
ISP will show you all you need to know). You also need to make payment
arrangements before you leave. You pay most ISPs on a monthly basis,
similar to your other utility bills. However, if your trip lasts more than a
month, you should set up an alternative payment option with your ISP to
avoid being cut off from service. Most ISPs want to help you out in any way
they can — it's a very competitive field, so customer service is held in high
esteem.

Roam around the world with iPass

Paying a monthly fee for an Internet connection doesn't make a whole lot of
sense if you're a frequent traveler who is constantly on the go and needs to
connect in multiple foreign countries — that is, unless your ISP is a member
of the iPass roaming network (www.ipass.com).

iPass developed a worldwide network of ISPs that allows you to access the Internet from virtually anywhere for one fee, with the same user name, and always with a local phone call.

Here's how the network operates: iPass created partnerships with ISPs all over the world. Through these partnerships, and by way of the iPass roaming technology, you can connect to the Internet from more than 2,700 access points in 150 countries. (iPass can assist you in finding an ISP that participates in the roaming program.) You then install some connection software on your laptop and use its list of participating ISPs to connect.

For example, if you are in Japan, you have several iPass partners to choose from. Dial the connection number (it should be a local call), and the software recognizes you as an iPass roaming member and forwards your connection to your home ISP.

The costs for using iPass roaming service vary, but they generally range between $0.05 and $0.25 per minute of use. The world is your oyster.

Connecting with the major online services

If you are an America Online, CompuServe, or Prodigy member, you should be able to connect from many countries around the world. Contact your service's help desk to find out what's available for international access.

Chapter 13

Chatting with Your Fellow Travelers

● ●

In This Chapter

▶ Using Usenet newsgroups to get travel advice

▶ Participating in e-mail mailing lists

▶ Chatting in real time about travel

▶ Translating tools to help you get by in foreign languages

● ●

*W*hen you think of the Internet, the World Wide Web usually comes to mind first. The World Wide Web has come to dominate the Internet to such a degree that many people forget that the WWW represents just a portion of what the Internet has to offer. The older components of the Internet — newsgroups, electronic bulletin boards, and e-mail mailing lists — are still very active and very good sources of all sorts of travel information. And, in contrast to a Web site, these forums offer true interactivity, the opportunity to exchange ideas and questions with living, breathing travelers.

In this chapter, I show you how to participate in Usenet newsgroups, how to find and subscribe to e-mail mailing lists, and how to use chat rooms to talk with real-life travelers. And, in the spirit of communication, I also include a couple of cool sites that translate languages. I'd hate to think of you not ordering breakfast just because you don't know how to ask for it.

Newsgroups as Travel Forums

Sharing stories about travels and journeys is one of humanity's oldest traditions. In the stone age, travelers clad in animal skins huddled around a campfire and sketched their travel tales in the dirt. Thank goodness that things have changed a bit since then.

For years, computer-savvy travelers have been using *Usenet newsgroups,* one of the oldest components of the Internet, to relate travel information. (See the sidebar "What's a newsgroup?" in this chapter if you need a little brushing up on newsgroups.) With the help of the Usenet newsgroups, you can probe the minds of hundreds of thousands of travelers around the world for the most up-to-date, first-hand travel information and experiences. Want to find someone who has trekked Annapurna in Nepal? The `rec.travel.asia` newsgroup can hook you up with someone who has been there and hiked the route with her own feet. Or maybe you just want to find others who share your love of Australian travel. `Rec.travel.australia` acts as a meeting place online for people who want to talk about travels Down Under.

Best of all, unlike those chat rooms available on the commercial online services, tapping into the Usenet newsgroups doesn't cost you a dime.

What's a newsgroup?

Think of Usenet as a gigantic, interactive bulletin board. On this gigantic bulletin board, people "post" messages about virtually every area of interest you can think of. (Currently, over 30,000 newsgroups exist, and people create new newsgroups every day.)

To make it easy to find all the messages on the bulletin board that focus on a particular topic, people post related messages into the same area, called a *newsgroup.* You can respond to any question or statement in a newsgroup, and, in turn, anyone can reply to your response. Often, provocative statements and questions illicit many responses; the resulting discussion is called a *thread.*

To access a newsgroup, you need one of the following:

✔ **Web-based newsreaders:** Several Web sites act as gateways to the Usenet. You can use these sites to search for newsgroup topics as well as to participate in specific groups. (Flip to the section "Reading and posting messages on dejanews" in this chapter for instructions on how to use Deja News (`www.dejanews.com`), the best Web-based newsreader and Usenet resource.)

✔ **A Web browser's newsreader functions:** Both Netscape and Internet Explorer have built-in newsreader applications. You must have access to a *news server* (most Internet Service Providers include this in their subscription package) to read newsgroups with your browser.

If your ISP doesn't offer access to a news server, you can hook up with a free public server. For a great rundown of how to configure your browser's newsreader and a current listing of public news servers, visit Rob's News Servers (`members.tripod.com~Robserver/servers.htm`). Rob's tutorial shows you step by step how to connect to a public news server.

✔ **An online service's newsreader:** The big, proprietary online services, such as America Online, Compuserve, and Prodigy, provide Usenet access. If you use these services, consult their help sections to find out how to access Usenet.

For complete information on using newsgroups, pick up a copy of *The Internet For Dummies,* 4th Edition, by John R. Levine, Carol Baroudi, and Margaret Levine Young, published by IDG Books, Worldwide, Inc.

Discovering travel newsgroups

A dedicated community of travelers regularly read and respond to "notes" posted on the numerous travel-related newsgroups. After you read a certain newsgroup for a few weeks, you will become familiar with some of the regular participants, allowing you to sift out who can offer the best recommendations and answers. But you need not be a regular to benefit from a newsgroup. You can drop in to ask a quick question about a particular restaurant or hotel or periodically scan the headers for topics that interest you.

You find the majority of travel newsgroups in the `rec.travel` or `soc.culture` hierarchies. The following sections highlight some of the most useful travel newsgroups. If you need to find additional newsgroups in order to get the travel information you need, turn to the section "Finding travel newsgroups using Deja News" later in this chapter.

Almost every newsgroup publishes a list of answers to frequently asked questions (FAQ) that provides a useful jumping-off point for an uninitiated user. The FAQ usually describes in detail which topics the newsgroup discusses, how to post questions and comments, and other newsgroup etiquette issues. The author of the FAQ usually posts the FAQ to the newsgroup on a regular basis, so that new entrants can view it. Numerous archived collections of Usenet FAQs exist on the Web, the best being The Usenet FAQ Archive (`www.faqs.org`). Search the Archive by the name of the newsgroup or browse through by hierarchy.

Unfortunately, I can't give you a very detailed description of the specific topics addressed in the following newsgroups (or any other newsgroups, for that matter). Newsgroups and the topics that they cover are constantly changing as people post new topics and other travelers respond to them. If you don't find a newsgroup very helpful to your travel planning on a certain day, check with the newsgroup a week later or post a question of your own. There's no limit to the number of topics that can be discussed in a single newsgroup.

Rec.travel newsgroups

Expect lively and timely answers to any queries posted to the following newsgroups in `rec.travel`:

- ✔ `rec.travel.africa`: Discussions of African travel.
- ✔ `rec.travel.air`: All topics pertaining to air travel.
- ✔ `rec.travel.asia`: Discussions of Asian travel.
- ✔ `rec.travel.australia+nz`: You guessed it — discussions about Australian and New Zealand travel.
- ✔ `rec.travel.bed+breakfast`: B&B discussions. You can find out whether B&B stands for Bed & Breakfast or Bed & Bug.

- ✔ rec.travel.budget: For all you cheapskates — I mean budget-conscious travelers.

- ✔ rec.travel.caribbean: Caribbean travel topics.

- ✔ rec.travel.cruises: All boats, all the time.

- ✔ rec.travel.europe: Talk about the Continent.

- ✔ rec.travel.latin-america: Que bueno!

- ✔ rec.travel.marketplace: Travel products for sale.

- ✔ rec.travel.misc: Any and all travel-related topics are fair game, the downside being that the discussion is pretty unfocused.

- ✔ rec.travel.usa-canada: North American travel discussions.

Other rec. newsgroups

The following newsgroups can help you find the answers to your questions related to specific activities:

- ✔ rec.backcountry: For hikers.

- ✔ rec.food.restaurants: Get advice from local eaters.

- ✔ rec.outdoors.camping: The skinny on campgrounds.

- ✔ rec.scuba.locations: Advice about underwater destinations.

- ✔ rec.skiing.alpine: Discussions of downhill skiing and resorts.

- ✔ rec.outdoors.rv-travel: Discussions about campers and recreational vehicles.

soc.culture newsgroups

Almost every country and nationality on the planet has a soc.culture newsgroup devoted to it. The people who visit soc.culture groups are a mix of expatriates desiring to connect with countrymen, natives, and travelers. In other words, the kind of people who can answer the questions you have about traveling to a particular place. However, the soc.culture groups tend to focus on cultural issues rather than purely travel-related topics.

The following newsgroups discuss some of the most popular travel destinations:

- ✔ soc.culture.african

- ✔ soc.culture.british

- ✔ soc.culture.canada

- soc.culture.china
- soc.culture.europe
- soc.culture.german
- soc.culture.french
- soc.culture.indian
- soc.culture.italian
- soc.culture.japan
- soc.culture.thai
- soc.culture.usa

A tiny newsgroup glossary

Newsgroup users have a lingo all their own. As you comb the Usenet newsgroups for travel information, you may run across the following terms:

- **Thread:** A conversation or discussion of one topic. A thread generally is initiated by a provocative statement or a subject introduced by an individual or a moderator. Threads are the essence of newsgroups.

- **Spam:** Any self-serving post that is unsolicited or otherwise blatantly promotional in nature. Be careful if you attempt to sell goods or services on newsgroups by posting unwarranted information. You may get *flamed.*

- **Flame:** A *flame* usually refers to any message or article that contains strong criticism, usually irrational or highly emotional. Often you can find long *threads* that have been initiated by an inflammatory statement.

- **BTW, WRT, LOL, and other acronyms:** Frequent newsgroup users have developed abbreviations for common phrases to speed up posting messages. *BTW* is shorthand for "by the way." *WRT* is "with respect to." *LOL* means "laughing out loud."

  If you ask a stupid question, you may get this response: *RTFM,* which stands for "read the flipping manual." (Many newsgroups have a frequently asked questions (FAQ) file, and all users are expected to have read it.

- **;-):** If you don't know what this is, tilt your head to the left. You should see a smiling, winking face, meaning you wrote something amusing. Or maybe you're being laughed at because you said something silly. In any case, when someone flashes one of these, it's generally in good humor.

Finding travel newsgroups using Deja News

Deja News (www.dejanews.com), Figure 13-1, is the premiere Web resource for reading and finding newsgroups. (I tell you all about reading newsgroups with Deja News in the next section of this chapter.)

Deja News compiles almost every Usenet newsgroup and discussion forum (there are forums, such as mailing lists and bulletin boards, that are not part of Usenet that you can locate through Deja News) on the Internet into a searchable database. If you're interested in a topic and want to find a place to talk about it, Deja News is the first place you should search.

On the Deja News home page, you find a search box at the top of the page. To search for discussions, just plug in some keywords and phrases into the search box and click Search. Deja News then goes through all the archived newsgroup articles looking for your keyword in individual messages. For example, if you search with the keyword **travel,** you won't exclusively find newsgroups about the kind of traveling you want to do; such a general search could pull up thousands of postings that contain the keyword **travel,** which could include messages related to basketball or space travel.

Figure 13-1:
The
Deja News
home page.

To ensure that you find newsgroups about travel and travel planning, click the Interest Finder button on the Deja News home page. This search method returns only newsgroups that have some relevance to your search term. For example, when I search the word **travel** in the Interest Finder, I get the more specific results I want, as shown in Figure 13-2.

You can also peruse the list of groups by using the Browse Groups function. Click Browse Groups, and Deja News presents you with a list of general categories. The site offers a separate category dedicated to the subject of travel; listed in this category are most of the newsgroups in which travel discussions take place. You can continue to browse by clicking on the sub-categories or by using the search box to limit your query to more specific travel topics.

Finally, Deja News also has a Travel section, Figure 13-3, that highlights interesting and timely discussions and travel-related topics. Start here if you want to get a feel for a variety of travel newsgroups.

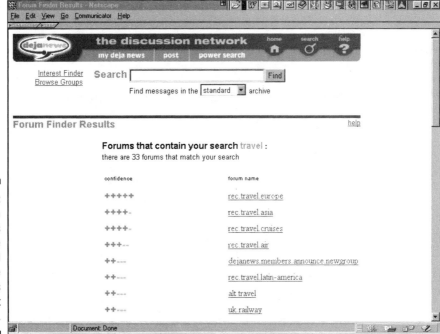

Figure 13-2:
Search
results
for the
keyword
travel in the
Deja News
Interest
Finder.

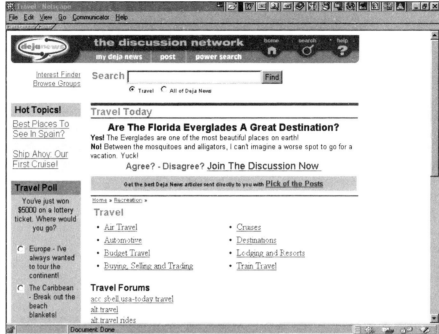

Figure 13-3:
The
Deja News
Travel
section
page.

Reading and posting messages on Deja News

After you find a newsgroup that interests you, use Deja News to read, respond, and post your own thoughts to the newsgroup. If you want to look through a specific newsgroup's topics, use either the Interest Finder or Browse functions to zero in on the group you wish to read. Then you just click on the subjects to read the postings.

To post a response or add a new message to the newsgroup, you need to do a bit of legwork. Follow these steps to ask that question about restaurants in Jakarta or libraries in New York City that you've been dying to ask:

1. **Click My Deja News at the top of any Deja News page.**

2. **Enter the required information into the form and choose a user name and password.**

   An e-mail address is essential.

3. **Click Register Me!**

   Deja News immediately sends a confirmation to your e-mail address.

4. **Check your e-mail for an e-mail from Deja News.**

   In the letter, you find a Web address.

5. **Plug the address into your browser (either click it or paste it directly) to confirm your registration process.**

   After Deja News confirms your request, you are fully operational. Go to My Deja News to choose newsgroups to which you want to subscribe. Click Add/Remove Forums to set up a customized newsreader for yourself, containing the forums that interest you.

After you register, Deja News works very much like an e-mail account. From a specific newsgroup, click Post Message (located at the top of the screen) to submit a message. Or, while you read a post, click Post Reply to submit a response that can be read by anyone. You can also use E-mail Reply to send an e-mail exclusively to the person who wrote the message. If you want to read the thread, that is, the line of discussion, click View Thread, which shows you all the posts relating to the topic.

Receiving Travel Info from E-Mail Mailing Lists

E-mail mailing lists, or *listservs,* like newsgroups, have been around since the early days of the Internet. These discussion forums, as you may have guessed, make use of e-mail as the communication medium.

A mailing list can be as simple as a weekly newsletter, such as the discount newsletters I tell you about in Chapter 9, to which you subscribe by submitting your e-mail address. After you subscribe, each week you receive information about a certain topic.

Interactive mailing lists also exist, which enable subscribers to converse, via e-mail, with a group of people who share an interest in a certain topic. These interactive mailing lists can be wonderful ways to research trips and find out accurate, firsthand travel info.

All mailing lists use a piece of software to relay messages automatically to the subscriber list, but some have a human moderator who filters the messages that are conveyed to the group (moderated). Some groups allow anyone to subscribe (open) while others require that the list manager approve you (approved). Whatever type of group you subscribe to, one thing's for sure: You'll be getting a lot more e-mail after you subscribe.

Tapping into travel mailing lists with Liszt

The best place to find a mailing list for all topics related to travel is a Web site called Liszt (www.liszt.com), Figure 13-4. At last check, the Liszt database contained 84,792 different mailing lists. Not only does Liszt catalog tons of mailing lists, it also features descriptions of the type of discussions that take place in many groups.

Searching Liszt

To search Liszt for a mailing list regarding a particular travel topic, enter your keyword into the search box and let her rip. You can set the search to filter junk, meaning you won't have esoteric or non-public lists returned by your search. The default filter setting is set on Some, meaning it automatically strips out lists that contain certain telltale signs/keywords that indicate a list of no interest. If you want more filtering, set the filter (by clicking the little circle next to the search box) to Lots. Then your results only contain lists about which Liszt has detailed information. If you want to see all the lists with no filtering, set the filter to None.

For example, when I search with the keyword **travel** using the default settings, Liszt comes up with a collection of all sorts of travel-related mailing lists, as well as the Liszt travel categories (Figure 13-5).

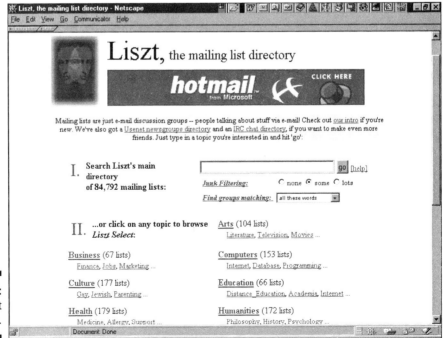

Figure 13-4:
The Liszt
home page.

Figure 13-5:
Search
results
for the
keyword
travel.

Liszt organizes its database into browsable subject areas that you can access from the home page by using the categories and subcategories. Though it's not listed on the home page, a travel category exists, which you can find under the Recreation heading and contains, at last check, 28 lists. Several other topics under the Recreation listing may interest travelers: Hiking, Camping, Fishing, Events, Railroads, and more.

Mailing list descriptions

Liszt color codes all the mailing lists in the database. The colors do more than just add a little flavor to each page. They tell you just how much Liszt knows about a particular mailing list, which could include whether the list is moderated, what topics are discussed, and who participates. The following colors have specific meanings at Liszt that could help you locate the travel information you need more quickly:

- **Green:** Lists that are coded green mean that Liszt has detailed info on the mailing list's subject matter, including the official *info file* (most groups publish an info file that outlines the purpose of the list).

- **Yellow:** Yellow means that Liszt knows some information about the group, but the site doesn't have a complete or official info file.

✔ **Red:** Red signals that Liszt doesn't have any info about the group. All you have is the name to go by.

✔ **White:** White means that Liszt doesn't know whether info exists about the mailing list; either it hasn't been requested or the group didn't reply.

Subscribing to a mailing list

After you find a group that sounds interesting in Liszt, click the name of the group to find out the subscription procedure. For example, you may want to subscribe to the Travel-L mailing list, a long-running, general travel discussion group. (Although Liszt codes Travel-L yellow, you can find all the subscription and topic info by clicking on the Travel-L link; see the preceding section for a discussion of this color-coding business.) As with many lists, the site provides an administrative address for people to request information.

Never send e-mail to the actual mailing list address; doing so will inevitably annoy everyone who receives the list; no one wants to read about your subscription requests. Always look for and use the mailing list's information address.

Because almost all mailing lists operate by way of specialized software, subscribing generally consists of mailing a specific command to a specific address. The subscription process usually goes something like this (Liszt tells you if you need to do something special to subscribe):

1. **Find the subscription address.**

   For example, the subscription address for TRAVEL-L is
   `listserv@vm3090.ege.edu.tr`

2. **Type** subscribe *name of newsgroup* **in the body of your e-mail.**

   Make sure to type only the word ***subscribe*** followed by a space and the name of the newsgroup. If you don't enter the information exactly as I show you, the subscription software won't be able to read your message, and you won't get hooked up with the mailing list.

   For example, if you were signing up for TRAVEL-L, you type **subscribe TRAVEL-L**.

3. **Send your e-mail.**

   After a few minutes, you get an automated response stating that you are subscribed to the list. The response also contains information on how to unsubscribe — make sure that you keep that info in a safe place.

You can usually request information about the mailing list from the automated e-mail response. For most groups, you can type **info** and the group's name (**info TRAVEL-L**, for example) into the body of the e-mail, and you soon receive information about the mailing list. Some lists also have a digest form of the mailing list, meaning that instead of getting an e-mail every time a message is posted to the group, you receive one e-mail that contains all the day's postings. The mailing list's info file should contain instructions for subscribing to the digest version. I always choose the digest form; opening your e-mail box to find 35 messages about arcane travel topics can drive a person to drink.

Useful travel-related mailing lists

Mailing lists generally focus on a fairly narrow subject, such as ecotravel or cruises. Give one of the following popular lists a try (I give you the subscription address in case you feel compelled to join up). What have you got to lose — it's easy to unsubscribe:

- ✔ **The B&B list:** A discussion of B&B accommodations around the world. Send the command *subscribe* to Majordomo@netconcepts.com

- ✔ **The Cruise Newsletter:** All about the art of cruising the high seas and the cruise industry. Send the command *subscribe* to listproc@lists.colorado.edu

- ✔ **The Green Travel newsletter:** This mailing list discusses "Sustainable, environmentally, and culturally responsible ecotourism worldwide." Send the command *subscribe* to mendicott@igc.org

- ✔ **Travel-Ease:** You find discussions of leisure travel for families and individuals. Send the command *subscribe* to Majordomo@kajor.com

- ✔ **Travel-L:** All travel topics are open to discussion, including tips on getting good ticket prices and what to pack for visiting places at different times of the year. Send command *subscribe* to listserv@vm3090.ege.edu.tr

In order for a mailing list to provide worthwhile information, participants need to be active. If you know the answer to someone's question, answer it!

Can We Talk? Online Travel Chats and Events

Newsgroups and mailing lists offer interesting ways to communicate with travelers, but they require a bit of patience. For those of you with shorter attention spans, an online travel chat may hold your interest.

Chats can range in subject matter from a simple open forum for travelers to speak their minds to a discussion of Mexican travel hosted by a travel writer. Some sites also sponsor ongoing travel events, such as the online travelogues that follow the ascent of Mt. Everest each year, various online discussions about travel issues, interviews with travel experts, and bulletins about travel happenings. All are good ways of hearing about the world.

Unfortunately (and paradoxically), in order to satisfy your need for instant gratification, a little planning is required. Travel chats happen at scheduled times: You can't just go online and expect to find a great travel chat. Chats are usually hosted by Web sites or online services — the same goes for the wide range of travel events. Often, a new Web site is created specifically to host an event, as happens with the Mt. Everest ascent.

How does it work?

You usually need some specific software to take part in a chat. Either you must have a Java-enabled browser (Netscape and Internet Explorer versions 3.0 and later) or a specific piece of chat software.

The sites that host online chats always provide a free download of the required software if you need it.

After you get set up to chat, the discussion takes place in *real time.* That is, you have a dialog box in which you type your statements; at the same time, you see a larger box that contains all the participants' statements.

Spend a little time reading and watching before you jump into a chat room: It quickly becomes apparent what type of discussion is taking place.

Finding a place to chit-chat about the world

The Internet is positively loaded with chat forums. However, surprisingly few focus on travel topics; it seems most people just want to talk about their love lives and other trivial stuff. Go figure.

Finding travel chats can be an arduous process. A bunch of sites serve as directories to online chat events, but pouring over these to find a travel chat will make you want to talk to a therapist instead of talk about travel.

Luckily, the following sites have done the work of finding travel chat for you, highlighting the top travel chats each day:

- **NetGuide TravelGuide** (`www.netguide.com/Travel`): Each day, the folks at NetGuide handpick the best chats and online events. Visit the TravelGuide to see the highlighted travel events each day (Figure 13-6).

- **Yahoo! Net Events Calendar** (`events.yahoo.com/Recreation/Travel`): Yahoo! has a great listing of daily and ongoing online travel events and chats.

- **Snap! Travel Events** (`www.snap.com/main/channel/events/0,45,home-tr,00.html`): Each day, Snap! lists the day's travel events. The site lists times, descriptions, and software requirements.

- **OnNow** (`www.onnow.com`): Use this massive directory of online events to search for travel chats. Although you're likely to come up with a fair amount of chaff, use the keyword **travel** to find some worthwhile events.

Travel chat on America Online

America Online has an extensive chat area devoted to travelers. If you are an AOL member, go to keyword **Travel Café** to join one of the many discussion forums for travelers. The chats are usually moderated by a travel expert and have a theme.

In contrast to the travel chats you have to search for on the Web, AOL's Travel Café sponsors regularly schedule chats and discussions — the site offers chat about a different topic every night of the week. The quality of the chat varies widely. It all depends on who is involved and if there are any travel experts participating.

Generally, the forums take place in the evening, around 9:00 p.m. EST. You can sign up to receive an e-mail newsletter that details upcoming chats and travel events on AOL.

Como se Dice? (How Do You Say . . .)

Every traveler, at some point in their journeys, runs into the inevitable language barrier. And if you try to decipher a Web site written in a foreign language, flipping through a translating dictionary can take hours. Luckily, some Web sites can take care of all your translating needs in a flash.

Travlang

One of the biggest challenges a traveler faces when abroad is being understood without speaking the native language. Ever try to describe a sickness to a doctor who doesn't speak your language? You could wind up getting a lobotomy when all you need is an aspirin.

Before your next trip, pick up some language basics by using Travlang (www.travlang.com), a site that translates over 60 languages into almost any language.

From the Foreign Languages for Travelers page (www.travlang.com/languages), select your native tongue and the language you wish to translate it into. After you submit your choices, you can choose to go through various useful phrases and common words.

Many languages also have a translating dictionary: Enter a word and moments later you have the translated version. And the coolest part: Click a phrase and Travlang speaks it for you.

AltaVista Translations

If you just need a phrase translated quickly, try AltaVista Translations (babelfish.altavista.digital.com). The site only allows you to work with the major European languages (such as French, German, and Spanish), but it works remarkably well.

Getting the information you need at this site is just a matter of a few simple steps:

1. **Type in a phrase and select the language conversion you wish.**

2. **Click Translate.**

   After a few seconds you see an approximate translation of the phrase in the language you selected. Now you have no excuse for ignoring the locals.

Part IV
The Part of Tens

In this part . . .

This part consists of two quick chapters, each full of helpful tips that I picked along the way. I guarantee that one chapter will save you money on airline tickets. The other chapter shows you a few cool tricks for making your time on the Internet more fun and productive.

Chapter 14
Ten Tips for Better Web Surfing

● ●

In This Chapter

▶ Setting your own start page

▶ Going to your favorite sites quickly and easily

▶ Searching done the easy way

▶ Using the right mouse button

▶ Cutting and pasting

▶ Avoiding eye strain

▶ Turning off graphics for faster downloads

▶ Tabbing between fields

● ●

*I*may be stretching things a bit to call surfing on the Web an art form, but refining your surfing techniques certainly makes your time on the Web smoother and more fruitful. This chapter shows you some tricks I've picked up along the way in my travels on the Web; these tips should allow you to spend less time online and more time enjoying the trips you plan.

As a note of caution, realize that the browser features I refer to are for version 4.0 of Netscape and Internet Explorer (the versions included on the CD-ROM), so if you use an earlier version, the commands may be slightly different.

Setting a Start Page

Every time you start your Web browser, it automatically shows the *start page*. The company that manufactures your browser (probably Netscape or Microsoft) sets its home page as the default start page. But you can set up your browser to use any page on the Web as your start page.

If you're an avid traveler, an online agency would work well as your start page — that way, you'll be sure to check for current deals at the agency every time you fire up your browser. Search engines, weather pages, and directories are also good choices for start pages. It's all up to you. Any single Web page can be your home page — it doesn't have to be the home page of a site.

If you use Netscape, select Edit⇨Preferences. The dialog box shown in Figure 14-1 appears. Type the Web address (URL) into the box and you're all set.

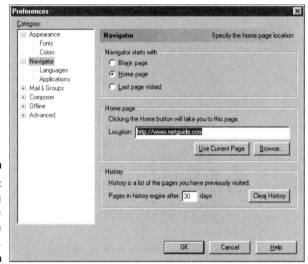

Figure 14-1:
Designating
a home
page with
Netscape.

If you use Internet Explorer, click View and then Internet Options. In the Home Page box, shown in Figure 14-2, enter the URL for the page that you want to be your start page.

Enter the URL to set the desired page as your start page.

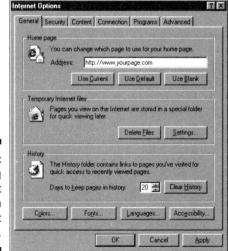

Figure 14-2:
Designating
a start
page with
Internet
Explorer.

Using More than One Browser Window

You're not confined to having just one browser window. Depending on the power of your computer, many browser windows can be open at the same time. (If you don't have enough power, using multiple browser windows decreases the speed of your already-slow browser.) With multiple browser windows, items can be downloaded (especially images) much more efficiently. For example, if you encounter a page with tons and tons of images on it (and many travel-related sites are packed with images), you can start your browser downloading the images, and while that rather mundane task takes place, you can open another window and browse on over to the next site you want to check out. In both Netscape and Internet Explorer, press Ctrl+N or choose File⇨New⇨Window to open multiple browser windows.

Bookmarking Great Sites

Your browser is equipped with features that allow you to quickly move between sites that you visit frequently. The most useful features for keeping track of sites that interest you are the Bookmarks (Netscape) or Favorites (Internet Explorer) files. These files are electronic address book entries to the Web sites you value. To revisit a cool site, add the site to your files.

With Netscape, click the Bookmark button (on Netscape version 4.0) and then click Add Bookmark or press Ctrl+D. If you use an older version of Netscape, click Bookmark Menu and then click Add Bookmark. Netscape adds a listing with the title of the Web site to your Bookmark file.

Internet Explorer users can press Ctrl+D or go to the Favorites menu and click Add to Favorites.

Both Netscape and Internet Explorer let you organize your Bookmark/Favorites files into hierarchical directories, using the familiar folder system used by both Windows and Mac operating systems. I bookmark almost every site that even remotely interests me; then I periodically organize the files into folders, as shown in Figure 14-3.

Having these bookmarks organized is the primary reason I am qualified to write this book; that is, I know where to find travel information on the Internet. You should keep your travel bookmarks together and even organize them into groups — online travel agencies, city guides, and so on.

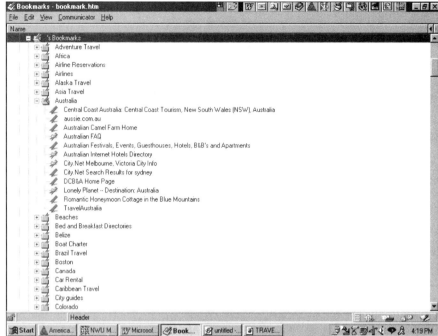

Figure 14-3:
Part of my
massive
bookmark
files
(Netscape).

Using the Go! Feature

Both Netscape and Internet Explorer have menus labeled Go. Use this feature to move between the sites that you visit during one session of Web surfing. Clicking Go lists the last ten or so sites you visited. To revisit a site, move down the list with your mouse and click that site's URL.

The box that displays the address of the current Web site performs a function similar to that of the Go menu. Click the arrow on the right side of the navigation box and the sites from previous Web sessions appear. Any site that you directly access by typing the address or pasting the URL into the address box is listed in this menu (the previous 14 sites are listed). So, each time you launch your browser, use this pull-down menu to quickly access the sites that you frequently visit. Check out Figure 14-4 to see what I'm talking about.

Adding an Infoseek Search Box

The popular search engine Infoseek (www.infoseek.com) provides a very useful tool for conducting speedy searches that works with any browser.

Figure 14-4:
The
pull-down
menu
under the
address box
(Internet
Explorer).

Go to the Infoseek home page and click the Infoseek Quickseek link. After you download the software and install the program (the site tells you how to do that), your browser's upper-right corner sports a small search box that allows you to enter keywords and perform a search at any moment during your surfing. To use the search box, enter your search terms then click the infoseek button. The search box pulls up the appropriate returns from Infoseek, which appear in your browser window.

Right-Clicking with Your Mouse

Almost all PCs now come with a two-button mouse. (Unfortunately, Macintosh users can't utilize the following info, because Mac mice have only one button.) You're probably well acquainted with the left button's capabilities — you've most likely spent many an hour using the left button to click on links. But, you may not know the full potential of the right button, which has some strange and wonderful powers when browsing Web pages.

For starters, use the right button to cut or copy and paste URLs (or any other piece of text, for that matter) from your browser without ever touching the keyboard or the Edit menu. Just highlight the appropriate text, right click, and choose the Cut, Copy, or Paste option, depending on what you want to do.

The right button also does some particularly cool things when it comes to links. For example, use the right mouse button to copy a link's location (the URL) without actually clicking the link (and consequently going to the URL's corresponding Web site). You'll appreciate this option when you're out on the Web combing for travel Web sites that you want to visit at a later time.

To copy a link's location, put the mouse pointer on the link so that the little hand appears then click the right mouse button. A menu pops up that looks like the one in Figure 14-5.

Figure 14-5:
Right-
clicking a
menu on
a link.

When the menu appears, choose Copy Link Location to put the URL in your computer's memory. You can then paste the link's URL into any document or another browser page.

In addition to copying link locations, other right-button options include the following:

- ✔ **Back and Forward:** These options allow you to move backward and forward from page to page with minimal effort on your part.

- ✔ **View Image:** You get this option only when you click an image. Choosing View Images allows you to view an image on a separate Web page, all by itself, totally unencumbered by text.

- ✔ **Add Bookmark:** If you plan to visit a particular site again, choose this option to add the site to your bookmarks. (For more about bookmarks, see "Bookmarking Great Sites.")

Cutting and Pasting from Web Pages

Whenever you come across fascinating, useful, horrifying, or titillating information on the World Wide Web, you don't have to commit it to memory or write it down by hand. Instead, use your mouse to highlight text on a Web page or newsgroup and then use your computer's Cut, Copy, and Paste capabilities to transfer the text to any document.

For travelers, cutting and pasting is most useful when you find some destination information that you want to take with you on the trip. After visiting a few sites about your destination, cut out the relevant part of each to compile a guidebook tailor-made to suit your needs.

If you prefer the keyboard to the mouse, PC users can make use of the following keyboard combinations:

- ✔ **Copy:** Ctrl+C
- ✔ **Cut:** Ctrl+X
- ✔ **Paste:** Ctrl+V

Mac users have the following keyboard choices:

- ✔ **Copy:** Command+C
- ✔ **Cut:** Command+X
- ✔ **Paste**: Shift+Insert
- ✔ **Paste:** Command+P

If you use Internet Explorer or Netscape on a PC, you can use the right mouse button to perform all of the above edit commands.

Saving Your Eyes Some Strain

Tired of squinting at the tiny text on Web pages all day long? Well, increase the font size!

If you use Netscape, look under the View menu and use the controls to increase or decrease font size.

For Internet Explorer, the toolbar features a button that allows you to control font size. The button has an A on it with an up arrow and a down arrow next to it. Click the up arrow to increase font size, and click the down arrow to decrease.

Turning Things Off for Faster Downloads

For me, the biggest drag about using the World Wide Web is waiting for pages to load. The wait is particularly pronounced on slow connections (28.8 bps or less).

One way to minimize the loading time for Web pages is to tell your browser not to automatically load images. You find graphics and photos on many travel sites, and they take much longer to load than text. If you're in a rush, turning off images speed things up a bit.

Netscape users:

1. **Under the Edit menu, select Preferences.**

   The Preferences dialog box appears.

2. **Click Advanced.**

3. **Deselect the Automatically loads images option.**

   Images now only load if you select Show Images under the View menu. Reverse this process to make images load automatically.

Internet Explorer users:

1. **Choose View and then Internet Options.**

2. **Click the Advanced tab.**

3. **Scroll down until you see the Multimedia section.**

4. **Click the check box next to Show Pictures to instruct the browser not to load images.**

Tabbing between Fields

During your Web surfing, you may come across many sites that ask you to enter information into input boxes, or *fields*. Whether it's an online travel agency asking you to enter some travel dates and cities or a mailing list that wants your e-mail address and name, you can speed things up a bit by using the Tab key to move between the various fields. Instead of taking your fingers off the keyboard to use the mouse, simply reach over with your left-hand pinky and hit the Tab key to jump from field to field.

For fields that require dates or information such as the state or province in which you reside, try highlighting the field and using the appropriate keystroke to scroll the options contained in the field. For example, if a field asks for your month of birth, typing the letter A once when the field is highlighted usually displays the month April in the field. Hit the letter A again and August pops up. This process works on most sites that use forms and fields.

Chapter 15

Ten Tips for Getting Cheaper Airfares

▶ Flying on the cheapest days

▶ Using all your options to get the best deal

▶ Choosing flights wisely

*T*he only thing better than a really good vacation is a really good vacation at a discount price. Because you usually shell out more for airfare than anything else when planning a trip, it *literally* pays to know how to get the best ticket prices from airlines.

Hundreds of fare classes exist for all flights; you can pay a wide range of fares for the same seat on the same flight. The advice I give you in this chapter helps you acquire the lowest-priced tickets on all airlines for travel in North America and some international routes. You can use my ticket tips both online and at your neighborhood travel agency.

Buying Your Tickets Well in Advance

Airlines know that a traveler who really needs to get somewhere on short notice doesn't have much of a choice about routes and ticket prices and thus will pay a higher fare.

To avoid the high ticket prices you get close to departure time, purchase your tickets at least 21 days before the flight (calling more than 21 days in advance may get you an even better deal). If you wait until closer to the departure date to buy, you will notice a steep rise in ticket price.

The 21-day rule is not set in stone; some airlines require more or less notice. To be on the safe side, call any airline you consider flying with and ask about their advance-purchase schedule. Even if you think you know an airline's advance-purchase schedule, it doesn't hurt to call. During some periods (such as during a fare war, when the airlines all try to beat each other out on ticket prices and services) an airline's advance schedule may be as short as 7 to 14 days.

Buying Your Tickets at the Very Last Minute

Airlines can usually estimate the number of empty seats on a weekend flight (a flight that leaves on a Friday, Saturday, or a Sunday) by the Wednesday preceding the weekend.

Airlines prefer to sell cheap tickets than have empty seats. To fill empty seats in a hurry, the airline offers last-minute fare sales, which I tell you all about in Chapter 9.

Of course, you must have a flexible schedule in order to take advantage of these great deals. But if you have breathing room in your travel time, you can save an incredible amount of money, sometimes more than 50 percent off the published fare, using these last-minute deals.

Signing up for e-mail fare alerts with ticket agents and the airlines is the best way to find out about last-minute deals. (Turn to Chapter 9 for more information.)

Catching Saturday Night Fever

An airline's number one priority is to fill planes with customers and make them pay the maximum amount possible for a ticket. To accomplish this insidious-sounding task, air carriers employ a little psychology when creating their fare structures. The airlines use some of their best psychology on the business traveler, the folks who typically pay the highest fares.

Airlines know that most business travelers want to be home for the weekend to be with the family. Good quality time with the family comes at a premium price — the airlines charge more for flights that don't include a stay over a Saturday night.

When you look for cheap fares, make sure your dates have you staying over a Saturday night, or be prepared to pay for the luxury of being home for the weekend.

Flying on Tuesdays, Wednesdays, and Saturdays

Because of the traffic patterns of travelers, flying on some days of the week costs more than others. On most major airlines, Tuesdays, Wednesdays, and Saturdays are the cheapest days on which to fly.

You can forget about my Tuesday-Wednesday-Saturday tip if the Tuesday, Wednesday, or Saturday you want to fly happens to be a holiday. This is an obvious one. Because everyone wants to get to grandma's house for the holidays, airlines know they can charge more for flights on (or even around) major holidays.

However, on certain holidays, usually of the three-day weekend variety, the airlines try to drum up business by offering deals and promotions. For Americans, Labor Day and Memorial Day are good examples of long week-end holidays when many airlines offer cheap fares for a short getaway.

In terms of international flights, you can usually expect to pay much higher fares when your travel falls during a holiday in your destination country, especially a holiday that has significance for expatriates of the destination country. For example, you can count on many Brazilians returning home for Carnival in Rio, allowing the airlines to charge more for flights to Brazil during this period.

Expanding Your Options

Finding cheap tickets requires a high level of resourcefulness. Don't expect the first combination of dates, airports, and flights to result in the cheapest fare. Getting good fares requires persistence and willingness to try many combinations and permutations of your options.

When you use an online travel agency to check fares, most give you an option of how many choices you want returned from each flight query. Set this feature to a maximum number of choices, allowing you to view a wide range of available flights. You have to sift through some chaff to find the wheat.

Flying on some days is more expensive than on others. When you input your flight info into an online agency flight query, try many different days of the week for all legs of the trip. It may surprise you how much one day can change your fare.

Trying All Airlines and Airports, Great and Small

Don't be afraid to fly smaller airlines. The little guys often have lower fares with fewer restrictions. You can use the Internet to find out about lots of smaller airlines that may not have a listing in your local telephone book.

In addition, when looking for a low airfare, you can't afford to play favorites with certain airports. If you live in a city with more than one airport (New York has La Guardia, JFK, and Newark, for example), check the fares going through each airport. Often, flights from different airports have very different fares for similar routes.

Flying the Same Airline on All Flight Segments

 Many online travel agencies list flights in terms of segments. Generally, the most expensive type of ticket is a one-way (one-segment) ticket. Buying a one-way on two airlines to complete a round-trip is far from cost-effective. In order to get the best round trip, flying your entire trip with the same airline usually gets you the best fare.

Looking for Flights with Plenty of Empty Seats

The inexpensive, less-restricted fares on a flight usually get snatched up pretty quickly. If you find a flight with just a few seats remaining, the seats you have to choose from are bound to be the expensive and restricted ones.

Most online travel agencies have features that show the number of seats remaining in each class (coach, business, first, and so on). Some agencies, such as 1travel.com (www.1travel.com), also list the seats remaining by the type of seat.

Seat types usually fall into four categories, each with its own *service class code,* which is denoted by a one-letter abbreviation. Although the codes vary widely from airline to airline and by region, several codes apply almost universally, including the following:

- ✔ **F:** First class
- ✔ **C:** Business class
- ✔ **Y:** Economy/Coach class
- ✔ **Q:** Economy/Coach Discounted class

Of course, each service level corresponds to a different fare rate. The closer you get to the departure date, the fewer types of fares are available.

Doing Your Homework

Even with all the advantages you get from planning your trip online, you still have to work for the cheap fares.

For starters, you first have to recognize a good fare for a particular flight before you can take advantage of it. In order to spot a good deal, you must be up-to-date on the current prices for a given route.

Use the prices listed in the Sunday newspaper travel sections to get a feel for the latest discount fares. In conjunction with the Internet, the newspaper travel section should keep you very informed about the going rate for a flight.

Doing your homework not only gets you the best flight — it also allows you to brag to your friends about a hot fare.

Talking to a Travel Agent

Even though this book is all about the Internet's travel planning virtues, you should still use online booking in conjunction with living, breathing travel agents. After you scout the Web for the best fares, call up your favorite travel agent and see what they can come up with. Who knows — they may better the deals you find on the Internet.

Part V
Appendixes

The 5th Wave   By Rich Tennant

"This afternoon I want everyone to go online and find all you can about Native-American culture, the history of the old west, and discount air fares to Hawaii for the two weeks I'll be on vacation."

In this part . . .

America Online, the world's largest commercial online service, offers a whole world's worth of travel advice. I devote Appendix A to showing you some of AOL's finer travel features. In Appendix B, I tell you what's on the CD-ROM that comes with this book and how the CD can help you with your travel planning.

Appendix A

A Guide to America Online's Travel Resources

- ▶ Using the America Online Travel Channel
- ▶ Making reservations on AOL
- ▶ Finding city guides and other travel tools

America Online (AOL) is unequivocally the single most popular Internet service in the world. The haunting "You've got mail" message is as well-known in Singapore as it is in San Francisco.

Because it's such a popular service, AOL can create loads of original content, host well-known companies' online services, and form partnerships with all sorts of great businesses. In terms of travel, AOL offers a bounty of useful features.

AOL members can use this appendix as a guide to its travel services. Those of you who don't use AOL, well, you can tear out the following pages and fold them into paper airplanes. Or maybe this appendix will convince you to give the AOL travel resources a try.

I present all the information in this appendix with the latest version of AOL, 4.0. If you use a different version of AOL, you may see things differently than how I describe them here. If you need help taking advantage of the travel offerings mentioned in this chapter, consult the Member Services Online Help feature available on AOL (you find it under a pull-down menu labeled Help). You can also pick up a copy of *AOL For Dummies,* 4th Edition, by John Kaufeld, published by IDG Books Worldwide, Inc.

The AOL Travel Channel

America Online organizes its travel content using a gateway known as the Travel Channel. You can access all of the AOL travel resources, including original content and pages from well-known travel companies, through the Travel Channel.

You can call up the AOL Travel Channel in a few different ways, including the following:

✔ On the Channel Guide, click the Travel box. (See Figure A-1.)

✔ Type keyword (Ctrl+K) **Travel**.

✔ Use the AOL Channels menu on the menu bar at the top of every AOL page. Use the pull-down menu to select Travel from the list of AOL channels.

Figure A-1:
The AOL
Channel
Guide.

After you arrive at the AOL Travel Channel, Figure A-2, you quickly see that AOL attempts to provide everything that a traveler needs to plan, research, and reserve every aspect of a trip. The service incorporates the offerings of many of the best known travel companies and online travel services into its own original resources, which I discuss in the following sections of this chapter.

Figure A-2:
The AOL
Travel
Channel.

Although you can get to all travel-related content by drilling down through the many areas of the Travel Channel, you can use separate keywords to access specific areas of the Travel Channel more quickly, such as **InsideFlyer** to reach the *InsideFlyer Magazine*'s AOL site. You can always find out the keyword used to access an area by looking in the bottom-right corner of the AOL screen.

The Reservations Center

You can reserve flights, hotel rooms, and cars on AOL by way of its partner, the popular online travel agency, Preview Travel (keyword **Travel Reservations**), which you find in an area called the Reservation Center. The reservation process at Preview Travel resembles that of Preview's Web site. (See Chapter 6 for more on Preview.)

To reach Preview Travel from the Travel Channel, click the Reservations Center box, or go directly by using keyword **Preview Travel**. Also found in the Reservations Center are links to Web sites where you can make reservations for bus, railroad, and vacation packages as well as buy tickets for American and Continental Airlines.

Searching and exploring

To acquaint yourself with the primary travel areas on AOL, use the Travel Search page (keyword **Travelsearch**). Brief descriptions and links to about 15 travel content areas are in the dialog box on the left. Scroll through them and see if any of the choices can help you accomplish your travel goals. You also find the following three links on the Travel Search page:

✔ **Best of AOL Travel:** Click this link to access a gateway page to the most useful travel sections on AOL. Click each area's link to view a brief description in the dialog box below the Go There! button. The areas include destination guides, bargain hunting, Preview Travel (reservations), and Today's Lowest Fares.

✔ **Destination Guides:** Click this link and a short advertisement for Preview Travel appears. A voice extols the virtues of online booking and destination research while photos of fabulous locales are viewed on the screen. A wonderfully useless feature.

✔ **Current Travel Spotlights:** Use this feature to check out timely and notable travel sections on AOL. An example: When I visited in September, I found a feature about how to be in the right place at the right time to view fall foliage.

From the Travel Search page you can also click the Find Central button to perform a keyword search that covers the entire AOL service — great for when you are looking for a very specific bit of travel info.

Destination Guides on AOL

Fodor's, one of the most popular travel guidebook series in the world, provides the destination guides on AOL (keyword **Destinations**). These guides are known for their excellent and comprehensive travel advice for all styles of traveler; you get information about accommodations, restaurants, and transportation for hundreds of destinations worldwide.

After you arrive at the Fodor's section, enter the destination that you want to read about or browse the destinations. You can also create a custom mini-guide by working through the checklists, selecting the travel information that you want to know about. Your customized guide has the information you want about any of the destinations covered by Fodor's Guides. (See Chapter 1 for an example of how a mini-guide works.)

Lonely Planet, the popular guidebook publisher, also has an area on AOL. Keyword **LP** brings you to an area rich with destination information geared toward independent travelers and other vagabonds. Lonely Planet guides are squarely aimed at independent budget travelers, however the country info and transportation options that LP details in its guides prove useful for anyone that likes to travel.

City Guides

For almost every major metropolitan area in the United States, AOL provides an interactive guide, called Digital City, that can help you find a restaurant or a good hotel. The guides let you choose the info that interests you — choose Weather if you want a forecast, use the yellow pages to find numbers for local businesses, or find the timetable for movies in any city. (AOL's Digital City also exists on the WWW; check out Chapter 1 for a full run-down of its many features.)

Plugging in the keyword **Digital City** brings you to a map of the U.S.; you can then click any city's name or use the city's name as a keyword to jump to the city guide. (To use a keyword to navigate AOL, type Ctrl+K at any time and then type the keyword into the box.)

Each city guide has a team of editors and writers who know their city intimately and dutifully report on the best that the city has to offer. Each guide keeps the pulse of its city with regular updates; the team delivers new articles every day, the weather forecast is always current, and the event guides are up-to-date. You may even find out some interesting stuff about your own hometown by checking out a Digital City guide.

The Resource Center

Clicking the Resource Center link on the Travel Channel brings you to an area focused on independent travelers (Figure A-3), those admirable folks who like to plan their own trips.

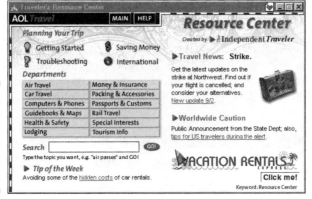

Figure A-3:
The main screen of the Resource Center.

The Center organizes the travel advice and resources by category. For almost any travel-related question you may have, the Resource Center contains the means to answer your questions; the Center offers tons of FAQs and links to Web sites that address your questions. Click a category button to access the info.

Also at the Center page you find timely articles that help with travel problems. For example, the last time I visited, the site featured an article about an airline strike.

The Tip of the Week is usually quite helpful, and you can use the search box to find a specific piece of travel advice in the Tip of the Week database.

Travel Interests Section

Click the Travel Interests link on the Travel Channel (keyword **Travel Interests**) to find information about the type of travel you want to read about. Each category of travel interests has a button on the main page of this section, including the following:

✔ Family

✔ Gay and lesbian

✔ Adventure

✔ Cruises

Each interest area connects to a section about that particular type of travel. In each section, you also may find links to additional areas on AOL, links to Web sites (AOL's browser automatically opens when you click a listing that has a little globe next to it), and photos, videos, and message boards related to your area of interest.

Messages and Chat

America Online offers more travel-related chat and message-board areas than any other online entity. The AOL Travel Chat (keyword **Travel Messages and Chat**), Figure A-4, offers an excellent means of getting firsthand advice and connecting with travel experts. Myself, I'm too shy.

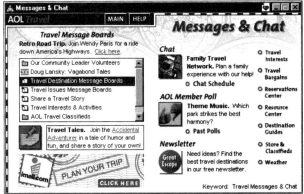

Figure A-4:
The
Messages
and Chat
area main
screen.

Click Chat Schedule on the Messages and Chat page (below the Chat graphic) to find out when chats take place. The following three travel areas regularly host chats on AOL:

- ✔ **The Family Travel Network:** Several times a month, the Family Travel Network (keyword **FTN**) puts on chats hosted by notable travel experts. AOL updates the schedule and descriptions of the chats regularly.

- ✔ **The Independent Traveler's Travel Café:** Each day of the week has a different topic in the Travel Café's nightly chats (keyword **IT**). The destination-based discussions generally start at 9 p.m. EST and are hosted by a moderator.

- ✔ **The Cruise Café:** These nightly chats (keyword **Cruise Critic**) explore all aspects of cruise vacations. Each night features a different topic.

In addition, the AOL message boards, Figure A-5, provide a place where you can post messages and read other travelers' musings about a variety of travel topics. Each topic has a number next to it denoting the number of subtopics or postings therein. The message boards are arranged into the following four general categories:

- ✔ **Destinations:** Find and share information about someplace you've been or someplace you're headed.

- ✔ **Travel Issues:** These message boards cover all sorts of topics — from airfare secrets to travel mishaps and everything in between.

- ✔ **Travel Stories:** Dying to share your experiences about your trip to Bali? Here's your chance to find an audience after your family and friends have lost interest.

- ✔ **Travel Interests and Activities:** Going on a honeymoon? How about an RV trip? Find kindred spirits in this area.

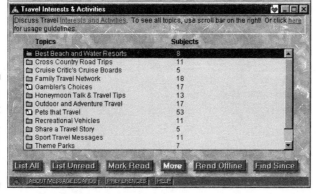

Figure A-5:
A topic list
on an AOL
travel
message
board.

After you find a posting to which you want to reply, click the Reply button and type your message. Or you can create a new subject by clicking Create Subject when you are in a topic area. But remember, your AOL screen name is attached to every post you make — so be prepared to get some mail if you voice a provocative opinion.

Business Travel

If you travel frequently for business, the AOL business center (keyword **Business Travel Center**) has some good resources (actually many of these resources are valuable to all types of travelers). For example, one section helps you find AOL modem access numbers for American cities as well as information about international access and connectivity problems. Other helpful areas include the following:

✔ Car and limousine rental

 ✔ Frequent traveler program information

 ✔ International business travel

 ✔ Maps and directions

 ✔ Weather and flight delays

Finding travel areas on AOL

If you want to see all that AOL has to offer for travelers in one convenient listing, use the Find feature. The Find button is located on the main toolbar, toward the left of the screen. Click the Find button and a screen appears asking you to type in a keyword.

Type the word **Travel** in the search box. The resulting list displays every travel-related area on AOL. At last check, the search came up with 68 travel areas. Not all of the areas focus strictly on travel; some areas, such as the Games Bookshelf, are useful for nontraveling folks, too.

You can also use the Find button to look for destination information. You simply use the name of your destination as the search keyword.

Appendix B
About the CD

The CD-ROM that comes with this book is loaded with nifty software designed to make your travels easier and more fun. For example, you get the following software, plus plenty more, on the *Travel Planning Online For Dummies* CD-ROM:

- MindSpring Internet Access, a popular Internet service
- AirMiles and MaxMiles, two great programs that keep track of frequent traveler award miles
- Road Traveler, a route planner for road trips in America
- Personal Passport, a program for finding travel deals and tour operators
- EuroData, a personal itinerary planner for European travel
- The Electronic Travel Desk, a fast way to look up flight schedules

Read this appendix to find out how to get the most out of the CD.

System Requirements

Before you try to access the programs on the CD, make sure that your computer meets the following minimum system requirements.

- A PC with a 486 or faster processor or a Mac OS computer with a 68030 or faster processor.
- Microsoft Windows 3.1 or later, or Mac OS system software 7.5 or later.
- At least 8MB of total RAM installed on your computer. For best performance, we recommend that Windows 95-equipped PCs and Mac OS computers with PowerPC processors have at least 16MB of RAM installed.
- For Windows, you need at least 120MB of hard drive space available to install all the software from this CD. For Macs, you need at least 60MB. (You need less space if you don't install every program.)
- A CD-ROM drive — double-speed (2x) or faster.

✔ A sound card for PCs. (Mac OS computers have built-in sound support.)

✔ A monitor capable of displaying at least 256 colors or grayscale.

✔ A modem with a speed of at least 14,400 bps.

If your computer doesn't match up to most of these requirements, you may have problems using the contents of the CD.

If you need more information on the basics, check out *PCs For Dummies,* 6th Edition, by Dan Gookin; *Macs For Dummies,* 6th Edition, by David Pogue; *Windows 95 For Dummies,* 2nd Edition, by Andy Rathbone; or *Windows 3.11 For Dummies,* 3rd Edition, by Andy Rathbone (all published by IDG Books Worldwide, Inc.).

Using the CD with Microsoft Windows

To install the items from the CD to your hard drive, follow these steps.

1. **Insert the CD into your computer's CD-ROM drive.**

2. **Windows 3.1 or 3.11 users: From Program Manager, choose File⇨Run.**

   Windows 95 users: Click Start⇨Run.

3. **In the dialog box that appears, type** D:\SETUP.EXE.

   Replace *D* with the proper drive letter if your CD-ROM drive uses a different letter. (If you don't know the letter, see how your CD-ROM drive is listed under My Computer in Windows 95 or File Manager in Windows 3.1.)

4. **Click OK.**

   A License Agreement window appears.

5. **Read through the license agreement, nod your head, and then click the Accept button if you want to use the CD — after you click Accept, you'll never be bothered by the License Agreement window again.**

   The CD interface Welcome screen appears. The interface is a little program that shows you what's on the CD and coordinates installing the programs and running the demos. The interface basically enables you to click a button or two to make things happen.

6. **Click anywhere on the Welcome screen to enter the interface.**

   Now you are getting to the action. This next screen lists categories for the software on the CD.

7. **To view the items within a category, just click the category's name.**

   A list of programs in the category appears.

8. **For more information about a program, click the program's name.**

   Be sure to read the information that appears. Sometimes a program has its own system requirements or requires you to do a few tricks on your computer before you can install or run the program, and this screen tells you what you might need to do, if anything.

9. **If you don't want to install the program, click the Go Back button to return to the previous screen.**

   You can always return to the previous screen by clicking the Go Back button. This feature allows you to browse the different categories and products and decide what you want to install.

10. **To install a program, click the appropriate Install button.**

    The CD interface drops to the background while the CD installs the program you chose.

11. **To install other items, repeat Steps 7 through 10.**

12. **After you finish installing programs, click the Quit button to close the interface.**

    You can eject the CD now. Carefully place it back in the plastic jacket of the book for safekeeping.

In order to run some of the programs on the *Travel Planning Online For Dummies* CD-ROM, you may need to keep the CD inside your CD-ROM drive. Otherwise, the installed program would have required you to install a very large chunk of the program to your hard drive, which may have kept you from installing other software.

Using the CD with Mac OS

To install the items from the CD to your hard drive, follow these steps:

1. **Insert the CD into your computer's CD-ROM drive.**

   In a moment, an icon representing the CD appears on your Mac desktop.

2. **Double-click the CD icon to show the CD's contents.**

3. **Double-click the Read Me First icon.**

   The Read Me First text file contains information about the CD's programs and any last-minute instructions you may need in order to correctly install them.

4. **To install most programs, just drag the program's folder from the CD window and drop it on your hard drive icon.**

Other programs come with installer programs — with these, you simply open the program's folder on the CD, and then double-click the icon with the words "Install" or "Installer."

Sometimes the installers are actually self extracting archives, which just means that the program files have been bundled up into an archive, and this self extractor unbundles the files and places them on your hard drive. This kind of program is often called an .sea. Double-click anything with .sea in the title, and it will run just like an installer.

What You'll Find

On the *Travel Planning Online For Dummies CD*, I give you a great collection of software that can complement both your online travel planning and your actual travels. Read on to find out how you can plan and organize your travels using some great software.

For the Internet

The following tools get you on the Internet (if you're not already there) and help you navigate it after you arrive.

MindSpring Internet Access Service

For Windows and Mac OS. In case you don't have an Internet connection, the CD includes sign-on software for MindSpring Internet Access, an Internet service provider.

You need a credit card to sign up for MindSpring Internet Access. The Registration Key for installing the Mac version of MindSpring is DUMY8579. Be sure to use all capital letters and type the key in just as it is shown here. (For Windows, you don't need to bother with the Registration Key.)

If you already have an Internet service provider, please note that MindSpring Internet Access software makes changes to your computer's current Internet configuration and may replace your current settings. These changes may stop you from accessing the Internet through your current provider.

For more information and updates of MindSpring Internet Access, visit the MindSpring Web site at `www.mindspring.com`.

Netscape Communicator 4.06

For Windows. This popular browser from Netscape enables you to view Web pages and perform a host of other Internet functions, including e-mail, newsgroups, and word processing. For more information on Netscape Communicator, visit the Netscape Web site at `www.netscape.com`.

Internet Explorer 4.0

For Windows and Mac OS. This browser from Microsoft enables you to view Web pages and perform a host of other Internet functions, including e-mail, newsgroups, and word processing.

This software, if run under Windows NT 4.0, requires Service Pack 3 to run. If you do not have Service Pack 3, please visit the Microsoft Web site at www.microsoft.com. You can also get more information about Internet Explorer at the Microsoft Web site.

For travel planning

The following software can help take the hassle and boredom out of researching and planning a trip.

Road Traveler v2.0

For Mac OS. With Road Traveler, you can plan road trips all over American road trips. The software features detailed information about routes, mileage, maps, states and cities, and much more.

For a full description of the software's capabilities, check out the Road Traveler Web site at www.roadtraveler.com.

Personal Passport

For Windows and Mac OS. Personal Passport attempts to alleviate some of the hassle of finding the right vacation. Use Personal Passport to peruse the offering of more than 1,200 travel suppliers, including cruises, tours, airlines, and hotels. You can also use Personal Passport to find out about current travel specials and discounts. Use the software's multimedia features to give you a better feel for a variety of travel opportunities.

Check out the Personal Passport Web site at www.personalpassport.com for more information.

EuroData

For Windows. EuroData, a unique piece of shareware software for Windows, enables travelers to plan European vacations and trips with ease. The interactive calendar lets you plan the dates of your itinerary and alerts you to holidays and other timely events. The Itinerary Budget helps you accurately plan your daily expenditures and automatically converts currencies. EuroData also has booking features for flights, hotels, car rental, and many more useful features.

Check out the Web site for more details (www.eurail.com/eurodata/eurodata.htm).

The Electronic Travel Desk

For Windows. The Electronic Travel Desk is a frequent flyer's best friend. This freeware program quickly looks up flight schedules and finds routes that some travel planning software may miss. You can also use the Electronic Travel Desk to purchase flights through a network of travel agents.

For more information, check out the Electronic Travel Desk Web site (www.TravelDesk.com/travel/free/Download.html).

For travel tracking

AirMiles v1.0

For Windows and Mac OS. AirMiles works in conjunction with hand-held computing devices, such as Palm Pilot. AirMiles allows you to track frequent flyer miles for 14 airline awards programs, as well as car rental and hotel awards. Because an estimated 20 percent of all travel awards points are lost due to clerical and other errors, a frequent traveler needs a way to manage all the programs associated with tracking these miles.

The AirMiles Web site (www.handshigh.com) has a detailed description of the service.

MaxMiles v3.0

For Windows and Mac OS. Manage all your frequent travel awards with MaxMiles' MileageMiner (a tongue-twister, I know). After you install the software on your computer, you input all your programs into the MileageMiner and the program then gathers all the awards info directly from the airlines, hotels, and credit cards. The software lets you know when it finds discrepancies and sends you a personalized report about your awards via e-mail.

Check out the MaxMiles Web site (www.maxmiles.com) for additional information about the program.

Accessing the links file

The links file on the CD saves you from the tedious task of typing in the URLs that I talk about in this book. If you want to visit a site I recommend, just click the links in the links file — that's much more fun than typing **www** and **.com** over and over again.

Follow these steps to use the links file:

1. **Insert the CD into your computer's CD-ROM drive.**

   Give your computer a moment to take a look at the CD.

2. **Open your browser.**

   If you do not have a browser, you can find both Microsoft Internet Explorer as well as Netscape Communicator on the CD.

3. **Click File⇨Open (Internet Explorer) or on File⇨Open Page (Netscape).**

4. **In the dialog box that appears, type** D:\LINKS.HTM **and click OK.**

   Replace the letter D: with the correct letter for your CD-ROM drive, if it isn't D.

If You've Got Problems (Of the CD Kind)

I tried my best to compile programs that work on most computers with the minimum system requirements. Alas, your computer may differ, and some programs may not work properly for some reason.

The two likeliest problems are that you don't have enough memory (RAM) for the programs you want to use, or you have other programs running that are affecting installation or running of a program. If you get error messages like `Not enough memory` or `Setup cannot continue`, try one or more of these methods and then try using the software again:

✔ Turn off any anti-virus software that you have on your computer. Installers sometimes mimic virus activity and may make your computer incorrectly believe that it is being infected by a virus.

✔ Close all running programs. The more programs you're running, the less memory is available to other programs. Installers also typically update files and programs. So if you keep other programs running, installation may not work properly.

✔ Have your local computer store add more RAM to your computer. This is, admittedly, a drastic and somewhat expensive step. However, if you have a Windows 95 PC or a Mac OS computer with a PowerPC chip, adding more memory can really help the speed of your computer and allow more programs to run at the same time. This may include closing the CD interface and running a product's installation program from Windows Explorer.

If you still have trouble with installing the items from the CD, please call the IDG Books Worldwide Customer Service phone number: 800-762-2974 (outside the U.S.: 317-596-5430).

Index

IDG Books Worldwide, Inc., End-User License Agreement

5. **Limited Warranty.**

   (a) IDGB warrants that the Software and Software Media are free from defects in materials and workmanship under normal use for a period of sixty (60) days from the date of purchase of this Book. If IDGB receives notification within the warranty period of defects in materials or workmanship, IDGB will replace the defective Software Media.

   (b) **IDGB AND THE AUTHOR OF THE BOOK DISCLAIM ALL OTHER WARRANTIES, EXPRESS OR IMPLIED, INCLUDING WITHOUT LIMITATION IMPLIED WARRANTIES OF MER-CHANTABILITY AND FITNESS FOR A PARTICULAR PURPOSE, WITH RESPECT TO THE SOFTWARE, THE PROGRAMS, THE SOURCE CODE CONTAINED THEREIN, AND/OR THE TECHNIQUES DESCRIBED IN THIS BOOK. IDGB DOES NOT WARRANT THAT THE FUNCTIONS CONTAINED IN THE SOFTWARE WILL MEET YOUR REQUIREMENTS OR THAT THE OPERATION OF THE SOFTWARE WILL BE ERROR FREE.**

   (c) This limited warranty gives you specific legal rights, and you may have other rights that vary from jurisdiction to jurisdiction.

6. **Remedies.**

   (a) IDGB's entire liability and your exclusive remedy for defects in materials and workmanship shall be limited to replacement of the Software Media, which may be returned to IDGB with a copy of your receipt at the following address: Software Media Fulfillment Department, Attn.: *Travel Planning Online For Dummies,* IDG Books Worldwide, Inc., 7260 Shadeland Station, Ste. 100, Indianapolis, IN 46256, or call 800-762-2974. Please allow three to four weeks for delivery. This Limited Warranty is void if failure of the Software Media has resulted from accident, abuse, or misapplication. Any replacement Software Media will be warranted for the remainder of the original warranty period or thirty (30) days, whichever is longer.

   (b) In no event shall IDGB or the author be liable for any damages whatsoever (including without limitation damages for loss of business profits, business interruption, loss of business information, or any other pecuniary loss) arising from the use of or inability to use the Book or the Software, even if IDGB has been advised of the possibility of such damages.

   (c) Because some jurisdictions do not allow the exclusion or limitation of liability for consequential or incidental damages, the above limitation or exclusion may not apply to you.

7. **U.S. Government Restricted Rights.** Use, duplication, or disclosure of the Software by the U.S. Government is subject to restrictions stated in paragraph (c)(1)(ii) of the Rights in Technical Data and Computer Software clause of DFARS 252.227-7013, and in subparagraphs (a) through (d) of the Commercial Computer–Restricted Rights clause at FAR 52.227-19, and in similar clauses in the NASA FAR supplement, when applicable.

8. **General.** This Agreement constitutes the entire understanding of the parties and revokes and supersedes all prior agreements, oral or written, between them and may not be modified or amended except in a writing signed by both parties hereto that specifically refers to this Agreement. This Agreement shall take precedence over any other documents that may be in conflict herewith. If any one or more provisions contained in this Agreement are held by any court or tribunal to be invalid, illegal, or otherwise unenforceable, each and every other provision shall remain in full force and effect.

Installation Instructions

To install the items from the CD to your hard drive, follow these steps.

For Windows 95 users

1. **Insert the CD into your computer's CD-ROM drive.**

2. **When the light on your CD-ROM drive goes out, double-click the My Computer icon (it's probably in the top left corner of your desktop).**

   This action opens the My Computer window, which shows you all the drives attached to your computer, the Control Panel, and a couple other handy things.

3. **Double-click the icon for your CD-ROM drive.**

   Another window opens, showing you all the folders and files on the CD.

For Windows 3.1 users

1. **Insert the CD into your computer's CD-ROM drive.**

2. **When the light on your CD-ROM drive goes out, double-click the Main program group.**

3. **Double-click the File Manager icon.**

4. **Double-click the icon for your CD-ROM drive.**

   The drive icons appear under the toolbar buttons. Your CD-ROM drive is probably called the D:\ drive. Another window opens, showing you all the folders and files on the CD.

For Mac OS users

To install the items from the CD to your hard drive, follow these steps.

1. **Insert the CD into your CD-ROM drive.**

   The *Travel Planning Online For Dummies CD* icon appears on your Mac desktop.

2. **Double-click the icon.**

3. **Read the Read Me First file and the License Agreement by double-clicking their icons.**

IDG BOOKS WORLDWIDE BOOK REGISTRATION

We want to hear from you!

Visit **http://my2cents.dummies.com** to register this book and tell us how you liked it!

- ✔ Get entered in our monthly prize giveaway.

- ✔ Give us feedback about this book — tell us what you like best, what you like least, or maybe what you'd like to ask the author and us to change!

- ✔ Let us know any other *...For Dummies*® topics that interest you.

Your feedback helps us determine what books to publish, tells us what coverage to add as we revise our books, and lets us know whether we're meeting your needs as a *...For Dummies* reader. You're our most valuable resource, and what you have to say is important to us!

Not on the Web yet? It's easy to get started with *Dummies 101*®: *The Internet For Windows*® *98* or *The Internet For Dummies*®, 5th Edition, at local retailers everywhere.

Or let us know what you think by sending us a letter at the following address:

...For Dummies Book Registration
Dummies Press
7260 Shadeland Station, Suite 100
Indianapolis, IN 46256-3945
Fax 317-596-5498

BESTSELLING BOOK SERIES